About America
Beyond the Oregon Trail

About America

Beyond the Oregon Trail

Editors
Dr. Manan Dwivedi
Dr. Raghubansh Sinha

Ane Books Pvt. Ltd.
New Delhi ♦ Chennai

About America: Beyond the Oregon Trail
Editors: Dr. Manan Dwivedi and Dr. Raghubansh Sinha

Pages: x + 164 = 174
Size: 6.25 × 9.5
Paper Quality (GSM): 80

Published by

Ane Books Pvt. Ltd.

4821, Parwana Bhawan, 1st Floor, 24 Ansari Road, Darya Ganj,
New Delhi - 110 002, Tel.: +91(011) 23276843-44, Fax: +91(011) 23276863
e-mail: kapoor@anebooks.com, Website: www.anebooks.com

Branch Office:

- Avantika Niwas, 1st Floor, 19 Doraiswamy Road, T. Nagar,
  Chennai - 600 017, Tel.: +91(044) 28141554, 28141209
  e-mail: anebookschennai@gmail.com, rathinam@anebooks.com

ISBN: 978-93-90658-88-6

Printed at : Trident Enterprises, NOIDA.

Prologue

"With Great power comes Great Responsibility". Thus, goes a maximalistic maxim. There was an avid and telling need of a think tank which could refurbish the academia in the nation with a well delineated approach in order to instill an Indic, India centric and national interest orientated flavor and characteristic to the IR academia in the nation. The think which has been spawned is titled as, CSIR: Center for the Studies of International Relations premised in Delhi with its chapters stretching out as an overarch across the length and breadth of the nation. The CSIR has envisaged and runs its American studies wing which is officially termed as the "American Meet" and informally referred to as the Avengers, premised upon the quintessential American narrative of "Make America Great Again (MAGA) and the stereotypical American Dream and the New American century Project and the geo strategic and diplomatic one uppance of the American Dream coalescing with the Indian credo of visceral Vishwaguru in these turbulent and changing times which our External Affairs Minister calls as the " Ides of Change" in his recent work on India's Foreign Policy.

The present Book is titled as, "About America: Beyond the Oregon Trail," which is a variegated amalgam of a multitude of aspects and geo political, geo economic and geo cultural tenets of the India –US trail of friendship, cooperation, bonhomie and camaraderie on the larger rostrum of the entire international system. There has been an avid distrust casting a shadow upon the reasonable and positive upkeep of cooperation between New Delhi and Washington. The edited Book intends to initiate a learned debate on the theme of the vilification of the conjoinetness of the Indian surge and the revival of the American Dream in the global firmament.

The strategically constituted research papers in "About America" showcase the larger idiom of the standard stricture of India US cooperation and a host of other attendant themes of the order of Indian Diaspora in the US homeland and their role play in giving a fillip to the "Bilateral", along with themes such as the Trade relations between India and United States. Other contributions hold sway over equally pertinent themes such as, the epistemological approach in the narrative of India US relationship, the Climate change divergences between India and United States and the charismatic leadership Idiom exemplified by Prime Minister Narendra Modi in the larger context of the India US partnership. The entire cavalcade of issues pertaining to the Indian indigeneity, spiritual finesse and the American homeland have been strived it in order to initiate a new sympathetic reading of all elements American and Indian in origin, shape and nature. Bon Voyage! The India-United States, Oregon Trail in the unchartered waters of an untested and unchaperoned Global firmament to be in sync with the mainstream nationalistic ethos and pathos of the grandeur of the Indian nation and its populace.

Editors

Acknowledgements

The work of labour and IR artifice spawned by the venerated contributors receives an one up thumbs up for having written, cared and thought and researched assiduously for "About America: Beyond the Oregon Trail". CSIR would extend its heartfelt thankfulness then on to its President, Prof. Ashwini Mahapatra, Dean, School of International Studies in the prestigious Jawaharlal Nehru University. He has been an unstinting and bright beacon of light and academic ebullience for the CSIR and the Avengers in their incipient phase of their birth and further down the road development. It would be similar to shedding light on the effervescent Sun if one delineates the profile of Sri Sunil Ambekar, noted and renowned Intellectual, writer and social activist, who chaperoned us and championed the cause of CSIR since its inception nearly a decade back.

Dr. Rajiv Nayan posted in the Manohar Parrikar Institute of Defense and Strategic Studies sheds his academic oeuvre through his crudition and perpetual guidance through his station in CSIR as the Vice chief of the ship since the last three decades and more. The entirety of the products and gifts of the thinking in IR and strategic affairs to the fold ensues from his generous and philanthropic thinking cap untiringly.

Dr. Abhishek Srivastava, Faculty in CIPOD, SIS, JNU has been akin to a stout backdrop for our work and strivings at CSIR with his impeccable intellectual and labourly efforts at sustaining and managing the ship that is CSIR and American Meet. Dr. Vivek Mishra, Dean, of Social Sciences at Gautam Buddha University has been an equally gifted gladiator and support system to our fledgling strivings at CSIR and the American Meet. I would take upon this proud opportunity to extejnd my obligation to Dr. Raghuvansh Sinha, Dr. Tirthessh Nandan, Dr. Sanjeev Srivastava, Dr. Soumyajeet Ray, Dr. Charu Ratna Dubey, Dr. Ajmeera, Dr. Vinay Garg, Dr. Gautum Jha, Dr. Vijay Yadav, Dr. Shonit Nayan and Dr. Pawan Sigh to serve the cause of free and liberal and INDIA CENTRIC IR thought and academics while the Book was being conceived and acted upon as everything was transforming in a post Taliban world and the post Trump international system. It's a grandiose and efficient team work at the in house portals of CSIR that the driving corpus of idea was conceived in its myriad brainstorming sessions though a decade.

❐

Contents

Prologue v

Acknowledgements vii

1. 9/11 Attack and its impact on Canada 1
   — Charu Ratna Dubey

2. Leadership in American Political System: Challenges Ahead 18
   — Dr. Neetu Jain
   — Tanushka Sharma

3. India-US Climate Change Policy Relations 27
   — Manisha Sarade

4. Research, Theory, and Pedagogy in the Indo-US Relations 37
   — Dr. Tirthesh Nandan

5. The Singularity of the India-United States "Bilaterals": An Investigative Exercise in Modi Doctrine and Public Diplomacy 55
   — Dr. Manan Dwivedi

6. The Panchashila of India-US Economic Relationship: Future Trajectory in a Post Pandemic World 69
   — Pritam Banerjee

7. President Trump's South Asia Strategy: An Analysis 80
— Dr. Vivek Kumar Mishra

8. Indian Diaspora's Standing in US in the aftermath of 2014 91
— Dr Shalini Saxena

9. Climate Change: A Prospect for India-U.S. Cooperation 100
— Dr. Shyamli Singh

10. US-Pak Relations in the Backdrop of Rising China 109
— Sudhir Singh

11. India-U.S. Cooperation in the Field of Education and Skill Development 118
— Dr. Vijay Kumar Yadav

12. India US Obfuscations on Intellectual Property Rights 128
— Dr. Pawan Singh

13. An Ode to the US Philanthropy Or Is It? 136
— Dr. Saket Bihari

14. America's 'Other War' with China on IP Theft 142
— Makhan Saikia

15. US-Afghan Relations: Uncertain Future 152
— Dr. Raghubansh Sinha

16. Bibliography on US Foreign Policy and US Culture 160
— Hemant Khare

9/11 Attack and its impact on Canada

Charu Ratna Dubey,
Guest Faculty, GBU,
Greater Noida, Uttar Pradesh

Introduction

After the collapse of the Soviet Union, the concept of security changed and the focus shifted from traditional security/ border security to human security. The protection of the life of the individual became the major area of concern as far as the concept of security is concerned. During this phase 'high' level issues such as—wars, safety and security of borders, military alliances were replaced by 'low' level issues, namely, protection of innocent civilians, coalition of willing for social development, environmental protection, safety and security of most vulnerable sections of society, i.e. women and children. The international community started to build new international norms and to an extent they succeeded in doing so by achieving Anti-personnel Landmines Ban Treaty (1997), establishing the concept of Responsibility to Protect in international discourse and also by developing Rome Statute (1998) which later culminated into the establishment of International Criminal Court (2002).

But, the international scenario changed with the terrorist attack on the United States, the only 'super-power', on 11th September 2001. The event not only changed the continuing discourse in the international order but also transformed the foreign policy priorities of different countries of the world. This attack transformed the geo-political equation in international politics. The subsequent war in Afghanistan (2001), the controversial attack on Iraq (2003) and the incidents of insurgency and civil war in different parts of Arab World are some of the examples of the impact of 9/11 terrorist attacks on the international political environment. As a close door neighbour sharing a porous border with the US, Canada faced an entirely new set of challenges after this attack on the North American soil.

Until 9/11 the international environment was relatively peaceful because there was no threat of 'expanding communism' before the US. The clash of ideologies of the Cold War era in international politics came to an end, and the US was celebrating its 'victory' over the Soviet Union. Suddenly, 9/11 gave a rude shock to the 'global hegemon', and an enemy in the form of non-traditional security threat emerged before the US. George W. Bush and his foreign policy advisors encountered a 'new threat' from internationally active Jihadi terror group called al-Qaeda. They had to respond to this newly emerged threat for the safety and security of common individuals and more importantly a sovereign nation. 9/11 shifted the entire focus from human security to border security. In fact, the safety of borders/territory from terror activities originating from a distant part of the world became the first and foremost important issue for countries particularly the United States.

After 9/11, vociferous protests against the terror groups operating in different parts of the world emerged, and every country came in support of the US and sent their emotional messages to grieving Americans. This attack on Canada's next-door neighbour had immediate and immense consequences for Canada. Around three thousand people were killed and six thousand injured in the attack. The dead included twenty-four Canadian citizens who were either travelling on those planes or were inside the building into which these 'human-guided missiles' crashed. After the attack on the World Trade Centre, Canadian officials decided that all the planes that could not return to their place of origin could land on Canadian soil. No one was sure that no further attacks would take place, but the Canadian officials showcased their bravery by allowing planes into the Canadian airspace. Due to lack of space planes landed on far-flung airports of Canadian territory. At some places, the passengers were housed in Canadian military bases. Moreover, Canada declared a national day of mourning after September 11. No doubt Canadians were the most affected individuals after the Americans. That is why Canadians responded in a very generous manner to the suffering of their neighbours.

This chapter examines how 9/11 terrorist attack on the North American soil influenced the foreign policy as well as domestic policies of Canada. A set of new questions emerged such as: What were the significant changes that took place in Canadian domestic and foreign policies? How have these changes in local policies impacted the lives of common citizens of Canada and the Canadian society as a whole? Did the new laws that came into force in Canada receive appreciation from citizens across the county and how the status-quoists reacted to these changes? Apart from these a very significant question arose: Was joining the 'War on terror' in Afghanistan (2001) nothing but a Canadian quest to play a new role in international affairs or was it an attempt to protect Canadian trade with the US across 49th parallel?

While these are important questions, it is worthwhile to have a look at the previous acts of terrorism that marked bloodshed on Canadian soil and how 9/11 was different from them. A section of this essay also discusses the new laws made by the Canadian government after the horrific attack and the debate that took place around these new laws.

Terrorism, 9/11 and Canadian Response

9/11 terror attack was different from other terror attacks that took place in the past. The first and foremost reason for this is that although the incident took place in one country, i.e. the US, the impact was immediately observed throughout the world. Secondly, the attack was carried out by a small group of individuals with the help of most powerful and sophisticated technology. Third, the buildings which were targeted were not ordinary buildings. The World Trade Centre was the symbol of world financial network whereas, the Pentagon is the symbol of the United States' military power. In this way, the 9/11 attack gave an idea of a globalised world where an incident in one part of the globe impacted the other regions as well.

Previous acts of Terrorism

It was not that Canada faced the wrath of terrorism for the first time, but 9/11 was different in many ways. In 1971 an Air Canada plane was hijacked. An Air India flight had been bombed in 1985. Writing about this incident Kent Roach said: "Terrorism took a deadlier turn with the 1985 bombing of an Air India flight from Vancouver, killing all 329 passengers on board" (Roach 2003: 4). Canadians had never experienced suicide hijacking on this scale ever before.

During the Cold War years, Canada faced a major internal security crisis popularly known as the 'October Crisis'. It was a horrific act of terrorism when in October 1970 the violent group *Le Front de Liberation du Quebec* (FLQ)[1] kidnapped the British trade commissioner James Cross and kidnapped and later murdered Quebec Minister of Labour, Pierre Laporte. This incident brought Canada into the global spotlight, and the crisis loomed large impacting the Canadian image before the world.

This was primarily a domestic crisis, and the Canadian federal government imposed the *War Measures Act*. According to Whitaker, Canada acted 'swiftly, forcefully and with no regard for civil liberties'. The provisions of the Act, which gave power to the police to arrest people without any warrant, came into force at 4 o'clock in the morning. In the words of Whitaker "the federal government placed Quebec under what amounted to a state of martial law. Extensive use of power was made available to the police to detain and interrogate without

[1] FLQ was a paramilitary separatist group of Quebec, influenced by the Marxist-Leninist ideology. The group was founded in 1963, and the goal was to establish an independent socialist Quebec state.

charge, without counsel, and without *habeas corpus*. The media was censored, and the FLQ was declared a banned organisation" (Whitaker 2010: 44). Kent Roach also pointed out how the FLQ was declared 'unlawful' by the Canadian Cabinet, and about 500 people were taken into custody simply because they were "guilty of the new offences of being a member and supporter of the FLQ" (Roach: 2003: 4).

In a developed democracy like Canada where public opinion impacts the decision of the government, the sentiment of the people was in support of the *War Measures Act*. Not only was the Anglophone community in support of the Actbut also a majority of the Francophone citizens were in favour of the way Canadian federal government handled the issue. William Tetley noted the widespread support of the *War Measures Act* by both the Anglophone and Francophone communities. He wrote that "In the Gallup Poll,[2] 89 percent of the English-speaking Canadians and 86 percent of French Speaking Canadians supported the introduction of War Measures Act" (Tetley 2014: 103).

Although the methods used by the federal government, were debateable, they produced some extraordinary results for the internal security of Canada. According to Whitaker, "the result was clear and unequivocal: the FLQ, and with it the entire terrorist tendency of the sovereignty movement of Quebec was eradicated" (Whitaker 2010: 45). Moreover, the execution of the Quebec Minister of Labour, Pierre Laporte by the FLQ proved a self-destructive move. The public support of the organisation particularly in Quebec came down sharply as soon as it was announced that the minister had been murdered by the group. With the destruction of the militant group, in the same year, the issue of Quebec nationalism was grabbed by the Parti Quebecois (PQ), but its means to achieve the goals were legitimate, lawful, peaceful and democratic.

9/11 Attack: How Different was It?

The terrorist attack of 11th September 2001 on the United States was a series of four coordinated attacks by the Islamic terrorist group al-Qaeda. Four passenger planes took off from American soil bound for California. These planes of two different airline companies (United Airlines and American Airlines) were hijacked by terrorists of al- Qaeda. Two of them were crashed into the North and South towers of the World Trade Centre in New York. The third hijacked plane partially hit the headquarters of the United States Department of Defense, popularly known as the Pentagon. The fourth plane crashed in the fields as it was approaching Washington D.C. This was a watershed moment for the world because it changed the course of action of several countries particularly, the countries of the West.

Canada had earlier taken part in the Cold War, which was a 'war against Soviet Communism', in alliance with the Capitalist bloc. After joining NATO,

[2] Gallup Poll was a public opinion poll took place in December 1970.

based on the concept of collective defence, Canada started defending against Communist expansion in North America and Europe. Canadian troops also took part in the Korean War to stop Communist expansion on the Korean peninsula. Its middle power diplomacy gave Canada a new identity, but its close connections with the United States made it a partner of the Western alliance in the Cold War. A few considered this partnership asymmetrical and termed Canada a 'very junior partner' in the Western alliance. During the same time, Canada continued its commitment to the United Nations and followed the policy of multilateralism.

The threat to the Canadian people due to the Canadian involvement in the Cold War period cannot be equated with the fear that emerged out of the 9/11 incidents. But Reg Whitaker argued that there exist some connections between the Cold War and the 'War on Terrorism' after the 9/11 attack. He said that "Just as Canadian troops have found themselves fighting 'terrorists' on the front lines in Afghanistan, Canadian soldiers in the Cold War soon found themselves battling 'communists' in Korea. Both wars included a home front and the identification of enemies within. Both wars involved Canada in ever closer integration with the Americans" (Whitaker 2010: 37-38). In this way, he drew parallels between the Cold War and the 'War on Terrorism'. Commenting on 9/11 terror attack in Special Session on Canadian Parliament in Ottawa, Canadian Foreign Minister John Manley said "On September 11, 2001, the world changed for Canada... We are a war against terrorism now... but it is unlike any war we have fought before" (Manley 2001). This statement by the foreign minister describes the panic that emerged out of terror event.

While describing the 9/11 attack as *déjà vu,* Reg Whitaker says that it had some different elements. According to him, "9/11 constituted a violent attack on American civil society" with the objective of spreading fear amongst the Americans. "Moreover, the targets have been publically designated in al-Qaeda pronouncements, as, any and all Americans, not being limited to state officials, military/security personnel, or corporate executives as was the case with some earlier terrorist groups" (Whitaker 2010: 47). In his article, comparing the 9/11 attack with the previous threat that emerged from the Cold War tight bi-polarity, he describes the threat as a "diffuse threat" that emerged out of the act of terrorism in the 21st century (Whitaker 2010: 48). After the attack on the United States, it became a common concern that how American centred unipolar world order will operate? Commenting on this and post 9/11 international scenario Andrew Cooper said "Empire and regime change through the use of force has come back in vogue" (Cooper and Rowlands 2005: 4).

Unlike the 'October Crisis', the popular sentiment of the public after the 9/11 attack was in favour of the total elimination of terrorist heavens. This led to pressure on governments to fight against the terrorists at any cost. Quoting

Globe and Mail-CTV-Ipsos Reid Poll Christopher Raj wrote that "The survey done between 17 and 20 September, found that 73 percent of Canadians favouring joining the United States in its battle against terrorism" (Raj 2007: 157). But being a close ally of the United States, the possibility of another terrorist attack could not be ignored by the Canadian government. Even the statements issued by the terrorist groups were aimed at Western countries particularly after the 'War on Terrorism' was launched against al-Qaeda and other jihadi groups. The bombing of the trains in Madrid, Spain and on the London Underground by the terrorist organisations in 2005 left other Western countries vulnerable to such acts of terrorism.

Although Canada did not take part in the Iraq War (2003) the Liberal government under Paul Martin and the Conservative government under Stephen Harper continued the presence of the Canadian military in Afghanistan to fight against the terrorists. This was because Canadians continued to sympathise with the United States after the 9/11 event and the general sentiment was against terrorism. But with respect to the Iraq War, the Canadian open-ended support of the actions of the United States came to an end. The two years long sympathy and similar opinion of the public of the two countries came to an end because Canadians were not in favour of the Iraq War and Americans had a firm belief that Iraq possessed weapons of mass destruction. Whitaker points out that the Iraq War draws a sharp line of demarcation between Canada and the United States, involving critical public opinion as much as, if not more than, official governments doubts about American judgement and intensions. The Liberal governments of Jean Chretien and Paul Martin were seen by many in Washington as 'Anti-American' and the Conservatives under Stephen Harper as more favourably inclined to the Bush administration (Whitaker 2010: 49).

Scholars of Canadian foreign policy gave very divergent views on the Canadian response to the 9/11 event. Undoubtedly, the security of the borders was the major and the primary concern of the Canadian government. On the other hand, the economic dependence on the United States was a major cause of concern for the business groups active on both sides of the border. No doubt Canada was fighting on two different fronts. On the first front, the Canadian government by becoming part of the coalition to fight against the terrorists was giving a message to the general public that the government was also worried about the safety and security of every citizen of Canada and would protect Canada from any terrorist attack and was also ready to do this at any cost. On the other front, which was less prevalent among common citizens, was the American interpretation of the need for national security on the border. The northern boundary with the United States which was important for Canadian exports and the flow of people was a significant issue for Canadian policymakers. Michael Grunwald (2001) in his article in Washington Post wrote that "Canada is the biggest player: more trade occurs between the

United States and Canada at the Detroit-Windsor border than occurs between the United States and the European Union". If tight security were imposed on this border by the United States, the economic interests of Canada would inevitably be impacted unfavourably, an outcome unacceptable for Canada.

The two fronts were interrelated with each other. This makes it even more difficult to understand the protection of Canadian economic interests as an aspect of the border security initiative taken by the Canadian government. Whitaker further argued: "Everything that Canada contributes to the 'War on Terrorism' and to maintain strong security against terrorism within Canada, tends to relieve pressure on the border" (Whitaker 2010: 50).

Canadian Response to 9/11

Canada responded quickly to the terrorist attack. On the occasion of the memorial service on 14th September 2001 at Parliament Hill, Prime Minister Chretien delivered a very emotional speech. In the presence of Paul Cellucci, the then American ambassador to Canada, he said "Our friendship has no limits. Generation after generation we have travelled many difficult miles together" (Chretien 2001). He assured the ambassador that Canada would be with the US in every possible way. In response to the words of Chretien, the US ambassador said that the tragedy had brought the two countries together. "It has once again shown us that the differences that divide us are far less important than the ties that bind us" (Sands 2002: 72).

Canadian response was not only quick as a neighbour but also as a member of the international community. Canada gave its full support to the United Nations Security Council Resolution 1373 which brought a new definition of terrorism. Moreover, Canada responded to the abuse of refugee status by the suspected terrorists by imposing barriers on the admission of all refugees. The boundary that Canada and the United States shared made Canada think tank twice about the free flow of potential terrorists across the border so that the porous boundaries between the two countries could not provide safe movement to suspected terrorists. Commenting on suspicion of the American public and policy makers Kent Roach said: "Canada drafted a new anti-terrorism law with an eye to American fear that it might provide a safe haven for terrorists" (Roach 2011: 361).

The response involved the pooling of resources in security and intelligence with additions in the budget, the development of a National Security Strategy, the formulation of a new umbrella Ministry of Public Safety and Emergency Preparedness Canada (PSEPC), more powers to the anti-terrorist law enforcement agencies and intelligence agencies and close coordination among the like-minded states. Such a large number of measures were taken for Canadian economic security by assuring the United States that Canada was taking the security of the US very seriously.

The Canadian government passed an act in the parliament of Canada very soon after the terrorist act on American soil, namely, the Anti-terrorism Act. Anti-terrorism Act is considered as the most important law that emerged after 9/11 incident. Kent Roach writes "A little more than a month after September 11, it (Canada) introduced a massive and hastily drafted Anti-terrorism Act (Bill C-36). The Bill included new legal concepts such as—investigative hearings, preventive arrests, broad motive-based crimes for participation in or support for terrorist groups at home and abroad, as well as new powers to list terrorist groups, deprive them of charitable status and take their property" (Roach 2011: 8). This act was enacted with UN Security Council Resolution 1373 in mind and defined crimes of terrorism under the Canadian Criminal Code. Roach wrote that the Anti-terrorism Act was "defended by the Liberal government as consistent with the charter and required to meet Canada's international obligation under resolution 1373" (Roach 2011: 376).

Although there was a consensus among the people from various walks of life with respect to the response to the terror activities, the Bill faced severe criticism from different quarters. Supporters of civil liberties, lawyers, unions, aboriginal people and the refugee community raised their voices against some of the provisions of the proposed Bill. Due to this opposition from the general public, some changes were made to the Bill. The Bill with these changes became an act on 18th December 2001 after securing royal assent. After passing the Anti-terrorism Act, the Canadian government came with another parliamentary Bill known as the Public Safety Act. The Bill proposed to provide new powers to the ministers in the government to declare military security zones around areas of protest. The Bill also provided more powers to control airport security but was withdrawn after vociferous criticism. The fear of biological and chemical attacks on Canada by the terrorist groups changed the environment, and the bill was reintroduced in parliament with some restrictions on the use of powers by the concerned authorities. Public Safety Canada formerly known as Public Safety and Emergency Preparedness Canada (PSEPC) came into being in 2005 after the passing of the Public Safety Bill. The government department was responsible for protecting Canadian citizens and maintaining a peaceful and safe society. The website of the Canadian government says:

> Public Safety Canada ensures coordination across all federal departments and agencies responsible for national security and the safety of Canadians. Public Safety Canada works with five agencies and three review bodies, uniting in the single portfolio and all reporting to the same minister. We also work with other levels of the government, first responders, community groups, the private sector and other nations (Public Safety Canada 2017).

In the same year 2001, the federal government announced a budget allocation of $ 8 billion for security. This allocation was popularly known as the 'security budget' and its spending was "devoted to policing, the military, increased airport security, and border and immigration controls but not to matters such as health care that many Canadians saw as a more immediate threat to their personal security" (Roach 2011: 10). The main impact of this budget was the increase in the numbers of police officers, security officials, immigration officials and border guards. However, Kent Roach believes that the "immediate concern for the many Canadians after September 11 was not distant events in Afghanistan, new legislation or even aviation security, but ensuring that the almost $ 2 billion in trade that crosses the American-Canadian border everyday continued to flow" (Roach 2011: 11).

The Department of Public Safety and Emergency Preparedness Canada (PSEPC) was a Canadian version of the US Department of Homeland Security. Christopher Raj in his edited volume writes "Ottawa also responded to the US government in creating in 2003 Canadian version of Department Homeland Security called Public Safety Emergency Preparedness Canada" (Raj 2007: 164). But the Canadian version of Homeland Security was not as large as the US one as it never received the required funds.

The government also made changes in its immigration policies. In 2002 the government replaced the old Immigration Act of 1978 with a new act called the Immigration and Refugee Protection Act (IRPA). The purpose of the act was to be "tough on those who pose a threat to Canadian security but maintain Canada's humanitarian tradition" (Department of Foreign Affairs and International Trade 2003: 2). The Canadian government felt that Canada should not fall prey to terrorist organisations due to its lenient immigration policies. The act primarily focused on the issues such as—immigration to Canada, refugee protection, enforcement and the Immigration Refugee Board. After the 9/11 event, foreign nationals were increasingly seen as 'terrorists' or threat to Canadian security.

Raj has pointed out that although the provisions of the act relaxed some restrictions, overall the "act conveys a negative tone". He writes that "rather than welcoming and fostering the integration of the immigrants and refugees, the act appears defensive in seeking to protect Canada by highlighting control, containment and regulations" (Raj 2007: 161). The act prescribed to immigration officers that the people who want to come to Canada should be thoroughly investigated and those who have been involved in serious crimes should not be given permission to come to Canada. Margaret E. Beare writes that "Background checks are performed, and the Minister of Citizenship and Immigration may issue a danger opinion that may allow the removal of the person from Canada and refusal of his application and issue security certificates allowing Citizen and Immigration Canada to remove a person posing a security threat" (Beare 2003).

In this way, the association of 'foreign nationals' and 'terrorists' encouraged the 'security threat' perception among the policymakers as well as the general public. This mentality drove the whole notion of preventing outsiders, i.e. people from other countries, entering Canadian territory. The PSEPC Bill when proposed in parliament echoed a similar mentality of a security threat from foreign nationals. It reads that 'the best way to stop terrorists from entering Canada is to stop them before they get here'. This also produced the sense that the threat to Canadian security was not from within but from outside. In other words, it was believed that the security threat to the Canadian people is from far beyond the borders.

Border Safety and Military Response after 9/11

The extensive debate and discussion that started in Canada after the horrific attack on 9/11 compelled the Canadian government to bring about new laws. Apart from the laws that were made by the Canadian parliament, it is also important to see how Canadian government responded with respect to the safety and security of the porous border with the United States across the 49th parallel. Similarly, when the countries of the world were joining the US for 'War on Terrorism' the government of Canada could not remain a silent spectator. In this section, we will also have a look at the military response by Canada.

Border Security Initiatives

The border between Canada and the US is considered as one of the busiest borders in terms of cross-border bilateral trade. The attack of 9/11 disrupted the flow of goods between the two countries amounting to a loss of around $ 2 billion every day. No two countries except Canada and the US are as dependent on each other for everyday trade. This could be observed by the argument made by Stephen Flynn. He reported that "just 36 hours after the September 11 attack, Daimler Chrysler announce that it would have to close one of its assembly plants because Canadian supplies were caught in an 18-hour traffic jam at the border. Ford then announced that five of its assembly plants would have to lie idle the following week" (Flynn 2002: 60). At that time closing down the border was the only option before the US government which later became a serious problem for the factories or plants which were dependent on supplies from Canada.

Those who incurred heavy losses out of the closing of border raised their voices and conveyed their concerns to the government of both the countries. The business communities of Canada and the US started lobbying for a new plan to make sure that such acts of terrorism in future in any part of the continent would not affect the interests of the business class. John Manly, the then Foreign Minister of Canada started discussing border-related safety and security matters with Tom Ridge, the newly appointed US Homeland security advisor and informed each other about the necessity of a mutually acceptable alternative to prevent any such situation in the future. After several rounds of talks, an agreement was signed between Canada and the US on 12th December 2001 popularly known as Smart Border Declaration. Commenting on the 9/11 attack and its impact on Canada-US porous border Daniel Drache wrote that "September 11 redefined not only the border but also North America as a geopolitical region.... In this new security age, every country is a potential partner (or enemy) for the US" (Drache 2004: 90).

The US had claimed that there were some terror groups active in Canada and the main reason for this was Canadian refugee and asylum policy. That is why, for the US, the prime objective of the Smart Border Declaration was the security of the US territory. The agreement was based on a 30-point action plan to avoid any terror incident originating from Canadian territory. Christopher Raj has argued that "30-point action plan was based on four pillars: (a) the secure flow of people; (b) the secure flow of goods; (c) secure infrastructure; and (d) information sharing and coordination in the enforcement of these objectives" (Raj 2007: 171).

The primary cause of concern for Canada was the protection of trade and commerce that took place across the border. Canadian policymakers had economy in their mind while dealing with the US on Smart Border Declaration. In an interview, John Manly told the *Toronto Star,* a Canadian daily newspaper that "I felt that the greatest risk to Canada as a result of September 11... was to the economy" (Toronto Star 2002: A6). Thus, the urgency with which he negotiated the 30-point border action plan with Tom Ridge was driven by economic necessities.

It is estimated that almost three lakhs people cross the border from both sides every day. Managing this large number of people had always been a tough task for both Canada and the US. After 9/11 it became vital to regulate the flow of the people at the border. The problem had been solved up to a great extent by using sophisticated technology for surveillance and screening. Who is eligible to cross the border by land and air was determined by a mutually acceptable programme called NEXUS. This programme made crossing easier with minimal inspection through dedicated lanes. Those who frequently cross the border had been issued electronic passes and were allowed to use the fast lane to cross the border. Those who are not the citizens of Canada and have the nationality of the third country are given Permanent Resident (PR) cards equipped with biometric identification to stop fraud and duplication. Raj claimed that "with these advances in technology Canada and the United States have moved towards a policy of harmonization and coordination on a number of issues including immigration systems and processes, refugee/asylum seekers and third country visa exemption and restrictions" (Raj 2007: 172).

To ensure the free flow of goods across the border a Free and Secure Trade (FAST) programme was concluded between Canada and the US. This programme is a clearance programme dedicated to the commercial traffic entering the US from Canada and Mexico. The official website of Department of Homeland Security of US reads: "Initiated after 9/11, this innovative trusted traveller/trusted shipper programme allows expedited processing of commercial carriers who have completed background checks and fulfil certain eligibility requirements" (Department of Homeland Security 2017). Thus, with the help of this programme approved importers, carriers, and registered drivers are allowed to cross the border with minimal inspection. Undoubtedly, this helped the businessmen from Canada and Mexico to conduct commercial trade relatively easier with the United States.

Canada's Military Response: 'War on Terrorism'

As soon as it became clear that the 9/11 attack had been orchestrated by a terror outfit called al-Qaeda from the safe havens in Afghanistan with the support of Taliban regime, William Maley and Jack Cunningham wrote that "it was only a matter of time before robust military action was taken to smash the al-Qaeda network and displace the Taliban regime that had provided it with a home" (Maley and Cunninghum 2015: 9). Canada's policy towards Afghanistan dominated Canadian foreign policy quarters after it became clear that the terror attack on the US had been planned in Afghanistan. Commenting on the importance of Afghanistan in Canadian foreign policy, Bill Graham who later became the Minister of Foreign Affairs in January 2002 wrote that "the issue of Afghanistan occupied a central place in our political environment. It figured very important in our foreign policy and our relations with our most important allies; it shaped the foreign dimension of our defense policy and procurement needs and provided an experience that had marked our military for a generation" (Graham 2015: 50-51). Undoubtedly, Canadian foreign policy also impacted domestic politics considerably.

Within a month after the attack, 'War on Terrorism' rhetoric proposed by the then President of the US George W. Bush became a reality. The Canadian contribution to this fight against 'evil' started as a part of its commitment to the concept of collective security of the North Atlantic Treaty Organisation (NATO). Highlighting Canadian commitment to NATO Bill Graham wrote that "After NATO Secretary-General Lord Robertson made that announcement on October 4, 2001, Canada was obliged to support American-led efforts to hunt down the al-Qaeda terrorist behind the 9/11 attacks and overthrow the Taliban regime that allowed them to use Afghanistan as a base of operations" (Graham 2015: 51). On October 7 2001, when the US and British warplanes started bombing in Afghanistan, Canadian Prime Minister Jean Chretien announced that Canada would join the US war against the terror-exporting hubs in Afghanistan. Soon after this announcement Defence Minister of Canada made it clear on the very next day that Canadian Armed Forces would take part in this battle against terrorism. Graham wrote, "As quickly as October 8, our defence minister, Art Eggleton, announced Operation Apollo, a Canadian operation in support of the American Operation Enduring Freedom" (Graham 2015: 51).

In this way, Operation Apollo was a Canadian operation in Afghanistan that took place from October 2001 to October 2003. Under Operation Apollo Canada sent its naval ships to the Persian Gulf followed by surveillance and patrol aircrafts. Apart from this Canada also sent armed forces of around 2000 troops to take part in the Operation. Canadian contribution was relatively small in comparison to other countries which were taking part in the campaign in Afghanistan. Commenting on Canadian contingent Raj wrote, "it represented nearly one-third of the country's naval fleet and was the largest combat force Canada had sent abroad since the Korean War" (Raj 2007: 165). By the end of November 2001, the Taliban regime in Afghanistan came to an end. In the very next month, UN Security Council recognised Hamid Karzai's government as the interim government in Afghanistan.

Canada's initial engagement was very limited. Before Canada decided to start Operation Apollo, the major focus of Canada was to build an international campaign against terrorism. It is important to note that Canada played a pivotal role in an international campaign which culminated in United Nations Security Council resolution 1368. But over a period of time Canadian engagement evolved. Operation Apollo was the first engagement which lasted until July 2003. After Operation Apollo Canada started its new commitment under the aegis of NATO-led International Security and Assistance Force (ISAF) which is popularly known as Operation Athena. Craig Stone describes Operation Athena as "presented by the Department of National Defense (DND) as a two-phase operation, with phase one involving operations in Kabul from August 2003 until July 2005, and phase two taking place in Kandahar from August 2005 until July 2011, when a transition force assumed responsibility for closing out Canada's mission in Kandahar" (Stone 2015: 133).

Canada's combat mission in Afghanistan came to an end on July 7, 2011. After Operation Athena came to an end in 2011, Prime Minister Stephen Harper announced at the NATO summit (2012) in Chicago that Canadian soldiers would continue to train and support Afghan National Army until March 2014. According to Stone, "Canadian contribution to Afghanistan was reduced from almost three thousand people to just under one thousand and repositioned to Kabul to focus on training Afghan National Army" (Stone 2015: 134). The estimated cost of Canadian presence in Afghanistan is subject to considerable debate. Canada continued to be involved in the reconstruction of Afghanistan through security programme and development assistance. On July 9, 2016, Canadian Prime Minster Justin Trudeau announced a comprehensive package of $ 465 million in security and development support to Afghanistan. In 2015 Bill Graham wrote that "a presence that endures today and has evolved the deployment of troops in many different capacities at the cost of C$ 14-18 billion" (Graham 2015: 50). Craig Stone also estimated total costs for Canada similarly. He wrote: "When looking at total cost for these areas (incremental costs for the mission, capital depreciation and liabilities of death and disability), the Afghan mission will have cost the Canadian taxpayer between C$ 15.6 and $19.5 billion" (Stone 2015: 147).

Apart from financial cost Canada also paid in terms of the lives of the members of its armed forces. During the combat mission in Afghanistan, 158 members of Canadian Armed Force died. The number of deaths was very low until 2005. The major turning point occurred when the Canadian government under the leadership of Paul Martin decided to join Kandahar province. After this, the number of Canadians killed in Afghanistan increased dramatically. "Between 2002 and the fatality in October 2011, the causes of death were as follows: IED's, roadside bombs, or landmines (ninety-six); combat or other hostile fire (twenty-three); suicide bombers (thirteen); and accidents (eleven). Also, six lost their lives in 'friendly fire' incidents; four died from non-combat related causes; three committed suicide; and two died in a helicopter crash" (Nossal 2015: 212).

Canadian involvement in Afghanistan took place after a very long time. Although Canadian forces were involved in peacekeeping operations under the aegis of the United Nations, the military operation in Afghanistan raised the question of its necessity. Public opinion on Afghanistan did change over a period of time. Graham wrote: "I believe that the mission had considerable support at the beginning, but it gradually eroded in the face of significant and mounting casualties, the lengthening commitment, and a sense amongst the Canadian public that we are carrying an unfairly heavy share of the burden in Afghanistan" (Graham 2015: 72). He further believed that there was "at the beginning, a resistance in significant part of the public to a combat role for Canada and a belief that Canada was better equipped for and historically committed to traditional peacekeeping operations" (Graham 2015: 72).

As soon as *Operation Enduring Freedom* campaign of the US in Afghanistan came to an end in 2002, the then President turned American attention and shifted the sources from Afghanistan to Iraq against Saddam Hussein. It had been argued by Nipa Banerjee that Canada enhanced its role in Afghanistan to avoid its engagement in Iraq. While discussing the lessons from Afghanistan, she claimed that "Canada joined the US-led war in early 2002 as compensation for not agreeing to join US-led operation in Iraq and to fulfil our obligations as NATO member once NATO had approved the mission" (Banerjee 2015: 178). She further said that "in absence of any evidence that the Taliban posed threat to Canada, the public continues to wonder if the war was necessary to protect the Canadians" (Banerjee 2015: 178). Resonating similar views, Craig Stone wrote: "With Canada and others having drawn down from Afghanistan in 2014, many of those whose lives have changed the most from this mission will continue to ask if it was worth the cost" (Stone 2015: 148).

Conclusion

It is difficult to conclude whether the invasion to Afghanistan was necessary or not, but, it is a fact that Canada proved itself a concerned neighbour by changing the course of domestic and foreign policy after 9/11 and also a defender of collective security as a NATO member by its twelve-year long military operation in Afghanistan. The changes made by the Canadian parliament in domestic laws were very extensive. Due to the introduction of the Anti-terrorism Act, the Canadian Criminal Code was also changed, and new offences were added. The primary purpose of the Anti-terrorism Act was to secure Canada from terror activities. The best way to eliminate terrorism is to cut the funding sources which will make such groups vulnerable and virtually handicapped. Forming a new department, namely, Public Safety Canada also known as Public Safety and Emergency Preparedness Canada (PSEPC) by the federal government which is responsible for the safety and security of the common Canadian citizens was a new initiative after 9/11. Similarly, bringing new legislation on immigration policy showed Canadian commitment to resolve the threat of global terrorism by stopping 'possible terrorists' on the border. These stringent laws did face protests but the issue of terrorism was very important to tackle, and it was felt that the Canadian government could not take chance by putting the lives of innocent civilians in danger.

On foreign policy front too, Canadian foreign policy makers made several changes. Canada took part in Afghanistan, but at the same time, it is also important to note that it did not agree to participate in the Iraq War (2003) because of the lack of evidence of the presence of Weapons of Mass Destruction (WMD) in Iraq. Describing the importance of Iraq, Bill Graham, the then Minister of Foreign Affairs of Canada, wrote in his memoir that "Iraq was a multi-layered problem. One level was Canada-US relations, another was multilateral relations, the third was domestic politics—all three were interacting each other all the time... If we started a war without authorization from the Security Council and without proof regarding the WMD, there could be terrible consequences" (Graham 2016: 273, 289). Undoubtedly, 9/11 changed the priorities of Canada. Before the terror attack, the Canadian government was focusing on human security and was taking innovative steps for the security of individuals. But after the attack, human security did not remain first priority for Canada. Instead, the safety and security of Canadian people from non-traditional security threats mainly from terrorism became more critical.

References:

- Banarjee, Nipa (2015), "Development: Lessons Learned from a Decade in Afghanistan", in William Maley and Jack Cunningham (eds.) *Australia and Canada in Afghanistan: Perspective on a Mission*,

Toronto: Dundurn.

- Beare, Margaret (2003), "Policing with National Security Agenda", [Online: web] Accessed 15 May 2016, URL: http://digitalcommons.osgoode.yorku.ca/reports/15/
- Cooper, Andrew Fenton and Dane Rowlands (2005), "A State of Disconnects- The Fracturing of Canadian Foreign Policy", in Andrew Cooper and Dane Rowlands (eds.) *Canada Among Nations, 2005: Splitting Images*, Montreal and Kingston: McGill and Queens University Press.
- Department of Foreign Affairs and International Trade (DFAIT), *Canada's actions since the September 11 Attack: fighting terrorism- A top priority for the Government of Canada* Page 2. Quoted in Erin Kruger et al. (2004) *Canada After 9/11: New Security Measures and 'Preferred' Immigration*, Edmonton: Prairie Centre of Excellence for Research on Immigration and Integration, University of Alberta.
- Drache, Daniel (2004), *Borders Matter: Homeland Security and the Search for North America*, Halifax: Fernwood Publishing.
- Flynn, Stephen (2002), "America the Vulnerable", *Foreign Affairs*, January-February 2002.
- Government of Canada (2003), *A Dialogue on Foreign Policy*, Department of Foreign Affairs and International Trade, Ottawa.
- Government of Canada (2017), *Public Safety Canada*, Accessed 5 June 2017, URL: https://www.canada.ca/en/public-safety-canada.html
- Grunwald, Michael (2001), "Economic Crossroads on the Line", *Washington Post*, 26 December.
- Graham, Bill (2015), "Afghanistan- Some Lessons Learned: A Personal Political Perspective", in William Maley and Jack Cunningham (eds.) *Australia and Canada in Afghanistan: Perspective on a Mission*, Toronto: Dundurn.
- Graham, Bill (2016), *The call of the World: A Political Memoir*, Vancouver: On Point Press.
- Maley, William and Jack Cunningham (2015), "Afghanistan and Its Challenges", in William Maley and Jack Cunningham (eds.) *Australia and Canada in Afghanistan: Perspective on a Mission*, Toronto: Dundurn.
- Nossal, Kim Richard (2015), "Shadows of the Past: Commemorating the Fallen in Afghanistan and Canada", in William Maley and Jack Cunningham (eds.) *Australia and Canada in Afghanistan: Perspective on a Mission*, Toronto: Dundurn.

- Raj, Christopher S. (2007), "Canada and International Terrorism Since 9/11", in Christopher S. Raj and Abdul Nafey (eds.) *Canada's Global Engagement and Relations with India*, New Delhi: MANAK PUBLICATIONS PVT.LTD.
- Roach, Kent (2003), *September 11: Consequences for Canada*, Montreal and Kingston: McGill-Queen's Press-MQUP.
- Roach, Kent (2011), *The 9/11 effect: Comparative counter-terrorism*, Cambridge University Press.
- Stone, Craig (2015), "The Cost of the War in Afghanistan: A Billion Dollar a Year and Counting", in William Maley and Jack Cunningham (eds.) *Australia and Canada in Afghanistan: Perspective on a Mission*, Toronto: Dundurn.
- Tetley, W. (2014). *October Crisis 1970: An Insider's View*. McGill-Queen's Press-MQUP.
- Thompson, Allan (2002), "Can Canada Still Lay Claim to be Glorious and Free", *Toronto Star*, Toronto, 9 September 2002.
- US Department of Homeland Security (2017), "FAST: Free and Secure Trade for Commercial Vehicle", [Online: web] Accessed 12 December 2017 URL: https://www.cbp.gov/travel/trusted-traveler-programs/fast
- Whitaker, R. (2010), "How Canada Confronts Terrorism: Canadian Responses to 9/11 in Historical and Comparative Context", in Karim-Aly S. Kassam (eds.) *Understanding terror: perspectives for Canadians*, Calgary: University of Calgary Press

❐

Leadership in American Political System: Challenges Ahead

Dr. Neetu Jain, Associate Professor, IIPA
Tanushka Sharma, Research Officer, IIPA

Introduction

Since the end of World War II, the traditional U.S. role in the world is generally designated as one of global leadership. The United States tends to be the first or most important country for classifying and edging international issues, setting an example for other countries to follow, organizing, implementing multidimensional efforts to address international issues, and enforcing international rules and norms. Having been involved extensively on the international front, the country has lately been pursuing an internationalist foreign policy; a foreign policy of global engagement or deep engagement; a foreign policy that provides global public goods; a foreign policy of liberal order building, liberal internationalism, or liberal hegemony; an interventionist foreign policy; or a foreign policy of seeking primacy or world hegemony.

Even though traditional U.S. role in the world was stable over the past 70 years, the specifics of U.S. foreign policy have changed in phases primarily due to changes in administration. The economic, political and security strategy that the United States has pursued for many decades now, under Democratic and Republican administration is today widely questioned by large segments of the American public. Many Americans no longer seem to value the liberal international order that the United States created after World War II and sustained throughout the Cold War and beyond, or perhaps they take it for granted and have lost sight of the essential role the United States plays in supporting the international environment from which they benefit greatly. The unprecedented prosperity made possible by free and open markets and thriving international trade; the spread of democracy; and the avoidance of major conflict among great powers: All these remarkable accomplishments have depended on sustained U.S. engagement around the world. Internationally, the U.S. is no longer a giant on the geopolitical front, a position it no longer occupies that it enjoyed soon after the collapse of the Soviet Union. However, it still has a better hand to play than any of its global competitor, with the world's best military and substantial spending on defence the U.S economy remains the most advanced and adaptable in the world, despite gross inequalities. The costs and profits of the international commitments are high, yet the disconnect on the part of citizens of America and between the diplomacy puts a halt to its successive growth abroad. The window for defining America's key role abroad will not stay open forever. The moment of opportunity depends largely on the commitment of the American Leader i.e., the President who can help create a muscle-bound nation of shared vision and purpose.

'America First'- Psychology of American Leadership

America has propped the "rule-based order," taking a neutral stand by acting as moral police for the world, but that certainly was not the case during the tenure of former President Donald Trump. During the past four years, Donald Trump's "America First" presidency has challenged the post-war spirit of cooperation more aggressively than any leader before him. One by one, he has defunded and abandoned the multilateral agreements and institutions created by his predecessors. His courtship of strongman leaders has allowed autocrats to exploit this extraordinary moment in time to further their own interests and roll back democratic freedoms in their countries. A research paper by Theodore Millon on 'The personality profile and leadership style of U.S. president Donald J. Trump in office' presented in the Forty-Third Annual Scientific Meeting of the International Society of Political Psychology Berlin, Germany (virtual conference), has outlined a comprehensive review of the leadership style of Trump's primary personality patterns which were found to be Ambitious/self-serving, Dominant/controlling, and Outgoing/gregarious, infused with secondary features of the Dauntless/dissenting pattern. Ambitious individuals are bold, competitive, and self-assured; they easily assume leadership roles, expect others to recognize their special qualities, and often act as entitled. For those who study leaders' personalities and how their actions affect situations domestically and internationally while in power, President Trump has really been a blessing, if well-disguised. For many of his opponents, turning a corner on the Trump Presidency is not just about changing his policies but also quieting his persona, removing the centre-stage megaphone of political office from the hands of a man eagerly keen to use it. The expressive and agreeable Joe Biden – perhaps average, risk-averse, and vanilla to his critics –is surely very different. There are many ways their leadership style diverges. President Joe Biden is much more cooperative in his dealings, believing in values by using more rewards and possibilities of keeping promises in his approach to others, seeing more value in using rewards and promises. Hilary Clinton shared some personality characteristics with fellow Democrat Biden, but in some ways, she was similar to Trump. Clinton's leadership style and decision-making skills are attributes of being well-versed in the art of Washington politics considering her background of being a political elite and her experience in diplomacy. She is not a great visionary, yet she came across as a person who knew what she was talking about, something which she must've developed over her years of contribution in public service. However, many of these leadership models identified do not incorporate the leadership characteristics of John F. Kennedy. Although he has been distinguished as an outstanding leader, many of the present candidates in line to be the president lack his leadership style, John F. Kennedy was known for his enduring abilities to make leadership look effortless and to see obstacles as opportunities.

Leadership and Policymaking: Virtues and Vices

Many leaders experience a growing number of adversaries because of the seminal decisions taken by them. A use of force on strategies involving risks by these leaders creates domestic/international political and economic diversions. As a consequence of these strategies one develops an image for policy makers, suggesting key psychological variable of the leader, their policy behaviour, and the willingness to engage in dicey situations. Among many different influences on Presidential foreign policy decision-making, the President's personal characteristics arguably hold the most influence. Fred Greenstein's framework of presidential leadership focused on how emotional intelligence, cognitive style, organizational capacity, public communication, vision, and political skill, capture both the internal and external aspects of presidential decision-making.

Donald Trump's political decisions are always under constant controversy and strong scrutiny. During his administration the scope of international relations and the field of American foreign policy have witnessed serious alterations. Trumps unpopularity during his tenure made a significant negative impact on America's overall image. Ratings for the United States plunged once he took over the White House in 2017, declined further in the next successive years, or at least majorly due to the widespread perception domestically and abroad on how the U.S. handled Corona virus Pandemic poorly. It is in two decades that the U.S. has achieved the lowest point in the public view. For example, 41% of adults in the United Kingdom expressed a favourable opinion of the U.S., the lowest percentage registered in any Center survey there. In France and Germany, ratings for the U.S. are essentially as low as compared to in March 2003, at the height of U.S.-European tensions over the Iraq War. U.S. favourability also reached all-time lows this year in Japan, Canada, Australia, the Netherlands, and Sweden. Also, there has been considerable opposition to many of the U.S. policies, including the decision to withdraw from the Climate Change agreements and the Iran nuclear deal. An ordeal to make 'America Great Again', Trump's harsh policies on migration had not only been unsettling for the citizens of diverse authenticity residing in the States for years but also for the ones that aspired to make it to the land of opportunities someday. Instead, a policy consensus around introducing a new form of role of U.S. global leadership could prove a turning point for shifting to peaceful development endeavours.

Renewing America's role in Global Leadership

Leadership matters the most at the times of crisis, or during strategic susceptibility or when the international circumstances are fluid. What is less understood and needs attention, is the leadership that takes up a consolidated collective action during the phases of transition. With the current global scenario, increasing power competition especially between the United States and China, and emerging economies like Brazil, Argentina, Indonesia, India, South Korea fuels concerns on the gradually declining international cooperation. Many scholars of International Relations commonly understand and conclude that a leadership vacuum is likely to develop in response to the increasing global challenges. The necessity to bind the interests and responsibilities between dominant and emerging power will be difficult to achieve in the near future.

Devising an approach for America in a post-primacy world is no easy task. Neither unthinking retrenchment nor the muscular reassertion of old convictions will be effective remedy in the years ahead. The American leaders will have to re-establish the balance of American foreign policy and its priorities to tackle the most concrete and pressing challenges and respond to the crucial and urgent threats. That will mean sharpening their attention on managing competition with great power rivals and using their capacity to mobilize other players to address twenty-first-century challenges, that ought to be infused with a bold and unapologetic vision for free people and free and fair markets, with the United States being more attractive than it is today. The task ahead is to provide the kind of leadership that many around the world seek and that the American public can support. For the past two years, under the support of many international organisations, U.S. has worked with a diverse, bipartisan group of Americans and representatives from other countries to put together the broad outlines of a strategy for renewed U.S. leadership. The strategies to sustain the present international order are much the same as the strategies that created it. But they need to be adapted and updated to meet new challenges and take advantage of new opportunities.

The most critical test of American administration and its leader is working on the competition with the Asian giant China, but for U.S., Asia must remain its priority. Bilateral cooperation, web of regional alliances, and institutions that strengthen the bond should continue to be moderated. The primary aim is not to compete or contain China or force the allies to choose sides, rather it is to create a scenario wherein China's growth doesn't come at the expense of everyone else's security and prosperity. The irony is that former President Trump and many of his predecessors have so far shown no or limited scope to device a vision like this. In Asia, Trumps sole focus was on highlighting Beijing's unfair trade practices, energetic theft of intellectual property and continuing militarization of the South China Sea. Along with which he abandoned and attacked with America's NATO allies, Mexico, Japan, and Korea, the Trans-Pacific Partnership; a trade agreement designed to strengthen the US position in Asia.

India- U.S.: Balancing Leading Power

India-U.S. bilateral relations have developed into a "global strategic partnership", based on shared democratic values, and increasing convergence of interests on bilateral, regional, and global issues. The emphasis placed by the Government in India on development and good governance has created opportunity to reinvigorate bilateral ties and enhance cooperation under the motto --- "Chalein Saath Saath: Forward Together We Go", and "Sanjha Prayas, Sab ka Vikas" (Shared Effort, Progress for All) adopted during the first two summits of Prime Minister Modi and President Obama in September 2014 and January 2015 respectively. The summit level joint statement issued in June 2016 called the India-U.S. relationship "Enduring Global Partners in the 21st Century".

United States has an eminent footing on the global existence therefore it comes as no surprise that the gradience of the effects of the administration is felt far widely, to an extent, that it reaches to another largest democracy halfway around the world: India. Like the United States, India too has its varying points although of a very different sort. Prime Minister Narendra Modi enjoys a very strong electoral mandate and high popularity ratings, reinforced by major wins for his party in state elections. The country has a large and capable military experienced in dealing with a broad array of security challenges, it enjoys a wide international diplomatic presence, and it boasts a globally competitive space program. India's demographic profile is also favourable, with an expected increase in the working-age population for the next three decades. The United States is India's most important global partner. The U.S. believes that India is a significant source for trade. Both the countries are involved in a range of initiatives to advance their countries development. The administration of Donald Trump and Narendra Modi had pursued an association that was blended with care and attention for a long-term commitment. During the first meeting between the two diplomats in 2017, on priority basis focus was given to security indicating a continued commitment for a long-term defence relationship, but at the same time the way in which economic issues were addressed, it indicated a more transactional relationship in the coming years. Former President Donald Trump has always referred India as a "true friend", and never left a chance to appreciate how the relations between the two countries have never been stronger and better. Trump has an assumption that both the countries share a common interest on edging Chinese hegemony in Asia. During Trump Administration, the expectation from India were to outweigh China, believing that India will pursue a foreign policy that would accommodate larger U.S. interests. Whereas Modi's clarion call for India is to assume a balancing role, his vision envisages India becoming a traditional great power by its actions domestically and choices internationally, wanting to creating itself as an authentic great power— a conclusion for the desire of multipolarity at the global level.

Yet in the words of the Indian Prime Minster the relationship with the U.S. has been regarded as the "most important partnership of the 21st century". At multiple events PM Modi has announced that both leaders have held discussion on every important aspect of US-India partnership, be it defence and security, energy, strategic partnership, trade, or people to people ties, and have also decided to upgrade ties to "Comprehensive Global Strategic Partnership". He has also highlighted the role of the Indian diaspora in the US, commenting on how professionals or students have strengthened the people-to-people relations between the two countries, nourishing and deepening ties by contributing to the U.S. Economy.

Biden and India

For first time the United States of America has a president who has been the Chairman of the Senate Foreign Relations Committee. Joe Biden was at the forefront of international diplomacy and policy making as a senator and later as vice president. He has represented U.S. in almost every part of the world: post-Cold War Europe, Balkans, Russia, China, Iraq, Afghanistan, South Asia, Asia-Pacific, Middle East, Africa, and Latin America. Having played an important role in shaping U.S. foreign policy for years, President Biden understands that with China's rising might, the power balance in the world is fast shifting - increasingly becoming bipolar. This is where U.S. and Indian interests converge.

A Democrat administration in the US will probably be more rational, mature and form a stand towards India, that is of an ally and not as a member country of an informal group of countries against China on the issues of trade, climate change, oil, and defence exports. In many areas, the relations with the Biden Administration would be easier in comparison to the Trump's transactional view of foreign affairs. Trade negotiations and agreements during Biden's term is expected to be smoother, with his approach not being similar to that of Trump's White House approach. Also, on immigration and H-1B visas the path would be shinier. Tech companies both in the US and India will get much-needed relief when the visa issue is cleared. Dr Joshua White, Associate Professor in John Hopkins University School, believes that the Biden administration will prioritise India. The Democrats are particularly worried about the growing tension between India- Pakistan and how they will need to play an important role in preventing and mitigating crisis if it emerges. More to it is that Biden-Harris administration has been very vocal on protection of civil rights and liberties, raising expectations of not only the citizens of the U.S. but across the world, given Bidens pledge that his administration will "restore America's role and voice as a human rights champion on a global scale". Both President and Vice President have on record taken a stand that makes it very clear that they back a liberal India. Biden has on certain platforms expressed disapproval of the Citizen Amendment Act (CAA) and the National Register of Citizens (NRC), and Kamala Harris' Words on the abrogation of Article 370 should alert the Central Government of its actions: "We have to remind the Kashmiris that they are not alone in the world. We are keeping a track on the situation. There is a need to intervene if the situation demands."

All things considered, Biden should be good for India, even if he's less enthusiastic to see relations with India in the personalised format that Prime Minister Modi prefers, and see them more as diplomatic government-to-government relations.

Conclusion

Throughout the twentieth Century, the United States drove the greatest economic expansion with its innovations that the world had ever witnessed. All the American citizens enjoyed with higher wages, better standard of living and greater opportunities. Unfortunately, this scenario fizzled off. For years now, there has been a national debate on what went wrong. As the world globalized, the U.S. traded to a great extent, significantly more than what it had done historically. Was the competitiveness and resiliency; a result of increased trade, represented a core strategic challenge in shaping the U.S. leaders domestically and internationally? Has the changing landscape of global scenarios pushed the American Electorates to no longer accept 'American role' of a world policymaker, which they have taken for granted for years while transitioning towards being the most developed power in the world. Or the only clear success of remaining the most powerful leader in the most developed country would be without incurring huge costs and risks that America bore in the conflicts of the last century, maintaining the most appealing image of an unchallenged, compassionate global leadership based exclusively on American values and democratic politics. But it hasn't worked out that way.

For a brief period, America's relations with other countries were not guided by the conviction that U.S. leadership is good for the country itself and the world, but by Trump's transactional approach. Several experts and politicians who are exhausted, frustrated and disappointed by the Trump administration and his style of leadership, are plummeted and convinced for the Biden's approach to boost efforts to rebuild the country's flagging image in terms of global leadership and pose a winning stance with respect to its foreign policy. But the harsh reality is the fact that President Joe Biden has been elected at the time where the global economic supply chains and the domestic well-being of almost every country is diminishing and the U.S.- China competition has casted a spell in almost all the institutions of the third world countries. With the world order being 'out of order', it charms an opportunity for other nations to start playing off the superpowers and push forward for the changes they have always wanted to pursue, but most importantly rebuild the cadre of leaders that have the staying power to follow through, considering the domestic as well as global governance the centre of all they intend to do.

Refernces

- Kagan, Robert, Daaldar, H.Ivo, The U.S. can't afford to end its global leadership role,Brooking, Monday,April 25, 2016

  https://www.brookings.edu/blog/order-from-chaos/2016/04/25/the-u-s-cant-afford-to-end-its-global-leadership-role/

- Dewan, Angela, America's role as global leader all but died under Trump. The world was outgrowing it anyway, CNN, November 1, 2020

  https://edition.cnn.com/2020/11/01/world/trump-us-global-leadership-election-analysis- intl/index.html

- Immelman, Aubrey, Griebie, Marie Anne, The Personality Profile and Leadership Style of U.S. President Donald J. Trump in Office, Paper presented at the 43rd Annual Scientific Meeting of the International Society of Political Psychology, Germany, July 14–16, 2020

  https://www.researchgate.net/publication/343400256_The_Personality_Profile_and_Leadership_Style_of_US_President_Donald_J_Trump_in_Office

- Saidemand, Steve, Leader Personalities: Trump vs. Biden, Duck of Minerva, October 27,2020

  https://duckofminerva.com/2020/10/leader-personalities-trump-vs-biden.html

- Neely, Victoria, Residential Personality and Foreign Policymaking, Hofstra University

  https://www.hofstra.edu/pdf/library/neelyulrawinner2015.pdf

- Wike, Richard, The Trump era has seen a decline in America's global reputation, Fact Tank, November19, 2020

  https://www.pewresearch.org/fact-tank/2020/11/19/the-trump-era-has-seen-a-decline-in-americas-global-reputation/

- J.Burn, William, Assessing the role of the United States in the world, Carnegie Endowment for International Peace, February 27, 2019

  https://carnegieendowment.org/2019/02/27/assessing-role-of-united-states-in-world-pub-78465

- Kagan, Robert, Daaldar, H.Ivo, The U.S. can't afford to end its global leadership role,Brooking, Monday, April 25, 2016

  https://www.brookings.edu/blog/order-from-chaos/2016/04/25/the-u-s-cant-afford-to-end-its-global-leadership-role/

- A Brief on India-U.S. relations, Ministry of External Affairs

  https://www.mea.gov.in/Portal/ForeignRelation/India_US_brief.pdf

- Jaishankar, Dhruva, India and the United States in Trump era: Re-evaluating Bilateral and Global Relations, Foreign Policy at Brookings, Policy Paper 37, June 2017

  https://www.brookings.edu/research/india-and-the-united-states-in-the-trump-era-re-evaluating-bilateral-and-global-relations/

- India and US Upgrade Ties, Agree to Start Talks for ' Bigger' Trade Deal, TheWire, February 25, 2020

  https://thewire.in/diplomacy/donald-trump-narendra-modi-delhi-ties-trade-deal

- Guha, Seema, Joe Biden will be good for India, The Outlook, November 6, 2020

  https://www.outlookindia.com/website/story/opinion-joe-biden-will-be-good-for india/363704

- Vij, Shivam, Biden as president will be good for India, perhaps not that good for Modi, The Print, November 2, 2020

  https://theprint.in/opinion/joe-biden-president-good-for-india-not-for-narendra-modi/535649/

❐

India-US Climate Change Policy Relations

Manisha Sarade,
MNLU, II year Student

Evolution of India's Climate Change Policy – A Glimpse of The Last Three Decades

As soon as climate change occurred as a global disquiet in the 1990s, the issue was projected as a diplomatic problem for India, reinforced by a narrative around climate ethics entrenched in India's minimal role in triggering the accumulation of Greenhouse Gases (GHGs). Although this continues to be a prominent theme, this idea has, over time, been accompanied by other viewpoints as knowledge and concepts about climate change have advanced. These modifications are more prominent around ethics, ideas of climate influence, links to Indian disputes around energy transition, links to larger ideas of sustainability, and implications of Carbon Dioxide Removal (CDR) for India's debates on forest policy.

In 1972, the then Indian Prime Minister Indira Gandhi addressed the United Nations Conference on the Human Environment. This speech began an intellectual ritual in Indian climate policy that pits socio-economic development against environmental protection and indicts the developed countries of the North for producing worldwide environmental issues.[1] In 1992's Rio Earth Summit, the ideological grounding of India's climate policy was further put in an important report by the Centre for Science and Environment (CSE),

[1] Vihma, A., Mulugetta, Y. & Karlsson-Vinkhuyzen, S., 2011. Negotiating solidarity? The G77 through the prism of climate change negotiations. *Global Change, Peace & Security*, 23(3), pp.315–334

named 'Global Warming in an Unequal World'. The report indicted developed countries of "carbon colonialism".[2]The report contended that developed countries bear the accountability for climate change given their historical emissions and that per capita allocation of emissions should be the metric for distributing responsibility for climate mitigation.[3]

A study of Greenhouse Gas emissions from 1850 to 2012 observed that cumulative emissions in that timeline from the USA, European Union (EU) and China will contribute to 50 percent of the temperature rise by 2100 with emissions from the US, EU, and China being 20 percent, 17 percent, and 12 percent respectively. India's emissions in that same timeline contribute to mere 5 percent. In the UNFCCC, these alterations in historical responsibility for causing the issue were recognized through the expression 'Common but Differentiated Responsibilities' (CBDR) in Article 3 of the Convention.[4]

The historical responsibility of the North and per capita rights to the global carbon budget were swiftly taken up by India's climate delegates as the foundation of India's position in the first climate change negotiations.[5]In the initial years of India's climate policy beginning with the UNFCCC in 1992, India associated itself with the Group of 77 (G77), i.e. developing countries who required developed nations to take action on climate change while contending that developing nations might only take on voluntary commitments conditional on receipt of technology and finance transfers from industrialised nations.[6] The ethics of equity being mirrored in the UNFCCC at Rio in 1992 through the phrases CBDR and Respective Capabilities (RC) were thus significant triumphs for developing nations and Indian negotiators claim significant influence over this intervention.

Subsequently, India continued to play a dynamic part in global climate negotiations and its endeavours were seen as vital to securing the Berlin mandate in 1995 which would direct two years of negotiating procedures for the legal instrument fixated on mitigation actions by developed countries. Eventually, the negotiations led to the Kyoto Protocol in 1997, which obligated Annex I parties of the UNFCCC, i.e., developed countries, to pledge to "quantified emission limitation and reduction objectives" while developing nations such

---

[2] Agarwal, A. &Narain, S., 1991. Global Warming in an Unequal World: A Case of Environmental Colonialism, New Delhi.

[3] Rocha, M. et al., 2015. Historical Responsibility for Climate Change – from countries emissions to contribution to temperature increase, Available at:http://climateanalytics.org/files/historical_responsibility_report_nov_2015.pdf [Accessed February 13, 2021].

[4] UNFCCC, 1992. Full Text of the Convention, Available at: https://unfccc.int/resource/docs/convkp/conveng.pdf.

[5] Dubash, N.K., 2013b. The politics of climate change in india: Narratives of equity and cobenefits. *Wiley Interdisciplinary Reviews: Climate Change*, 4(3), pp.191–201.

6 Dasgupta, C., 2012. Present at the creation: the making of the UN Framework Convention on Climate Change. In N. Dubash, ed. Handbook of climate change and India: development, politics and governance. New Delhi: Routledge.

as India were relieved from legally obligatory commitments.[7] For other G77 nations, and India, the Kyoto Protocol highlighted the constant significance of the distinction between developed and developing nations regarding the weight of responsibility for climate action. India was able to effectively protect its room for socio-economic development, at the same time propelling developed countries to take on more responsibilities.

The first commitment period of the Kyoto Protocol was to run from 2008-2012. Negotiations throughout 2007-2009 concentrated on the agreement of a post-2012 climate governance regime. During this period, high economic growth in the initial years of the new millennium for developing countries such as China, Brazil, India and South Africa (collectively denoted as BASIC) had led to a growing anticipation on these countries to take the centre stage in shaping the upshots of global governance.[8]These countries started to be labelled 'emerging economies'. They were also differentiated from the G77[9] bloc based on their economic power and carbon footprint. As a consequence of their economic development, there was some pressure to take on climate commitments. So, the BASIC countries started to follow negotiating strategies, separately from the G77[10]and more carefully synchronize their climate policies with each-other.

What came as a surprise at Conference of Parties (COP) 13 in Bali in 2007, India acknowledged that developing countries should join in the worldwide mitigation effort, at best on a voluntary basis matched with their abilities.[11] On a domestic level, India also announced its National Action Plan on Climate Change (NAPCC) in 2008. Also, ahead of the Copenhagen summit in late 2009, India along with other BASIC countries announced voluntary targets to lessen the emissions intensity of its GDP by 20-25 percent against 2005 levels by 2020 and never surpass the per capita emissions of Annex I countries. More importantly, at the Kyoto Protocol negotiations, India had openlydeclined any idea of voluntary commitments. In due course, the COP summit at Copenhagen was a let-downwith regard toreaching upon a new climate agreement to substitute the Kyoto Protocol.

---

[7] UNFCCC, 1997. Kyoto Protocol. Available at: https://unfccc.int/resource/docs/convkp/kpeng.html [Accessed February 13, 2021].

[8] Hallding, K. et al., 2013. Rising powers: the evolving role of BASIC countries. Climate Policy, 13(5), pp.608–631. Available at: http://dx.doi.org/10.1080/14693062.2013.822654%5Cn.

[9] The G77 does not include China but China has frequentlylinked itself with the G77 on many issues resulting in the grouping sometimes being termed G77+China.

[10] Kasa, S., Gullberg, A.T. &Heggelund, G., 2008. The Group of 77 in the international climate negotiations: Recent developments and future directions. International Environmental Agreements: Politics, Law and Economics, 8(2), pp.113–127.

[11] Michaelowa, K. &Michaelowa, A., 2012. India as an emerging power in international climate negotiations. Climate Policy, 12(January 2013), pp.575–590.

At COP 19 in Warsaw in 2013, the concept of Nationally Determined Commitments was introduced and ultimately led to the final form of Intended Nationally Determined Contributions (INDCs) which was espoused by countries at COP 20 in Lima. Preceding COP 21 in Paris, all countries were requested to submit INDCs highlighting their plans for climate action up to 2030.India, in its NDCsubmitted in October 2015, outlined its commitment to installationof clean energy capacity equivalent to 40 percent of the total installed electrical capacity in the country by 2030, vowed to decrease the carbon intensity of its economy by 33-35 percent by 2030 compared to 2005 levels, and declared an objective to set up carbon sinks worth an additional 2.5 to 3 billion tonnes of Carbon Dioxide equivalent through additional forest and tree cover by 2030. The Indian Government put across its NDC as 'fair and ambitious' even though India's involvementin climate change is 'limited'. India also set up the global solar alliance observing COP 21, and is furthering for enlargement of its renewable energy program. Prime Minister Modi has declared a domestic objective of 175 GW renewable energy by 2022 in 2014, which if accomplished would further establish India's headship in global climate action.[12]

Climate Crisis — A New Realm For Us-India Cooperation

The United States (US) and India constitute for nearly 20 percent of global GHG emissions. While the two countries vary distinctly in both per capita emissions and incomes, India and the US should take up roles as per their capabilities to bring about solutions that can enhance economic development and alleviate the costs of climate change. Both the US and India have taken important steps together to further their strategy and partnership in the realm of climate action and policy. Yet, current efforts bank mainly on a gradational approach to addressing climate change, that are inadequate. As the world fights COVID-19 pandemic, we are recapped with the human and economic limitations linked with frail international collaboration, deferred action, and the scarcity of investments in paramount infrastructure and capabilities. Climate-generated disasters may make the current pandemic look docile, and the world could overlook this hazard at its own risk. Therefore, it is imperative for India and the US to advance efforts in bringing about structural change, overcoming institutional bars, and overcome the inactivityimpeding green growth and development.

[12] Allianz Climate Solutions, New Climate Institute &Germanwatch, 2017. *What do current policy developments in China, India and the US mean for investing in renewables?*Available at: https://newclimateinstitute.files.wordpress.com/2017/04/allianz-climate-and-energy-monitor-deep-dive-2017.pdf [Accessed February13, 2021]

US withdrawal from Paris Agreement – Implications for India

On November 4, 2020, the United States initiated the course of withdrawing from the Paris Agreement, informing the United Nations of its withdrawal from the climate deal. A press release from a US State Department said that the withdrawal will come into operation one year after the delivery of the notification. Once it exits, the US will be the only non-signatory in this protocol. During his presidential campaign in 2016, Donald Trump had said the Paris Agreement was "unfair" to US interests and assured to sign out of the Agreement if he was elected.

His dispute emanated from his impression that China and India produce more CO2 emissions than the United States, and asserted that the deal punishes theU.S. instead of those countries. A differingview to the president's contentionwas offered in the 2015 EuropeanCommission's Emissions Database for Global Atmospheric Research. It reported that indeed Chinaproduces the globe's highest level of CO2 emissions (total kilotons), but the country that immediatelyfollows is the U.S. and not India. The United States' *per capital* CO2 emissions exceed thejoint total of both China and India at 16.07 tons *per individual* compared to 7.73 and 1.87tons per individual respectively. Therefore, while the USmay not be the onlyculpritof CO2 emissions, they definitely contribute a huge amount and one cannot disregardthis contribution.

In 2015, India played a decisive role in forming the agreement through the BRICS (Brazil, Russia, India, China, South Africa) and LMDC (Like-Minded Developing Countries) country groups. In October 2015, before the annual Conference of Parties in Paris, India had declared its aspiring INDCs. It promised a decrease in its emissions concentration of its Gross Domestic Product by 33 to 35 per cent by 2030, below 2005 levels. Importantly, it declared that by 2030, it would raise the share of non-fossil fuels in the installed energy capacity to 40 per cent. Additionally, it set a mark of creating an additional carbon sink to absorb 2.5 to 3 billion tonnes of carbon dioxide by raising its forest and tree cover by 2030.

India's climate action designwill remain as per the idea even as they termed the US departure as a measure that would result inissues in reducing emissions globally."We have already said that we stand by the agreement and we will fully implement our INDCs, so that will not change with the position of the US," remarked Ravi Shankar Prasad, Additional Secretary, Ministry of Environment, Forest and Climate Change and the country's main negotiator at the 2019 annual climate conference that too place in Madrid, Spain.He added that the departure of the United States is a global problem as they are the prime historic emitters and high-volume accumulators of GHGs. "Mitigation is important and if they do not cut their emissions drastically, it will affect all of us. They have also reduced their funding. Though it does not affect our ongoing projects, having more international funding through Green Climate

Fund is good for the agreement," Ravi Shankar Prasad stated.Ajay Mathur, Director-General of The Energy and Research Institute (TERI) and country's key spokesperson at the 2015 Paris conference highlighted that the United States continues to be a member of the UNFCCC, under which the Paris agreement was sanctioned, and therefore will partake in the yearly conferences where countries discuss on climate change.

Biden-Harris Administration's strategy towards Climate Cooperation with India

With the nomination of John Kerry as Special Presidential Envoy for Climate, the Biden-Harris Administration is hinting at their commitment towards climate action in the United States and globally. Highlighting the climate exigency by the new administration is an imperative to drive worldwide determination in the prologue to the fifth anniversary of the Paris Agreement. Undoubtedly, no other country presents a bigger opportunity for climate cooperation for the Biden-Harris Administration than India.Collaborating on climate change with India should be an early move for the Biden-Harris Administration as it makes climate change anurgencyin USA's foreign policy.

Huge damage has been done at the domestic level and to international relationships by the United States backpedalling on climate measures over the last four years. The international community[13] has carried the burden of a U.S. government going in the mistakenway on climate action. Mending these relationships won't be facile. The Biden-Harris Administration has a lot of work in hand ahead to recuperate climate cooperation and to work toward attaining the Intergovernmental Panel on Climate Change's call for the "rapid, far-reaching and unprecedented changes"[14]required to restrict global warming to 1.5°C.

One hopeful place to begin rebuilding trust globally for the USA is with India. Despite the last four years, the networks between people, the private sector, civil society, states, and other actors between the world's two largest democracies continues to be firm. Economic progress, job growth, climate change, trade, and national security are pressingissues for both nations.Indian Prime Minister Modi highlighted India's strong commitment[15] to the Indo-US strategic partnership and shared priorities— "COVID-19 pandemic, climate change, and cooperation in the Indo-Pacific Region."

---

13 Guy, B., Schmidt, J. 2020. An International Climate Agenda for the Biden Administration. NRDC. Available at: https://www.nrdc.org/experts/jake-schmidt/international-climate-agenda-biden-administration.[Accessed February 14, 2021].

14 IPCC, 2018. Summary for Policymakers of IPCC Special Report on Global Warming of 1.5°C approved by governments. Available at:https://www.ipcc.ch/2018/10/08/summary-for-policymakers-of-ipcc-special-report-on-global-warming-of-1-5c-approved-by-governments/ [Accessed February 14, 2021].

15 Ibid.

It is projected that India's energy requirements and emissions in a business-as-usualsituationwill doubleby 2050, despite the current COVID-19 economic slump. While per capita emissions are little at present, India is currently the third largest single-country emitter of GHGs and has the second largest population in the world at over 1.3 billion. India's metropolises are swiftly urbanizing making sustainable cities with healthy communities a central priority.

India is a frontrunner in clean energy, particularly solar and wind energy. India is heading in the right direction to meet two of its Paris Agreement targets[16]—to decrease emission intensity by 33% to 35% of its gross domestic product by 2030 from 2005 levels and accomplish 40% of installed power capacity from non-fossil fuels by 2030. The country aims to install an ambitious 175 gigawatts (GW) of renewable energy by 2022 and 450 GW by 2030—20% more than India's current electricity capacity of 372 GW. India is halfway on the road to meeting its 175 GW by 2022 goal, with renewables reaching 89 GW, representing 23% of India's total installed capacity. On its third target, generating an additional 3 billion ton "carbon sink" by 2030, the Indian government identifies the necessity to increase efforts.India is a highly influential in international negotiations. India is efficaciously the lead representative among the developing world. Accomplishingprolific U.S.-India bilateral cooperation can go a long way in moving toward a common pathway to climate change, with respect to the pressures of global inequality.

The United States and India have established scientific and research partnerships that have resulted in advances in climate science and clean energy advancement. Both countries accommodate a giant market for clean energy technologies and investment prospects. The people of the US and India have a shared camaraderie from a big Indian diaspora in the US as well as many knowledge-exchange programs, for instance the Nehru-Fulbright program and the Fulbright-Kalam Climate Fellowship. Thus, India is an indispensable partner to the United States in making growth on climate change.

To facilitate climate cooperation with India, the US Administration should schedule a high-level US-India bilateral summit with climate change as thedominant agenda issue. Extending the former U.S.-India Joint Working groups and 2016 Joint Statement: The United States and India: Enduring Global Partners in the 21st Century[17], the countries should evaluate the programs to revitalise and generatenovel programs.

---

[16] NRDC, 2020. The Road from Paris: India's Progress Towards Its Climate Pledge. Available at: https://www.nrdc.org/sites/default/files/road-from-paris-202009.pdf [Accessed February 14, 2021].

[17] The White House, Office of the Press Secretary, 2016. JOINT STATEMENT: The United States and India: Enduring Global Partners in the 21st Century. Available at:https://obamawhitehouse.archives.gov/the-press-office/2016/06/07/joint-statement-united-states-and-india-enduring-global-partners-21st. [Accessed February 14, 2021].

Clean energy plans should be enlarged, for instance, the Partnership to Advance Clean Energy, concentrated on energy effectiveness and solar and wind energy, as well as electric vehicles, battery storage and renewable grid-integration that align with India's preferences. New zones for cooperation should be established, such as climate resilience, infrastructure, sustainable finance, air quality, electric mobility, and others. Global partnerships should be reinforced, as well aslarger ambition under the Paris Agreement, ratification of Montreal Protocol's Kigali Amendment to slow down hazardous hydrofluorocarbons (HFCs), development of the International Solar Alliance (ISA), growth of USAID cooperation on energy, facilitating Mission Innovation, and so on. Climate finance should also be increased sharply,encompassing investments and trade with India and evolving markets to assist clean energy through the International Development Finance Corporation (IDFC), U.S. Export-Import bank and other international forums, such as the Green Climate Fund.Further, Subnational climate action at the state- and city-levels should be nurturedwith effective funding create opportunities forcapacity building and execution on the ground.

The rampant COVID-19 emergency in both countries traverses with majorproblems such as growth rate of the economy, public health structures, employment, and climate change. Potentially,plans on green inducement, climate resilience, and disaster management could aidstrengthen a green and resilient recovery. Improved government action on climate change, besides climate-oriented agencies to largergovernment involvement, including national security, economic governance, bilateral diplomacy, trade, etc., can also play a role in furthering avigorous climate relationship between the United States and India.

At this critical juncture with the globe facing numerous intimidations – Pandemic, economic despair, and the climate crisis; the world requires leadership, support, assistance, cooperation and action, exclusively from two of the world's topmost energy consumers. A strong U.S.-India strategic cooperation on climate change is critical for boosting and promoting low-carbon economies, fostering energy security, and devising mechanisms for the worst consequences and implications of climate change. Robust,combined, cooperative and well-planned action can help put us on a pathway to a better tomorrow, a more sustainable future that surges economic growth, generates employment and improves the life of humanity at large.

References

- Agarwal, A. &Narain, S., 1991. *Global Warming in an Unequal World: A Case of Environmental Colonialism*, New Delhi.
- Allianz Climate Solutions, New Climate Institute &Germanwatch, 2017. *What do current policy developments in China, India and the US mean for investing in*

- Dasgupta, C., 2012. Present at the creation: the making of the UN Framework Convention on Climate Change. In N. Dubash, ed. *Handbook of climate change and India: development, politics and governance.* New Delhi: Routledge.
- Dubash, N.K., 2013b. The politics of climate change in india: Narratives of equity and cobenefits. *Wiley Interdisciplinary Reviews: Climate Change*, 4(3), pp.191–201.
- Guy, B., Schmidt, J. 2020. An International Climate Agenda for the Biden Administration. *NRDC.* Available at: https://www.nrdc.org/experts/jake-schmidt/international-climate-agenda-biden-administration.[Accessed February 14, 2021].
- Hallding, K. et al., 2013. Rising powers: the evolving role of BASIC countries. *Climate Policy*, 13(5), pp.608–631. Available at: http://dx.doi.org/10.1080/14693062.2013.822654%5Cn.
- IPCC, 2018. Summary for Policymakers of IPCC Special Report on Global Warming of 1.5°C approved by governments. Available at: https://www.ipcc.ch/2018/10/08/summary-for-policymakers-of-ipcc-special-report-on-global-warming-of-1-5c-approved-by-governments/ [Accessed February 14, 2021].
- Kasa, S., Gullberg, A.T. &Heggelund, G., 2008. The Group of 77 in the international climate negotiations: Recent developments and future directions. *International Environmental Agreements: Politics, Law and Economics*, 8(2), pp.113–127.
- Michaelowa, K. &Michaelowa, A., 2012. India as an emerging power in international climate negotiations. *Climate Policy*, 12(January 2013), pp.575–590.
- NRDC, 2020. The Road from Paris: India's Progress Towards Its Climate Pledge. Available at: https://www.nrdc.org/sites/default/files/road-from-paris-202009.pdf [Accessed February 14, 2021].
- *renewables?* Available at: https://newclimateinstitute.files.wordpress.com/2017/04/allianz-climate-and-energy-monitor-deep-dive-2017.pdf [Accessed February 13, 2021]
- Rocha, M. et al., 2015. *Historical Responsibility for Climate Change – from countries emissions to contribution to temperature increase*, Available at: http://climateanalytics.org/files/historical_responsibility_report_nov_2015.pdf [Accessed February 13, 2021].
- The White House, Office of the Press Secretary, 2016. JOINT STATEMENT: The United States and India: Enduring Global Partners in the 21st Century. Available at: https://obamawhitehouse.archives.gov/the-press-office/2016/06/07/joint-statement-united-states-and-india-enduring-global-partners-21st. [Accessed February 14, 2021].

- UNFCCC, 1992. *Full Text of the Convention*, Available at: https://unfccc.int/resource/docs/convkp/conveng.pdf.
- UNFCCC, 1997. Kyoto Protocol. Available at:https://unfccc.int/resource/docs/convkp/kpeng.html [Accessed February 13, 2021].
- Vihma, A., Mulugetta, Y. & Karlsson-Vinkhuyzen, S., 2011. Negotiating solidarity? The G77 through the prism of climate change negotiations. *Global Change, Peace & Security*, 23(3), pp.315–334

❐

Research, Theory, and Pedagogy in the Indo-US Relations

Dr. Tirthesh Nandan,
Senior Journalist, ABP News

Introduction

There is an old saying. One should use as many languages to be properly understood. Choice of the right word is particularly important in diplomacy. The 2014 Indo-US summit when Indian Prime Minister Narendra Modi met the then US President Barack Obama somehow proved this proposition. The two countries incorporated few Hindi phrases in the Vision Statement for the Indo-US Strategic Partnership. During the September 2014 meeting of PM Modi and Obama the phrase was 'Chalein Saath Saath'- meaning together we go forward. "Our strategic partnership rests on our shared mission to provide equal opportunity for our people through democracy and freedom," a White House release after the meeting elaborated.[1]

In the January 2015 meeting between these two leaders 'Sanjha Prayaas, Sabka Vikaas - Shared Effort, Progress for All,' was the statement declaring the intent of friendship. "Each step we take to strengthen the relationship is a step towards shaping international security, regional and global peace, prosperity and stability for years to come," read the statement of Prime Minister's Office in India.[2] The use of Hindi phrases in two consecutive summit statements is so far were rare in the diplomatic history of both countries. Addressing the news

[1] Vision Statement for the U.S.-India Strategic Partnership, White House release September 29, 2014, available at URL: https://obamawhitehouse.archives.gov/the-press-office/2014/09/29/vision-statement-us-india-strategic-partnership-chalein-saath-saath-forw, accessed on 2 December 2018

[2] India-U.S. Delhi Declaration of Friendship, Press Information Bureau, Government of India, Prime Minister's Office, January 25, 2015, available at URL: http://pib.nic.in/newsite/PrintRelease.aspx?relid=114954, accessed on 30 November 2018

conference after the summit in New Delhi, President Obama spoke few lines in the Hindi. "Namaste. Mera Pyaar Bhara Namaskar- Hello, my greetings with affection", was his opening remark at a news conference.

In the town hall meeting at the Siri Fort Auditorium in New Delhi, Obama charmed everyone by quoting Shah Rukh Khan's famous line 'Senorita, bade bade deshon mein...'. This was from a blockbuster Bollywood movie Dilwale Dulhania Le Jayenge.

Experts believe that the incorporation of Hindi phrases in the diplomatic engagement is the sign of 'Soft power' equation. Harvard University's professor and political scientist Joseph Nye coined the term 'Soft power' in the late 1980s. However, tapping the soft power by the US government is not a recent phenomenon. Records suggest that pushing diplomacy through 'soft power' approach is a tried and tested formula which is being used for over 100 years. According to Nye, "The soft power of a country rests primarily on three resources: its culture (in places where it is attractive to others), its political values (when it lives up to them at home and abroad), and its foreign policies (when they are seen as legitimate and having moral authority)."[3] Through the use of soft power, a country tries to win the hearts and minds of people. In recent years the Indo-US relations have moved far ahead on a friendly tracks. Starting from the state of 'distrust' in the Cold War era, today the two countries are partners in strategic, political, economic, science and cultural diplomacy. The rise of Indian community in the US has had a profound impact on US diplomatic engagements with New Delhi. The other reason is India's booming economy - the country has shed the tag of 'Hindu rate of growth' and is now among the fastest growing major economies.

Language is a sine qua non of communication. India and the US have rich language sources spoken by diverse people. According to the Indian Census of 2011, the number of mother tongues or dialect spoken in India is 19,569.[4] Nine out of every ten Indian identifies his/her mother tongue as one of the 22 scheduled languages. The US Census Bureau in its 2015 report states that at least 350 languages are spoken in their country.[5]

---

3 Lin Li & Leng Hongtao, "Joseph Nye's Soft Power Theory and Its Revelation Towards Ideological and Political Education", Humanities and Social Sciences 2017; 5(2): 69-74, available at URL: http://article.sciencepublishinggroup.com/pdf/10.11648.j.hss.20170502.13.pdf, accessed on 22 November 2018

4 Language - India, States and Union Territories, (Table C-16) Census of India 2011, Paper 1 of 2018, published by Office of the Registrar General, India, available at URL: http://www.censusindia.gov.in/2011Census/C-16_25062018_NEW.pdf, p. 4., accessed on 13 November 2018

5 Press release of US Census Bureau in 2015, "Census Bureau Reports at Least 350 Languages Spoken in U.S. Homes", available at URL: https://www.census.gov/newsroom/press-releases/2015/cb15-185.html, accessed on 14 November 2018

So, what is the reason behind using Hindi phrase in the diplomatic text? "A country can co-opt the cooperation of others if its culture, political ideals, institutions, and broad domestic and external policies seem attractive; the country will have to exert less political capital than if it had to use coercion or payments."[6]

Diplomatically, Indo-US relations grew stronger only in the first decade of the 21st century. But India has made its connection to the American mind in the middle of the 19th century. An average American was aware of India during the rule of East India Company and the subsequent regime of British Crown that followed the Company and the control of several Maharajas and Zamindars.

Americans Academic Interest in India

The American universities in the early decades of the 19th century started a global curriculum by 1830s and included the languages and philosophies of world's oldest civilization in their curriculum. In the 19th century, there was literally no connection between India and the United States. Sanskrit language, Indian religion, and philosophy became the gateway of American academia connection to India. The American connect to India started with teaching of Sanskrit in 1836 at the City University of New York. Isaac Nordheimer taught the subject at the City University of New York and become a pioneer in this field. The earlier teachers in the United States, who taught Indian languages, neither had a background on India, nor they had visited the country. Nordheimer studied Sanskrit as a part of philology course at the University of Munich in Germany.

Sanskrit had already captured the imagination of Germans during the early 19th century. A noticeable publication (first book) of German scholar Dr. Freidrich Rosen (1805-1837), Rigveda Samhita, came after his death in 1838. Rosen studied Sanskrit at Berlin. He wrote his thesis in 1826 on Specimen of the Chief Sanskrit Roots. Another German scholar, Rudolph von Roth (1821-1895) wrote a book titled 'On the Literature and History of the Veda'. Freidrich Max Mueller (1823-1900) whose contribution to Vedic studies and Sanskrit language is significantly hailed needs to introduction in India or the western world.

The early exponents of Sanskrit language in the United States studied in Germany. The Sanskrit language was part of American Oriental Society which was formed in 1842 in Boston. Soon the Orientalism was to transform into a professional discipline. In 1841 Professor Edward Elbridge Salisbury inducted Sanskrit as a language in the curriculum of Yale University. The appointment

[6] Bush, Richard C., On the Eve of Obama's Inauguration: American Soft Power in Asia, Op-Ed in *Brookings*, Monday, January 12, 2009, available at URL: https://www.brookings.edu/opinions/on-the-eve-of-obamas-inauguration-american-soft-power-in-asia/, accessed on 19 November 2018

for the chair for Arabic and Sanskrit was first of its kind in the United States. Salisbury, who had had studied Arabic in Paris and Sanskrit in Berlin was one of the earliest members of the American Oriental Society. Salisbury's contribution to the Society and the Journal of the American Oriental Society is seminal in the growth of Sanskrit in America and US academia's future connection with India.

The academic interest on India grew after the Yale University's pioneering Sanskrit programme. What Sanskrit gave to the United States? It gave a pathway to understand the rich literature, history, religion, and the various aspects of Indian culture.

However, the US curriculum on Sanskrit was not evolved from the Indian tradition. American scholars emulated the German philological tradition, built upon a scientific approach to grammar and linguistic analysis.[7] Benjamin R. Foster wrote about Salisbury contribution in his 1997 article. "We must remember that in 1841 there was no such entity as the 'professional scholar' as the term is now understood; there were no universities, no research in the colleges, no graduate schools or degrees; no 'doctrine of expertise' in higher education or academic specialization; no professional societies or periodicals in what are now called the humanities ... no 'research libraries' with collections of Orientalist books, periodicals or manuscripts," he wrote.[8]

Salisbury had two students who studied Sanskrit under him - James Hadley and William Dwight Whitney. The latter succeeded Salisbury as professor of Sanskrit at Yale when first separate Chair of Sanskrit was created in 1854. Among the main works produced by Whitney included, "A Sanskrit Grammar" in 1879, and "The Roots, Verb-forms and Primary Derivatives of the Sanskrit Language" in 1885.

In 1856, Whitney edited the Atharvaveda-Samhita with the German Sanskritist Scholar Rudolph von Roth that was published from Berlin in 1856, another German connection to the Sanskrit language in the United States. Whitney popularized the Sanskrit courses in the United States. His students spread the language to other universities of the United States in the second half of the 19th century. It was like a domino effect, as one university after another introducing Sanskrit language. The second half of the nineteenth-century was a moment in the intellectual history of America during which Sanskrit seemed to offer a new means of intellectual and cultural independence from Europe.[9]

---

[7] Sinha, Mishka, "Orienting America: Sanskrit and Modern Scholarship in the United States, 1836-1894", in Anna Bernard, Ziad El-Marsafy, David Atwell (eds.), *Debating Orientalism*, Palgrave Macmillan 2013, P. 80

[8] Yale marks 175th anniversary of Arabic and Islamic studies with exhibit, public events, September 5, 2016, available at URL: https://cmes.macmillan.yale.edu/news/yale-marks-175th-anniversary-arabic-and-islamic-studies-exhibit-public-events, accessed on 19 November 2018

[9] Sinha, p.78

James Morris Whiton earned his doctorate in 1861 from the Yale University in 'Classics.' He was one of the three candidates to be awarded Ph.Ds in the United States. Whiton's doctorate is important because he took Sanskrit as one of the papers. His final examinations included Sanskrit apart from Latin, Greek and German. He had studied Sanskrit under Professor Whitney. Charles Rockwell Lanman, another student of Whitney taught Sanskrit at Johns Hopkins University from 1877-1880. He then moved to Harvard, becoming University's first Wales Professor of Sanskrit in the Department of Indo-Iranian Studies. Maurice Bloomfield, a student of Whitney, replaced Lanman at John Hopkins. Lanman was instrumental in publishing first edition of Sanskrit Reader- a standard text for English-speaking students. The religion of the Veda: the ancient religion of India (from Rig-Veda to Upanishads) is another seminal book written by Maurice Bloomfield. The first US Diplomat who had a background in Sanskrit was William Woodville Rockhill (1854-1914). He had studied Tibetan and Sanskrit. It is believed that Rockhill referred to William Dwight Whitney for any Sanskrit language book.

Whitney was instrumental in popularizing Sanskrit in the 19th century America. This coincided with the period when the country was emerging as the world's intellectual capital. The burgeoning intellectual base took interest in Indian culture, philosophy, and religions. Ralph Waldo Emerson and Henry David Thoreau studied Indian philosophy. Emerson was a towering personality who took serious exploration in the Indian philosophy. Emerson also inspired Thoreau who extensively read Hindu scriptures including the Bhagavad Gita. Thoreau published selected passages from the Laws of Manu from a French version of the Sanskrit Harivansa in The Dial.

From the East-Coast at Yale University in New Haven, Connecticut, Sanskrit spread to other regions of the US. In the Midwestern US states, the first Sanskrit course at the University of Michigan was offered in 1879, by Calvin Thomas. It was followed by University of Chicago where first classes on Sanskrit were held in 1892. Carl Darling Buck taught Sanskrit at the Chicago University. The University also held numerous Sanskrit and Indic philology books during 1892. At another east state, University of Pennsylvania started Sanskrit teaching in 1890 and had a full chair by 1912. Franklin Edgerton was appointed Sanskrit chair and he continued till 1926.

Sanskrit made further inroads and reached the West-Coast in 1897 when the language was inducted in the curriculum of University of California, Berkeley. Almost a decade later, Arthur Ryder joined the university as an instructor of Sanskrit language and went on to become professor. When hardly one thousand Indian immigrants were present in the United States, Ryder took pains to translate Kalidas famous works 'Shakuntala' and 'Meghaduta' in English. He also translated Panchatantra, the Hitopadesha, the Mahabharata, and the works of Bhartrihari.

In 1899, the American Oriental Society (AOS) created a special section within the Society for the historical study of religions and India was well represented here, too.[10]

Sanskrit fascinated American Orientalists. "Through Sanskrit teaching, they wanted to understand "the original source-language of the civilized world," a central aim of the contemporary comparative philology. In 1900, seven American universities comprised the "Sanskrit Club": Yale, Harvard, Johns Hopkins, Penn, Columbia, California, and Chicago."[11] To quote Stephen N. Hay: "The writings of Emerson, Thoreau, Whitman and of the Sanskritists Hopkins, Lanman and Whitney, helped instill in 19th century Americans a respect for India's cultural heritage.[12] The University of Michigan writes the need of Sanskrit as a language, "The historical understanding of languages such as English requires some understanding of Sanskrit."[13]

Edward D. Perry was University of Columbia's first professor of Sanskrit in 1891. His book, 'A Sanskrit Primer' in 1885 provides a complete introduction to the language.

The School of Theosophy founded in 1900 in Point Loma, California by the Theosophical University also offered courses in Sanskrit literature. Charles Johnston was the mainstay of Sanskrit studies in the University. Born in Dublin, Johnston later immigrated to the United States, and also advertised the Sanskrit course on the inside back cover of Theosophy magazine published in September 1897. He also translated the Upanishads, the Bhagavad Gita, the Yoga Sutras and the works of Sankaracharya into English.

The Connect to India – From 1900 to 1947

The 19th century interest in India among American scholars emanated from Sanskrit and was influenced by German scholars. The approach was different in the 20th century. Now, the American researchers took active interest in India by visiting the country then ruled by the British. Starting from Sanskrit, they were now curious about many more subjects that the ancient civilization was offering. Some of the Indian Maharaja took active interest in the US education and its content. The concept of library in India was borrowed from American Universities. The Baroda state among the pioneers. In 1910 Maharaja Sayyaji Rao Gayakwad, the ruler of the Erstwhile Baroda State invited American Librarian WA Borden who was based in New Haven. During

[10] Novetzke, Christian Lee (2006), "The Study of Indian Religions in the US Academy", *India Review*, 5:1, pp. 91-121

[11] South Asia at Chicago: Fifty Years of Scholarship, Institutional history - World War II and Its Aftermath, available at URL: https://www.lib.uchicago.edu/e/su/southasia/50yrs1.html, accessed on 28 November 2018

[12] Stephen N. Hay, "Ravindranath Tagore in America," *American Quarterly*, No. 3 (Fall 1962): p. 439.

[13] https://lsa.umich.edu/asian/language-and-academic-programs/south-asian-programs.html

his three year tenure starting from 1910, Borden established a central library and trained a number of city librarians. Hence kick starting India's library movement.

American scholars of that period made a priority to visit India to explore subjects that stretched far beyond Sanskrit. James B. Pratt made his first trip to India in 1913-14 to study Buddhism. Pratt, a philosopher from Williams College made several follow-up trips in the decade of the 1920s and 1930s. Helen Moore Johnson became a scholar of Jainism with her trips to western India over a period of more than thirty years. John Clark Archer, professor of comparative religion at Yale, is known for his study of Sikhism. He visited Amritsar in 1937 to research for his book on the religion. In 1937-38, David Mandelbaum visited India for ethnographic work.

The malaria research was sponsored in the 1930s by the Rockefeller Foundation. It was one of the earliest American foundations to contribute to the development of public health in India. The foundation provided funding for the establishment of an All India School of Hygiene and Public Health in 1932. The foundation also helped in starting nursing education in India. Such academic engagements continued despite there was no full diplomatic ties between the two nations.

William Norman Brown was among the first Americans who studied Sanskrit in India. In 1926, he took over from Franklin Edgerton, popularising Indian studies on the University of Pennsylvania campus. Brown was the founder of the first academic department of South Asian Studies at the University of Pennsylvania and the United States.

Brown visited India as a young boy with his parents in 1900 as a part of the missionary of the Christian Church. He studied in the schools at Harda and Jubbulpore, Central Provinces, learned Hindi language and enjoyed folk tales. The Brown family returned to the United States in five years after establishing a lifelong connection with the country. His father George William Brown was also a scholar of Sanskrit and Hindi. His son, Norman Brown, completed his Ph.D. in Sanskrit studies under Maurice Bloomfield and topic for his doctoral thesis was 'Panchantantra and Modern Indian Folklore.'Brown wrote, "India and Humanistic Studies in America" as an introduction to a survey of the field "Indic Studies" commissioned by the American Council of Learned Societies. His work was published in the society's 1938 bulletin. By 1935, the University of Pennsylvania had about 2,700 manuscripts on Indic language, making it the largest collection of manuscripts in America at that point in time.

In the 1940s, Brown knew that India would soon gain its freedom from the British; he asked his colleagues in 1939, "It takes no gift of prophecy to predict that [during the second half of the twentieth century] the world will include a vigorous India, possibly politically free, conceivably a dominant power in the Orient, and certainly intellectually vital and productive. How can Americans who have never met India in their educational experience be expected to live intelligently in such a world."[14]

During World War II several thousands of American soldiers were stationed in India. By the end of 1942 alone, 17,000 American troops had arrived in India. They were posted in Calcutta, other parts of Bengal, Assam, Manipur, and Nagaland. In another three years more troops came from America. Naturally they had to be acclimatized with the Indian subcontinent. The American troops had to be versed with Indian condition and taught Hindustani. In total, the Second World War took 100,000 Americans to South Asia from 1942 to 1945.

"By the end of the war, the US Army Specialized Training Program was created to train personnel in the languages and cultures of the areas to which they were posted, and Penn (University of Pennsylvania) became the national site for the India program in 1943-44. Using this program as a model, Brown devised a summer program that provided an interdisciplinary view of India's culture, history, politics, and economics."[15]Under the guidance of Professor Brown, the University of Pennsylvania was instrumental in promoting India related studies. As India was gearing up for her independence in 1947, the University of Pennsylvania came up with "India: A Program of Regional Studies" as an experimental summer programme. Substantial grant was provided by the Carnegie Corporation of New York, and the Rockefeller Foundation to further India and South Asian studies at the campus. Brown remained active with his effort at the Penn. "Brown continued to be an important figure in the national effort to define, organize and implement "international area studies" on an interdisciplinary model, and lobbied for the continued support of Area-Studies by the US Department of Education."[16]

The Library of Congress is America's oldest federal cultural institution. A research wing of the US Congress, it is the world's largest library with a rich, diverse and enduring source of knowledge with millions of books, recordings, photographs, newspapers, maps, and manuscripts in its collections. It appointed its first Indic specialist in 1938, nine years before India got independence. Horace Poleman was a Sanskritist at the Library of Congress and was sent to India for a year (1939-40) on an acquisitions trip that included locating and microfilming Sanskrit manuscripts. Poleman earned his doctorate in Sanskrit from the University of Pennsylvania in 1933. He wrote his thesis on the Aurdhvadehika-paddhati, a medieval Sanskrit text on death ritual.

[14] Brown, William Norman & Horace Irvin Poleman & Elmer H. Cutts, Indic Studies in America, American Council of Learned Societies (American Council of Learned Societies Bulletin, 28), Washington (D.C.), 1939, p. 358.

[15] South Asia Studies of University of Pennsylvania, available at URL: https://www.southasia.upenn.edu/about/department-history, accessed on 28 November 2018

[16] Ibid.

Poleman's contribution is considered immense in the United States' understanding on India. Poleman, with the encouragement of the Committee on Indic and Iranian Studies (CIIS), thus laid the groundwork for the postwar massive collection effort under US Library of Congress (LC) auspices - the so-called PL 490 acquisitions program.[17] Few American anthropologists also turned to India for research work. One of them was David Goodman Mandelbaum, who collected data on the Kota tribe in the Nilgiri Hills of Southern India from 1937 to 1938. He returned repeatedly to Southern India to continue his fieldwork with the Kota and Toda tribes. Mandelbaum was the first American Anthropologist to do academic fieldwork in India.

In July 1946, US Congress passed a bill allowing naturalization for Indians. The Luce-Celler Bill reinstated naturalization to Asian Indians and allowed an immigration quota for Indians coming to America. With the enactment of Luce-Celler bill as part of the Immigration Act of 1946, Indians could gain citizenship, own property and vote.

The United States was among the first major countries to immediately recognize India on August 15 1947, soon after it got independence. Interestingly, the diplomatic relations were established a year before India's freedom. The US Department of State had raised the American Embassy in New Delhi on November 1, 1946, formally starting formal relations between the two nations. During the Indian freedom struggle movement, Mahatma Gandhi's message of nonviolent resistance 'Satyagraha' was discussed in the American Universities. Prominent Indians like Rabindranath Tagore, Kamaladevi Chattopadhyay, Ram Manohar Lohia, and Vijaya Lakshmi Pandit traveled and lectured in the United States talking about India's freedom struggle movement.

The US Academic Interest in Post Colonial India

After independence, India followed its independent foreign policy and remained neutral in the Cold War. It kept distance from both super-power blocks. The Nehru government was critical of American Cold War policies. After 1947, the United States was slow to implement Public Diplomacy policies in India, and it struggled to counter Indian criticisms of Washington's Cold War foreign policies and the practice of racial segregation in the American South.[18] Despite the sluggishness in terms of relations, the United States academic interests remained unabated in India. The Ford Foundation dispensed one grant to the Allahabad Agricultural Institute in 1948, and the Carnegie endowment gave funds to the University of Pennsylvania and Cornell in support of their

[17] Maureen, L. P. Patterson and Joseph W. Elder (2010), "*A HISTORY OF THE AMERICAN INSTITUTE OF INDIAN STUDIES, 1961 to 1998*", available at URL: https://minds.wisconsin.edu/bitstream/handle/1793/38774/History%20of%20the%20AIIS.pdf?sequence=6, accessed on 26 November 2018

[18] Graham, Sarah Ellen, "*Engaging India: Public Diplomacy and Indo-American Relations to 1957*", Los Angeles: Figueroa Press, 2012, p.5

anthropological and linguistic research work in India.[19]

Three years after India gained independence, the Indo-U.S. bi-national agreement on the educational exchange was signed in 1950. It established the United States Educational Foundation in India (USEFI) to administer the Fulbright Program in India. The Fulbright Scholarship is named after former Senator J. William Fulbright of Arkansas, who introduced legislation in 1946 that later became a law. The US Department of State's Bureau of Educational and Cultural Affairs sponsors the Fulbright scholarship. Throughout the 1950s and 1960s, the coordinating office for the Wheat Loan at the US embassy in New Delhi was also able to channel U.S. philanthropic funds into Indian libraries and educational institutions.

Apart from plain philanthropy, there were other reasons for American generosity for India. The Ford Foundation had provided $2.8 million to the Indian government in the agriculture sector in 1952. Later it also provided grants in the health sector for malaria research. This generosity had a hidden intention. Paul Hoffman, who was the president of the Ford Foundation from 1950 to 1953 wanted "India, one of the two Asian giants, and the non-Communist one, to become the reason's focal point for serious investment from the US...Assistance to India would demonstrate what free men with wealth and wisdom could do to help other men to follow them down the same...path of development."[20] Poverty alleviation, according to Hoffman, would "put Indians firmly in the Western camp."[21]

There was a general struggle to maintain cosy relations between India and the United States. The mistrust was obvious as in the early 1950s US-Pakistan relations started on a good note. While at strategic level Indo-US relations were going on a downhill track, on the public diplomacy front the Ford, Rockefeller, and Carnegie Foundations all offered funds to US universities to develop their South Asian Studies programmes. By the late 1950s, the Ford Foundation contributed to aid in rural development, medical projects and urban planning initiatives in India.

The formation of the American Institute of Indian Studies in 1961 had a ripple effect. In the decade of the 1960s, the Bengali Studies Conference (1965), the Research Committee on the Punjab (1966), the Maharashtra Studies Group (1968), and the Society for South Indian Studies (1968) were formed.[22] Now the American universities were entering into more micro-level study of India.Immense contribution from the American academician also had a lasting

[19] Ibid, p. 23

[20] Ibid, p. 28

[21] Ibid.

[22] Patterson, Maureen L. P., "Institutional Base for the Study of South Asia in the United States and the Role of the American Institute of Indian Studies," in Joseph W. Elder, Edward C. Dimock Jr. and Ainslie T. Embree (eds.), *India's Worlds and US Scholars: 1947–1997*, New Delhi: Manohar Publishers & Distributors: American Institute of Indian Studies, 1998, p. 45

impact on policies of the Indian government. Economist and Professor John Kenneth Galbraith was appointed as the high-level consultant to the Indian government on problems of economic expansion. Galbraith stayed in India for two months to advise on the goals of India's Second Five Year Plan. Later, he was appointed as US Ambassador to India during the presidency of John F. Kennedy.

Indian Institute of Technology (IIT) at Kanpur was formed with help coming from the United States. Nine leading institutions of the United States assisted IIT-K in the setting up of the academic programs and development of laboratories for instruction as well as research for a decade (1962-1972). These were California Institute of Technology, Carnegie Institute of Technology, Case Institute of Technology, Massachusetts Institute of Technology, Ohio State University, Princeton University, Purdue University, University of California at Berkley, and University of Michigan.

The Indian Institute of Management (IIM), Ahmedabad was established in 1961. For the initial five years, the Harvard Business School helped the IIM-A in developing its teaching curriculum that included the case method of teaching. Similarly, IIM Calcutta was established in collaboration with the Sloan School of Management (MIT), with the help from the Ford Foundation.

Today IIT Kanpur and IIMs are India's best institutes in terms of providing high-quality education. There was a huge agriculture collaboration between India and US Universities. "The Agricultural Universities in India set up on the 'land grant' pattern of USA have contributed immensely to human resource development as well as enhancement of agricultural productivity and production in the country over the years. The system of education in Agricultural Universities was basically taken from USA pattern that greatly enabled incorporation of a number of diverse subjects in the courses. The provision of hands-on practical experience to the students is also borrowed from American Universities."[23] The result was the establishment of India's first agriculture university of the nation, the GB Pant University of Agriculture & Technology in 1960. It was greatly influenced by the pattern of Land Grant Agriculture Universities of the United States and the University of Illinois which signed a contract in 1959 to assist the university in Pantnagar. The blueprint for the university was prepared HW Hannah who was the Dean of the University of Illinois. The university also offered the services of its scientists and teachers.

The American 'hand' in the Green Revolution is now part of folklore. The 1960s were the decade of frequent droughts and during this time Borlaug visited New Delhi in March 1963. He worked extensively and after six months

[23] Draft document on National Agriculture Education Project in 2012 by Indian Council of Agricultural Research Department of Agricultural Research & Education, available at URL: https://icar.org.in/files/NAEP-Projec-documentt.pdf, accessed on 16 November 2018

sent IARI four selected varieties of his dwarf wheat. His effort made India- a food deficit country (during 1960s-70s) became self-sufficient in an amazingly short time, saving hundreds of millions of lives.

Broadening 'Indic' Courses in US Universities

On the diplomatic front, India was not aligned to exclusive club governed by the US and naturally the State Department had little interest in the country. At the same time, the American universities were showing increasing interest in India. There was great demand by the public in the United States in the 1950s to increase the country's technological prowess in the light of the Soviet Union's launch of Sputnik satellite in 1957. The National Defense Education Act of 1958 became one of the most successful legislative initiatives in higher education. It established the legitimacy of federal funding for higher education and made substantial funds available for low-cost student loans, boosting public and private colleges and universities.[24] This greatly benefitted not only the flow of students in science and mathematics but helped them join foreign language courses in the universities.

The House report recommending passage of the bill stated: "It is no exaggeration to say that America's progress in many fields of endeavor in the years ahead—in fact, the very survival of our free country—may depend in large part upon the education we provide for our young people now."[25] But the main benefits happened to the US universities, where South Asian centres were already functional. A century ago, an initiative to study the Sanskrit language was taken by few academic enthusiasts in the United States. By 1960, the US federal funding helped area studies to grow at American universities. If in 1842, Yale University took initiative in forming Sanskrit chair at the university, a century later the University of Pennsylvania took lead in South Asia centre where India studies became the focal centre. If Salisbury gets credit for the formation of Sanskrit in the United States, the contribution of W. Norman Brown in establishing 'Indic Studies' is also well known.

During the 1950s and 1960s, Brown formed the nucleus of Indic studies and promoted area studies. In the decades of the 1960s, Richard Lambart succeded Brown at University of Pennsylvania. Lambart was votary of South Asian studies and made a name in this field. Richard Park, who created Modern India project at the Berkley South Asia Programme moved to University of Michigan in 1959 and created a major role in the formation of South Asian studies. Around the same time, Milton Singer created the Chicago civilizations project at the University of Chicago. At the University of

---

[24] Senate document on Sputnik Spurs Passage of the National Defense Education Act, October 4, 1957, available at URL: https://www.senate.gov/artandhistory/history/minute/Sputnik_Spurs_Passage_of_National_Defense_Education_Act.htm, accessed on 16 November 2018

[25] National Defense Education Act, August 21, 1958, available at URL: https://history.house.gov/HouseRecord/Detail/15032436195, accessed on 5 November 2018

California Berkley, Anthropologist David Mandelbaum continued research on Kota and Toda tribes of the Nilgiri Hills by visiting India for research. Another Indic specialized anthropologist, Bernard Cohn, trained at Cornell University, later joined the University of Chicago in 1964 and wrote extensively on the Indian caste system. In the 1950s, he came to India on research grant provided by the Fulbright programme and as a Rockefeller Foundation Fellow.

"Cohn's work, in particular, provided a new understanding to India's caste system. His work revealed that although the caste system had existed in India much before the British took control, the system took on new meaning when the British established laws to codify it."[26] Cohn developed an interdisciplinary approach to study on India.

The other universities that took lead roles in encouraging South Asian studies in the 1960s were – Universities of Pennsylvania, Columbia, Chicago, Michigan, Washington, Minnesota, Virginia and Texas. This encouraged other universities in America to create area studies on the South Asia.

At Columbia University, Ainslie Embree was a known Indologist and shaped the thinking of a generation of South Asian scholars in the US. As a key Historian, Embree's work on 'Sources of Indian Tradition' is considered a masterpiece for all those who study India. Another India specialist, Joseph W. Elder at the University of Wisconsin-Madison played a key role and edited volumes on Indian Civilisation. Another professor at the University of California, Berkley Leo Rose specialized in the Himalayan region of the Indian sub-continent. He wrote extensively on India, Nepal, Bhutan, and Sikkim.

Lloyd and Susanne Rudolph - called as the Rudolphs were known for scholarly contribution to India during their six decades of intellectual discourses. Hired by the Chicago University in 1964, they turned the University into a leading centre on South Asia. The Rudolphs co-authored eight books. One of their works, 'The Modernity of Tradition (1967)', they mention about the modernisation of Indian society.

Mc Kim Marriott, anthropologist at the University of Chicago used the structural-functional approach in his study of village India. He wrote extensively on rural India with his new "alternative social sciences for studying differing cultural realities, using formal modeling and simulations".[27] At the same University, Ronald Inden taught History and South Asian Languages. Inden's early work focused on 'Bengali culture' and in his book 'Imagining India', he concluded that West's major depictions of India are dominated by imagination rather than reason. He investigated "Indian class formations

26 Title, "Bernard Cohn, 75, studied colonialism, India's caste system", The University of Chicago Chronicle, December 11, 2003, vol.23, No.6, available at URL: http://chronicle.uchicago.edu/031211/cohn-obit.shtml, accessed on 9 November 2018

27 McKim Marriot biography in the University of Chicago Website, available at URL: https://anthropology.uchicago.edu/people/emeritus-faculty/mckim-marriott, accessed on 4 November 2018

in relation to changes in world ruling classes and the ways in which people have tried to articulate these changes with intellectual practices encompassing national and ethnic "identities" in the twentieth century."[28]

At the University of Michigan, Thomas R. Trautmann taught and researched on History and Anthropology especially focusing on ancient India kinship and marriages. His area of work included anthropology of kinship, history of anthropology, history of Orientalist scholarship in British India, history of racial thought in India and Europe, concepts of time and environmental history of India. He also wrote a book on 'Kautilya and the Arthashastra'. Burton Stein, an American historian specializing in India taught first at the University of Hawaii and later in London. He wrote and worked on pre-modern and colonial South India. They were the visionaries in the American University campuses who spread the direction of Indic studies from Sanskrit to different socio-cultural, historical and anthropological studies.

In 1960, the population of an Indian born resident in the United States was only 13,600. It was minuscule when compared to the country's total population. After, the United States passed the 1965 Immigration Act. On October 3, 1965, it opened the doors for the immigrants from different parts of the world including Indians. From 1960 to 1980, the population of Americans of Indian descent rose to 387,223. In just 20 years, Indian descent population rose by thirty times.

From 1960 to 1980 several universities which included Indian studies programme went a step ahead to include Indian language course in its course. The teaching in Hindi in the American Universities grew phenomenally in 1950s. Tamil Studies is part of the University of Chicago and UC Berkeley for the last forty years. Punjabi language was introduced in Columbia in 1989 and followed by other universities too. Similarly, languages like, Bengali, Gujarati, Tamil, Marathi have been added to the university pedagogy. With the growing number of Indian courses in the Universities, US publishers too started focusing on India with the new journals. Prominent US authors and teachers specializing on India started writing on the subject prominently. The US publishers that focus entirely on India or South Asia as a region in the journals included India Review (Routledge), South Asian Popular Culture (Routledge), Contemporary South Asia (Routledge), Journal of South Asia Studies (Routledge), South Asia Research (Sage), as well as Comparative Studies of South Asia, Africa, and the Middle East (Duke University Press).[29]

After 1965, when the doors of immigration were opened, highly qualified Indian from different walks of life entered the United States. They went to the American universities to pursue world class knowledge, skills and also follow

---

[28] Ronald Inden biography in the University of Chicago Website, available at URL: https://history.uchicago.edu/directory/ronald-inden, accessed on 8 November 2018

[29] Novetzke, P. 108

the 'American dream.' Indians value their education; want their children to inculcate best of it. By the 1980s and 1990s, with their good education background, a huge number of Indians joined the faculty in different US Universities.

High educational attainment distinguishes the Indian diaspora population from the US general population as well as diaspora from other countries. The Indian diaspora is one of the most educated of the 15 groups in the RAD analysis.[30] Several Indian origin academicians are now heading American Business schools. They are also well placed in different departments of US universities. The Indian origin people's median income is more than average Americans. Households in the United States that were headed by a member of the Indian diaspora had a median annual income approximately $39,000 higher than the US national median ($89,000 versus $50,000).[31] (Quote) The children of immigrants who moved after the change in immigration act of 1965 developed interests in South Asian studies.

"The growing relationship between South Asian Studies and South Asian Americans has been a great boon to the field, and has provided both a constituency and an urgency to a field that had previously been restricted for the most part to graduate studies and undergraduate courses in religion and philosophy." In the last one and half decade, as the relations between India and United States has grown, there has been increasing collaboration on knowledge front. Four kinds of initiatives are adding to this collaboration. Firstly to preserve the culture and heritage Indian origin people in the high-income groups have been donating to the US universities in form of endowments and community gifts. Indian Americans donated $1.2 billion to 37 US universities between 2000 and 2018.[32] According to an Indiaspora research of publicly available information 68 such donations were over $1 million.[33] The University of California at Berkeley, Santa Cruz and Santa Barbara, Indiana University, University of Michigan, University of Pennsylvania have chairs endowed by Indian origin people. The Harvard University has Mehra Family Professor of South Asian Studies at the Department of South Asian Studies. At few places, Indian origin academicians are heading such chairs. There are also Americans who are heading such chairs. For example, Rick Rossow is the Wadhwani Chair in U.S.-India Policy Studies, Center for Strategic and International

[30] Migration Policy Institute document prepared for the Rockefeller Foundation - Aspen Institute Diaspora Program (RAD), "The Indian Diaspora in the United States", January 2014, P. 7, available at URL: https://www.migrationpolicy.org/sites/default/files/publications/RAD-IndiaII-FINAL.pdf, accessed on 13 November 2018

[31] Ibid, p. 8

[32] PTI story in the Financial Express, "Indian Americans donates USD 1.2 billion to 37 US universities from 2000 to 2018", available at URL: https://www.financialexpress.com/india-news/indian-americans-donated-usd-1-2-billion-to-37-us-universities-from-2000-to-2018/1326930/, accessed on 3 November 2018

[33] Ibid.

Studies.

Secondly few Indian Industrialists are also donating to the US Universities. Anand Mahindra's gift to the Harvard University is Mahindra Humanities Centre'. In 2008, Tata Industries' Ratan Tata gifted $50 million to his alma mater, Cornell University in New York. The personal initiative from Tata was to help recruit top Indian students to support joint research projects with Indian universities in the areas of agriculture and nutrition. India's tech company Infosys co-founder NR Narayana Murthy also donated US$5.2 million to form the Clay Sanskrit Library at the Harvard.

Thirdly Government of India is also increasing its footprints in the US universities. In 2012, with a $1.5 million endowment grant, the Ministry of Culture created 'Vivekananda Visiting Professorship' in the University of Chicago for the study of teachings and philosophies of the Swami. These include Indian philosophy, politics, and social movements. The Columbia Law School's B.R. Ambedkar Professorship in Indian Constitutional Law was created by Government of India in 2010. The two sides are also enhancing the cooperation for faculty development and on India's Global Initiative of Academics Network (GIAN). Under this network, the MHRD creates a channel for US professors in science, technology and engineering to teach in Indian academic and research institutions on short-term exchanges.

Devesh Kapur of University of Pennsylvania writes that there has been a considerable increase in India-related work in the social sciences. He writes, "The social science field has become much more empirical and India offers several advantages for a researcher: large sample sizes, heterogeneity in multiple dimensions, relatively low cost of gathering data, and weak official oversight (which, in any case, is unlikely to be enforced). It would be hard to do many of these trials in the US or China. As a result, custom-designed household surveys and randomized control trials have proliferated, most supported by external funding, which have generated new understandings about the country."[34]

Fourthly few US universities have been heading towards India and opening their centres on the Indian soil. The University of Chicago opened a centre in Delhi in 2014. In the same year, Virginia Polytechnic Institute and State University, popularly known Virginia Tech, opened its centre. Harvard Business School has an Indian research centre in Mumbai. In order to encourage young American leaders to study in India, the US Department of State and the Ohio State University launched the new Passport to India initiative.

[34] Kapur, Devesh, "*The Study of India in the United States*". India in Transition (IiT) is published by the Center for the Advanced Study of India (CASI) of the University of Pennsylvania, available at URL: https://casi.sas.upenn.edu/iit/deveshkapur2018, accessed on 7 November 2018

Altbach and McGill state, "Higher education has always served as an international force, influencing intellectual and scientific development and spreading ideas worldwide"[35]

Conclusion

At the dawn of the 21st century, two things happened in terms of Indo-US relations. Firstly, India with its decade of liberalization emerged as a strong emerging market in the world. In the due process, the economic voice of India was heard in all major corners of the globe and this includes the United States. Secondly the Indian diaspora which maintained a low-key affair has emerged as a strong voice in the country. The turnaround in the Indo-US relations also took place with the US President Bill Clinton visiting India in 2000. In the last 17 years, there has been a significant improvement of relations between two countries which was earlier marked with uncertainty and distrust.

The United States diplomatic relations is not just based on government-to-government relations. Its foreign policy is also shaped by key actors like the diaspora community, the intellectual base in the universities and think tanks. In 1939, the famous Indologist Norman Brown had said, "How can Americans who have never met India in their educational experience be expected to live intelligently in such a world." Eighty years after what Brown had prophesized, America has met India countless of times, the two nations have collaborated, there has been exchange of ideas as well as academic exchanges in different fields.

Despite favouring Pakistan at diplomatic level, the US Universities did not stop collaboration with India and its institutions. Despite their government's cold attitude during the Cold War, there were no stopping on 'Indic', 'Indian languages courses', and Indian religion and philosophy studies and programmes in the US universities. The courses on Sanskrit grew in more US universities. This was followed by the entry of other Indian languages in their University curriculum. These languages include Hindi, Punjabi, Gujarati, Tamil, and Telugu not only made an entry, students too opted for the course making India relevant.

As India grows and progresses, the country remains relevant and important for the World and the United States. In the nineteenth century, when a Sanskrit language course was started in the fledgling university, no one knew that indic study in the US will reach its present height. During the Cold War, when the University of Pennsylvania started the South Asian programme, it was beyond imagination that India and the US would collaborate at this level.

[35] Altbach P.G. & P. McGill-Peterson, "Higher Education as a projection of America's Soft Power" in Y. Watanabe and D.L. McConnell (eds.), "*Soft Power Superpowers: Cultural and National Assets of Japan and the United States*", Armonk, NY, USA and London, UK: M.E. Sharpe, p. 37

Even in the US Congress, India commands a positive strength. India has the largest country-specific caucus in the House of Representatives. It is also the only country-specific caucus in the Senate. The unthinkable has happened and shaped by Universities which created platforms for moving information, money, and people across state boundaries.

❒

The Singularity of the India-United States "Bilaterals": An Investigative Exercise in Modi Doctrine and Public Diplomacy

Dr. Manan Dwivedi,
Faculty, International Relations and
American Affairs, IIPA

Introduction

Cultural portrayals lead to the reflection of the reality and the attendant myth pertaining to any nation state particularly and in a region to be generally inclined. The cultural landscape of a nation can serve as the spawning centre for the political and social unison of a region within the context of its constituent political units. The myriad nations in South Asia also revolve around these parameters of a Mediascape generated discourse which apart from congealing the rubric of a nation state or a region, also, tends to create a divisive trend. The various myths and the historical facts attached to the lore of conflicts in the context of the India-Pakistan- China triumvirate serve a dual purpose which the paper will attempt to delineate in the form of a visual and cultural narrative.

The paper will dwell upon the context of media generated hype and also about the much needed constructs of nationalism and patriotic themes which do not actually militate against the conjoined theme of Public diplomacy with United States. The Government of the day in New Delhi with its recent overtures towards a 'near –to-Friendly' policy will form another argument in the proposed research paper. The paper would develop the idea of Public Diplomacy as it being visibly attempted by the Prime Minister Modi's foreign policy dispensation. The role which the nation's Mass Media can play in firming up the case of state led Public Diplomacy, will, be further elaborated and investigated upon through a brief content analysis of the Media reports in India through a selective utilisation of prominent national dailies and national satellite Channel networks all across the mediascape of India and United States. The Media and the Public diplomacy apparatus can be equated with the all pervading commonality of national interest which will figure in the paper's narrative.

Making of a myth or the myth making function is an essential component of the idiom of a national interest seeking foreign policy making and implementation of the selfsame. As a precursor element, the western nations embarked upon a strategy of serving potential national interest oriented specificities, where-in, the respective establishments attempted to make the 'rest' swoon over and cooperate with their specific nationalities and national aims and objectivities. In a quintessential proactive and positive framework ordaining policy making, the spawning of a myth becomes a prerequisite for the cementing of a narrative at a national and localized keel.

Wither Public Diplomacy and What is It?

Public Diplomacy is the creation of certain images and visages in order to spawn a sub set of an exteriority in order to simplistically and in a plane jane manner augment the national interest of a nation state. And, its an American construct forged as part of American soft power Diplomacy in the interregnum between the two World wars. Public diplomacy can be defined as a "Communication with foreign publics for the purpose of achieving a foreign policy objective."[36] The Internet and social media tools have given U.S. public diplomacy practitioners a new venue for such communication. Without the valuable on-the-ground presence of a diplomatic mission however, its online presence is currently the chief route of direct access to Iranian citizens.[37]The establishment of this online presence has been in line with the State Department's development of a virtual diplomacy strategy – entitled 21st Century Statecraft – which includes efforts to establish an online apparatus for nearly all U.S. diplomatic missions.[38] Manicheasm seems to be the order of the day where-in, the satanic and Evilesque narration and an intentional projection of a specificity of an image leads to the fulfilment of a national interest ordained objective of a nation.

---

[36] Wallin, Matthew. "The New Public Diplomacy Imperative." American Security Project. 2012. Available at: http:// americansecurityproject.org/featured-items/2012/the-new-public-diplomacy-imperative/

[37] U.S. Department of State Official. Telephone Interview. 2013, April 12.

[38] Hanson, Fergus. "Revolution @State: The Spread of eDiplomacy." Lowy Institute. 2012. Available at: http://lowyinstitute. cachefly.net/files/hanson_revolution_state_web.pdf

Still, what needs to be realised is that the origin and the praxis of the nom de plume of Public Diplomacy is not about a mere bland satanization and vilification of the other, but, rather it is a larger than life exercise to establish a national sentiment upon the vestiges of the global firmament. It definitively involves the propagation of a myth but the question which needs to be asked is that what is wrong in the creation and the sustenance of a national myth with the all apparent notion of providing an international platform for the history, tradition, economic, trade, societal and political achievements of a nation state such as United States and maybe India in the contemporary context of South Asia. One cannot deny the fact that it is the American diplomatic establishment which created the first effective edifice and a superstructure in order to propagate the national objectives. India too has followed suit with the Media and Diplomatic Blitzkrieg initiated by Prime Minister Modi since the inception of the Delhi denomination in the momentous month of May 2014. The Modi denomination is attempting to develop a transformation between this diplomatic myth and reality in the Indian and the American context.

Public Diplomacy in United States

The art of selling and marketing a product, a theme or a cause is not chiefly attributable to a marketeer of the market or a corporate salesman. The lore and praxis of marketing one's country and its history, tradition and linguistic construct, also is a fulltime vocational engagement. The myth about India or United States as a nation has to be globally and perforce propagated all across the public sphere in the international firmament. The ides of Global politics perpetuated United States's involvement in the World Politics and led to its disembarkment from its traditional isolationist perch, where-in, the American founding father's myth of "staying away from the entangling European alliances' was relegated to the political backburner. In the same continuum, it was through the auspices of President Franklin Delano Roosevelt, in the year 1936 that the "Good Neighbour Policy" was initiated in the South American context which was a continuation of the quintessentially American in origin, nature and functionality , i.e, Monroe Doctrine.

It so transpired that President Roosevelt visited the Argentine capital, Buenos Aires in 1936 with an impressive motorcade leading the way to the Argentine Parliament. An assurance was given to the Argentine nation and the rest of the Western hemisphere that the nations could continue with their daily humdrum routine along with larger Umbrella of the American 'superpuissance' in the region. A messaging was given to the rest of the World that the South American and the Latin American region was United State's preserve and had to be sustained with the American presence and large hearted philanthropy. The larger issue of regional hyper power was reinstated with another significant development.

The art of Public Diplomacy was soon to be honed by the foreign policy establishment of the United States of America. During the period of World War-II, also, the American war office and the State Department, were, given directions to mount a global campaign through the Public management mechanisms. Such a global campaign would arraign all the American Media and the Cinematic apparatus which would amplify the fact of' America being the most powerful and the richest nation in the international polity.' Other issues such as United States of America being the repository of fundamental freedoms, egalitarianism, decolonization along with the dignity and freedom issues of humankind were also paraded and portrayed globally by the US war office in conjunction with the American mainstream Media. A conclave was developed between the Cinema producers, comic artists, pamphleteers and national dailies and Radio in order to transmit combative messages against the Nazi Germany and later on against the Soviet Union, led, by Stalin which soon assumed manicheastic dimensions as the quintessential Cold war confrontation was cemented right across the Iron curtain all the way from river Trieste to Sienne tearing across the European heartland.[39]

Thus, Public Diplomacy emerged as an instrumentality to advance American national interest globally through deft message campaigns thus bringing to the fore, the MIM (Military Media and Industry)[40] complex in the United States. The American instrumentality of Soft war was unleashed all across the global firmament with a subterranean motif of propagating the all pervading omniscience and the "City atop Mount Sinai" analogy which caught the larger World's and especially the imagination of the developing nations. The aura and the halo of the supersession and the invincibility of the American Republic was soon to become one of the quint essential narratives in the Third and Middle world.

As an instance, the creation of the superhero genre in form of Superman, Captain America and Avengers through DC comics was soon to become the emblem of the grand American stereotype. In the context of the super hero termed as Superman, the narrative involves the idea of the. " Other" which reaches Earth from the planet Krypton in order to grow up as an earthling after the fact that planet Krypton explodes in one self destructive crescendo and there emerges a space capsule carrying a two year old boy child, Kal El41 who on reaching the Earth's atmosphere soon metamorphoses into a mutant super power wielding earthling. He assumes the name of Clark Kent as his father teaches him to hone his super powers and hide it from the world and utilise it when he turns into the Man of steel and the caped crusader which is the name by which the American and global Media learns to call him. The

[39] Henry Kissinger, "Diplomacy," (New York: Simon and Schuster, 1994) Page No. 40-60

[40] Ben H. Bagdikian, "The New Media Monopoly" (New York: Beacon Press, 2004) Page No. 10-20

[41] Richard Donor, " Superman: The Movie" Warner Brothers, 1978

myth of Superman is the precursor element in the context of the American state's soft power Diplomacy which was further strengthened with other facets in the propagation of the power, pelf and the efficiency of the grandiloquent American Dream.

As the Clark Kent character grows up he fights manifold menaces and villains and soon emerges as an American and global beacon of liberty, non proliferation, disarmament, peace, stability, democracy and all that is appreciable in the American liberal tradition and largely the American Dream. In the recent Hollywood release, Man of Steel, Superman's mother cajoles him after he has vanquished marauding villains as his initial foray into saving men, that, " Now son, that you have vanquished the evil Zod and saved Earth, how would you support yourself in the world. So better look for a job once the job of saving the mankind is over!"[42] Some motherly suggestion! Thus, the appellation of United States of America being the international supercop with all the quintessential American beneficence becomes the "Ragtime raga" of the American experience. It is this do-gooder instinct and US being the symbolic custodian of human rights and world peace which was astutely propagated through the World War II and the dreary Cold War days as the world very often reached the edge from where the World War III, was very often not a forgone possibility.

Public Diplomacy though Indian and South Asian lens

It is in the same context of international razzmatazz that Prime Minister Modi has reinvented the artifice of Public diplomacy in the Indian and the South Asian context. His first message reflected the importance that New Delhi attaches to the immediate neighbour in the form of the South Asian countries despite the nagging and minute differences which India shares with some of them. The presence of all the South Asian and SAARC heads of state at the Modi inaugural in May 2014 was all about India according primacy to the SAARC comity of nations. The visits to Japan, Fotaleza, Bhutan and Nepal too portrayed a developing world perspective. The presence of President Obama on the occasion of the Republic day celebrations in New Delhi too depicted the growing convergence between the Indian Union and United States of America as several significant agreements were inked along with the ironing out of the details of the Nuclear Civil Liability Bill in India. All these formed part and parcel of an Indian striving which was much more than a standard Photo opportunity with a trail of agreements and treaties to follow. What was awe inspiring was the India centric justification of this novae genre of media Diplomacy which was under taken very deftly by the Indian foreign policy establishment in order to erase out the previous memories of reactive and larger policy paralysis of the previous regime in New Delhi.

[42] Zack Snyder, " Man of Steel" Warner Brothers, 2011

Public Diplomacy: Known Frontiers in United States

Though the term Public Diplomacy has been part of the Foreign policy skill set of Washington since the inception of two World wars, still some scholars attribute it with an innovation of the cold war years. In one such enumeration, Jomane Chahine hailing from the McGill University contends that, "The term—public diplomacy‖ only entered the lexicon of political and international affairs in the Cold War environment of the mid-1960s. It could however be argued that the essence of the practice –government communication with foreign publics— is as old as history itself."[43] The author further contends that, "The primary purpose of this dissertation is to argue that public diplomacy, as the specific form taken by the practice of government communication with a foreign audience in the latter half of the twentieth century, is a distinctive product of the development and ultimate intersection of several discrete though somehow connected concepts in social and political thought."[44]

Public Diplomacy is an artifice which is part of the mechanics of Foreign Policy in the country. The Government of the day attempts to circumvent the internal dissensions in order to bring forth the objective of national interest in order to promote the avowed national interest of the nation. Diplomacy did not have an element of, "Immediacy" in the classical and the traditional times. With the rapid upsurge in technological advancements and with the advent of geo economic interdependencies, the idea of how a nation and its foreign policy was perceived and analyzed by the international organizations and actors, metamorphosed over the years.

In a preeminent work on Public Diplomacy, the author attempts to delineate the inception of the idea of American Public Diplomacy which later on went to become the cornerstone of the policies of various foreign policy establishments in the world. 'The American Dream mythology,'[45] too, gets more than a reference in the work. It was John Truslow Adams who initiated upon and theorised upon the notion of the " Grandiloquent American Dream."[46] Justin Hart beautifully ekes out a detailed analysis of the notion of how Public Diplomacy was incepted in the American context with the visit of President Franklin Delano Roosevelt in 1935 in order to implement the, "Good Neighbor Policy" of United States. [47]The author narrates that the various shenanigans of

43 Joumane Chahine, "Public Diplomacy: A Conceptual Framework" Department of Art , History and Communication Studies, Mc Gill University, Montreal, 2010

44 Ibid

45 James Truslow Adams, "The Epic of America," New York: Simon Publications, 2001 , Page No. 1-20

46 Ibid

47 Justin Hart, " Empire of Ideas: The Origins of Public Diplomacy and the Transformation of US Foreign Policy" (London: Oxford University Press, 2001) Page No. 20-40

the Office of war and the Intelligence agencies, which were in their incipient stage, led to the firming up of the Washington's effort in creating a 'specificity' about the general visage and the demeanour of the American Republic. The narrative is rich in details and ably investigates the 'internal workings' through a study of memos and correspondence in the American foreign policy making establishment. The power struggles and the clashes of the men at the helm of Affairs, is sketched very evocatively and pithily within the historical setting of Public Diplomacy.

Justin Hart, the author clinically brings out the internal clashes of personalities and the cloak and dagger nature of the earlier setting, which soon became commonplace and arrived in public view with the advent of World War-II. The American war effort along with the cold war propaganda of John McCarthy,[48] too, evoke an academic and policy interest in the receptive index of the reader. The entire 'cleaning up' instrumentality of the American establishment aimed at the communists too is too elaborately narrated in this work on US Foreign Policy. The work examines the communications strategies of the American Government along with analyzing the origins of the American, "Soft Power". The Book includes interesting and vivid portrayals of personalities such as Henry Luce, Archibald Macleish[49] and other framers of the initial edifice of American image making efforts, culminating in the larger framework of Public Diplomacy. The entire diplomatic striving attains significant prominence with the pinpointing of original sources and primary research material which sheds more than an able light on the subject matter. The twilight zone of the American overarch in the World War-II years and the confrontation years in the Cold war years, too, gets an efficient rendition in the tradition of being a true blue researcher.

The Public Diplomacy Quest?: An Innovative Policy Prescription"

In the same tradition of myth making, one can scarcely forget the J P Dutta directed war movie, "Border" in which a lot of gargantuan developments take place. One of those which can be cited happens to be the consternation of the male actor, Jackie Shroff who is an air force commander. He realizes that if the Longewalan post in the desert has to be protected in the face off with a strong Pakistani thrust, then, the Gnats, hawker hunters and Mig 21's, had to be flown in to bombard the enemy tanks and armed cordons who had laid siege to the Longewalan post. Night falls while the 23rd Battalion of Punjab Regiment led by Major Kuldip Singh Chandpuri is still found fighting for its life. Jackie Shroff, as, the Air man shouts out in exasperation that, " Bloody

[48] MACRYTHISM refers to an American historical tradition, where-in, the idea of culling out of practicing and active communists was to be metamorphosed into a realistic Government paradigm, where-in, artists, playwrights, actors and authors, University professors and Academics and other public personages were targeted and were questioned and castigated for their communist linkages as part of the larger program of Global and domestic containment.

[49] Ibid

these birds (planes) cannot fly in the night.

Thus, as first light hits the sky, the bombers decimate the Paki advance in a surreptitious slight of a flight. On the other hand, the Lt. Dharamvir Bhan's personal battle to come to terms with his father's memories as a decorated war veteran and his visage as his mother (Rakhee) turns up as a fleeting vision in order to adorn Dharmveer with the Sehra, (the Bridegroom's head dress) while Dharmveer breathes his last inclined against a destroyed tank. Thus, apart from the chilling portrayal of Chushul during the epic India-China war, the battle of the Longewalan post too enters the annals of military history as an indelible and remarkable page in the entirety of the patriotic tome. It is this myth making which can be deftly utilized with the pantheon of daredevilry and the razzmatazz of the war heroes who laid down their lives or else survived as lasting testaments to the grit and determination of the Indian soldier. The Indian soldierly tradition can be aptly and effectively functionalised as the warring and determined myth of the nation and utilized judiciously as the star spangled, tri-colored buntings fading into one another as E. L. Doctrow would write in his historical novel, "Ragtime".[50] Doctrow writes in his work that, "Tracks! Tracks! It seemed to the visionaries who wrote for the popular magazines that the future lay at the end of the parallel rails. There were long distance locomotive railroads and interurban electric railroads, street cars and elevated railroads, all laying their steel stripes on the land crisscrossing the hearts of the indefatigable civilization".[51] All these details of a twenty first century United States on the move resonates with the provisions of the New Deal and the initializing of the gargantuan projects such as the Tennessee Valley Project being played out as pristine infrastructure all across the length and breadth of United States of America. Thus, as the Public Diplomatic agencies portrayed the capitalist and the market prowess coupled with the cultural strength and awe of the land of milk and honey, South Asia and India in particular can too take a leaf out of the book of Public diplomacy as practiced by United States of America though in a peacemaking tradition much befitting the land of Mahatma Gandhi and Gautama Buddha.[52]

The Indian American Parable of Public Diplomacy

The tale of Prime Minister Narendra Modi has enthralled the numerous nations through his Shuttle and Cultural Diplomacy which gets an ample reflection in the larger frame of the relationship with United States. The speech given by PM Modi at the plush environs of the Madison Square Garden is an ample reflection of the myth and the lorish intent of the New Delhi denomination vis –a-vis the stately Capitol Hill. Prime Minister spoke

[50] E L Doctrow "Ragtime," (New York, Random House, 2007) Page No. 1-10

[51] Ibid

[52] Dipanjan Roy chaudhary,"PM Modi Makes Strong Pitch For India's Permanent Seat in UN Security Council", Economic Times, April 15, 2015

eloquently much recently quoting from the songs of Bob Dylan which reflected the coming of age of the Indian people and its attendant youth segment. PM Modi spoke that, "Today as I call upon the youthful segment of the American population, I can feel the sting of electricity which abounds in the cityscape of New York. In India, we are no longer the land of Sadhus and Serpents, though our cultural oeuvre remains intact. We play with the invention of the mouse now in the sense of its computer usage. In India, we are going to send rockets in space and along with this innovation society, we, are going to build toilets for impoverished masses in the deeply seated Rural hinterland of India as a proud nation."[53]

Thus, the larger-than-life diplomatic quantification by a deft diplomatic legerdemain by PM Modi has largely metamorphosed the reactive foreign policy of the nation into a brightly vibrant notion of proactive Diplomacy. The marketing and selling of the larger visage of the nation has been hailed globally and domestically as the telling difference between the Diplomacy of the Congress Regime and the seething charge of Public Diplomacy by an astute diplomat which Prime Minister Narendra Modi has transformed himself and his external affairs entourage into. Thus, it is the novae foreign policy draft of PM Narendra Modi which scores as the soft power aspect of India's foreign Policy.

President Trump's coming into the saddle of power in United States will see a transformation in the way the bilateral relationship develops between the twin nationalities. Sadanand Dhume, an eminent observer of India-US Relations writes very pithily in the American national daily, the Wall Street Journal that, " Can Donald Trump and Narendra Modi yoke their countries more closely together in a common fight against radical Islam? The early signs look promising, but there's no guarantee of success. India needs to think more globally about the problem, while the U.S. must pay more attention to India's regional concerns."[54]Still, going by an issue specific analysis of the India US relationship, the countervailing role of India as a nationality containing PRC and the two legislative Bills and Executive Orders signed by President Trump in his first policy decisions can augur well for an Indian national security concern of curbing the menace of cross border Jihadi Terrorism from across the nation's northern and western frontiers. This American disdain for Global Terror modules and concerns of an unadulterated Immigration Policy hold bright future prospects for a grandiloquent convergence between India and United States in the near future of the larger international system.

President Trump declared in a Radio Chat show that, "India is one of the oldest Democracies of the world and is a natural ally of United States of

53 "PM Modi's Speech at the Madison Square Garden," URl: https://www.youtube.com/watch?v=tKx3OlHrV9I *(Online: Web), Accessed on 1 February, 2017*

54 Sadanad Dhume, "The Promise of a Modi Trump Alliance, " The Wall Street Journal, December 5, 2016

America. All efforts of my Government will be aimed at forging "better" ties with India but in the near future I can assure India that the nomenclature of the Indian nation as being a better friend will soon be changed to, "the best friend" which United States can expect to have." In the similar vein, President Trump gave the campaign trail clarion call to the Indian Americans by addressing the Hindutva denomination of the Indian settlers with the catchy and efficient call of, "Abki Baar Trump Sarkar" in tandem with the Modi denomination's call to the nation of the order of, "Ab Ki Bar Modi Sarkar." This makes the genre of Public Diplomacy as a clarion call in the garb of, "New/ Sound Byte Diplomacy" which brings out a historical, cultural and economic convergence between India and United States.

Since the early engagement, between the New world and India, negative precedents have been established which were not conducive for cooperation and amalgamation between India and the New World, North America. The American President Franklin Delano Roosevelt attempted to convince the British Prime Minster during the victorious days of World War-II to free India. In the contemporary context, India and United States are nations presently poised at an interesting liberal cusp. Idealism has a say in the way "interdependence" is being supported and has been increasingly witnessed in the relationship between India and United States. There-in, both the nations are compatriots in the odyssey to mar the destabilizing intent of the forces of terrorism as an example. In the Idealist bandwagon, Democracy, Constitutionalism, Rule of law and unbridled individual entrepreneurship, are, the cornerstones of the American Dream and its attendant founding myth. The idea of India, too, as a nation premised upon the democratic founding fathers such as Gandhi and Patel, partook of the demos-pathway immediately in the aftermath of the freedom struggle. Some foreign policy observers do not attach much significance to the aspect of Democratization facet of the American foreign policy, vis-à-vis, nations all across the global firmament. Still, the fact remains that two democracies seldom go to war with each other and are much more friendly with each other.

In the context of the Indian nation, US used to relegate India to the strategic and diplomatic backburner, as, the larger South Asia was described by the US State Department as " a mere blip on the radar screen of the American Policy thought". The statement of Assistant Secretary of State, Robin Raphael in the early nineties blaming New Delhi with atrocities in the state of Jammu and Kashmir, too, served as part of the "negative narrative" of the India-US relationship. Much before the India-US dissonance on the Nuclear cooperation front, the hyphenation of India with Pakistan soured the pitch of the India-US Relationship before it could grow out of the shadow of the Cold war. Prime Minister Narendra Modi has too declared that "these shadows of hesitance between the twin nations should be done away through the C's of candor and convergence."[55] The American President has too termed the India-US "bilaterals" as the "defining partnership of the century". One American President who was a Democrat, went against New Delhi's national interest in the sphere of Nuclear issues, in the form of Bill Clinton. Hillary Clinton, the other Democrat is poised for a showdown with the unpredictable and presumptive candidate amongst the Republicans, that is, Donald Trump.

The recent visit of the American Secretary of State to India, too, made the Indian External Affairs Minister to question the Diplomat, when, the Minister raised the theme of the neighborly contributions in the context of terror activities in Indian territory. The pinpointing of Lashkar-Ai-Toiyaba and Jaish Ai- Mohammad by the Indian Minister made the American Secretary of State take notice of the Indian concern.[56] As a positive development from US, the country has also lobbied for making New Delhi's entry a convenient reality in the Nuclear Suppliers Group. India too has been open to a friendly handshake and is doing a quid pro quo. New Delhi has pledged one billion dollars for various sectors in Afghanistan which has been well received in the American quarters.[57] The American standpoint in working towards conflict resolution in Afghanistan will receive a fillip from these Indian steps. As India has emerged as one of the largest donors of civilian aid to Afghanistan, the State Department spokesperson has contended that India is helping Kabul defend itself better and restore security for its people.

Apart from raising the complaint of cross border terrorism with US, one of the post-May 2014 foreign policy standpoints of the New Delhi have been the intelligent coupling of the Defense and the Commercial aspects of the partnership. According to Professor B M Jain in his work, titled as, "The Age of Uncertainty",[58] in the year 2016, the role of "Complex Interdependence" in the firming up of the partnership between India and United States, has been taken up energetically. The work utilizes the thesis of "Alter casting," where-in, both the nations can begun to be cast in each other's selves, in the larger perspective of the relationship. Signalling, brandishing of a sword, a forceful march-on, a retreat into the high-up hills, (If the terrain of the battle is akin to Balaclava)[59] or the fluttering of a white surrender flag, are part of the diplomatic acts. This posturing has to be carried out in any exchange between two nations.[60]

---

[55] Shubajit Roy, " Shedding Hesitations of History: PM Modi Points to Future in his Address to US Congress," Indian Express, June 6, 2016

[56] "On Terror and Pak, Meeting of Minds With US: Sushma Swaraj" Indian Express, 6 December, 2016

[57] "India US Relations" URL: https://www.mea.gov.in/Portal/ForeignRelation/USA_15_01_2016.pdf (Online: Web), Accessed on 2 February, 2016

[58] B M Jain, " Indo US Relations in an Age of Uncertainty: An Uneasy Courtship," (New York: Routledge, 2016) Page No. 2-20

[59] Alexander Wendt, "Anarchy is What States Make of it: The Social Construction of Power," International Organization, Volume 46, No.2 Spring 1992, Page No. 391-425

[60] Ibid

The MEA release reports that there were major exchanges in the year 2015 before the visit of President Obama in January 2016, as, the state guest in New Delhi. The relationship's foundation was laid in cordial terms in the form of the "electricity" generated by PM Modi in his speech at the UN General Assembly in September 2015 along with his oratory at the Madison Square Garden. This innovative style of Public Diplomacy transpired much before the San Jose-Shark tank event with the American software firms being asked to invest in India. The MEA release further reports some of the 2015 engagements, "There were a number of high-level delegations in both directions in 2015. In January, Secretary of State John Kerry led the U.S. delegation to the Vibrant Gujarat Summit in Ahmedabad. In February, US Secretary of Treasury, Jacob Lew visited India, for, the fifth meeting of the Economic and Financial Partnership Initiative with our Finance Minister. U.S. Secretary of Transportation Anthony Foxx and the Secretary of Defense Ashton Carter, too, visited India in the middle of 2015."[61]

Finally, the South Asian Millue

The latest entrant to SAARC that is Afghanistan which is culturally linked to India as the story of the eternal Kabuliwala engrosses us with the memories of the dry fruits trader in Kolkata. It is the supine Kabuliwala selling his dry fruits one hot afternoon in Kolkata and remembering his daughter as he befriends a girl of the age of his daughter in Kabul. The Indian connection with Kabul persists with the idea of India lending a helping hand of support, succor, aid and capacity building assistance to a war ravaged Afghanistan including the entire edifice of the Gwot[62] and the Indian stance and policy on it. The torched and tarred memories of the gory partition also keep India and Pakistan in an inconvenient truce despite having fought four wars. The Indian recrimination of the plight of personages like Mallala[63] in the interstices of a failing Pakistan and the threat which it poses to a stable and increasingly progressing India, remain as matters of regional and global concern as SAARC too objectifies to attain the collectivity as practiced and enjoyed by the likes of MERCOSUR and the European Union. Individually nations such as Bhutan, Nepal, Bangladesh and Maldives can partake of their respective social-cultural pies and move on to a larger collective both bilaterally and also as pegs in a larger regional order.

Prime Minister Modi's B2B clarion call can ignite the interests of the so called micro states in South Asia where-in, the sobriquet of a benign hegemon

[61] MEA Document on US Visits to New Delhi, 2016

[62] The GWOT can be comprehended as the Global War on Terror which was initiated by President Bush's Foreign Policy establishment in the aftermath of the September 11 attacks. It was a creation of a string of pearls in order to encircle the entire gamut of nations and civilities affected by the menace of global Terrorism.

[63] Mallala Yousufzai" I am Mallala: The Girl who stood up for Education and was shot by Taliban," (Liitlebrown and company, 2013)

can be done away by the Indian foreign policy making the establishment. The relationship between India and Bhutan is historic. The new government is committed to make this even stronger. Strength of a democracy is very important for that region and its people. The stronger India will be, the better it is for Bhutan and other SAARC nations. A strong and stable India is needed to make sure that we can help our neighbours with their problems." [64]Prime Minister Modi ignited the passions during his first visit in his uncanny Public diplomacy pattern, where-in, he stated that terrorism divides but culture and Tourism unites in the context of the hilly billy Kingdom of Bhutan.[65] The significance attached to Bhutan conveys a stolid message that the conundrum caused by the benign neglect in the Indian establishment is a development of the past and the new dispensation in New Delhi considers the South Asian nations as being second to none. Bhutan and Nepal being the correct instances in the context of regional cooperation.

In the context of Bangladesh, the issue of the enclaves has been considered anew by the Modi Government, where-in, stark resemblances can be drawn between the 1971 Land Boundary Protocol and the 2011 land boundary agreement with Prime Minister Manmohan Singh. Also, the Indian help to Maldives during the regime of Abdul Gayoom along with the help rendered to the island nation in the 2004 Tsunami and the stance related to Nasheed's political fortunes shed ample light to the India- Maldiv 'bilaterals.' Sri Lanka too has rescinded with agreements on the exchange of the fishermen and the Indian federalized touch in its regional foreign policy too has come into prominence in the context of the Bengalis in Bangladesh and Tamils in relation with the Emerald Isle with India lending all the vocal support for the promulgation of legislation to end the Executive and autocratic Presidential system in Colombo. The regional-Federalism paradox has been conveniently picked up by Prime Minister Modi as he intends to provide autonomy to the states as they interact with their immediate neighbors in South Asia.

To Conclude

The pre eminence imparted to a small South Asian nation states was to serve as an ideal staple mechanism for the Modi Government to flag off issues, ink agreements and solve differences with the neighborhood while the larger Look east policy adorns the regional mantle as the' "Act East" Policy. The entire striving of the New Delhi dispensation can be further buttressed by the content of the speech which PM Modi delivered at the Madison Square garden in Manhattan. The Speech can be related as thus, " He brought the roof down with crowd pleasing jokes about how a country that was once regarded as a land of snake-charmers was now spinning the world around its finger with a

[64] India Today Correspondent, "Modi addresses Bhutan's Parliament, Says a Stronger India Better For Bhutan too," India Today, June, 2014

[65] Ibid

(computer) mouse and how India had sent a spacecraft to Mars for seven rupees a kilometre when it cost 10 rupees a kilometre in Ahmedabad." [66] The Indian Prime Minister further narrated that, "It was the idea of Sulabh Shuachalayas ruling roost in India. Also, the air of new York has a peculiar electricity about it which only the proactive elders and the agile youngsters can bring to a city."[67]

Thus, apart from all this diplomatic razzmatazz, the act of delivering the United Nations General Assembly Speech in Hindi too served as an avidly observed and commonly commented upon ***'First'*** dovetailing with the Republic day visit of President Obama to the Indian capital winding up in a much televised spectacle of, "Chai Pe Charcha". The act of quoting from Bob Dylan also brought into context the changed facets of a traditionally ensconceds Indian diplomacy in the Nehruvian mould since the days of the decades of Congress rule. Observers and Pundits might be quick to belittle these steps and diplomatic initiatives as being too much in the higher end and being devoid of substance and being all about spectacularity, still the novae and fresh nature of the Diplomatic approach leaves an indelible mark on the foreign policy motifs of the India Union. It is this quaint quest with the amalgamation of the local with the Global which has ignited the fancy and the expectations of the Global polity and geo economics. If the 'visceral' and 'the color, verve, vibrancy and the gaiety' of the Cultural conjoindness can be eclectically firmed up and reach a converging fruition, then, the quest for a feasible and functional Public Diplomacy strategy can be on the anvil in the relationship with United States of America, with, India leading the odyssey with a 'benign benefaction.'

In the larger context, in the month of April 2015, Prime Minister Modi unveiled his Rawls Theorization by claiming to post Indian objectives as being supportive of weakest nations in the larger chain of the developing and developed world. He reiterated as part of his drive in Paris and with the Rafale manufacturers in Tolouse, France, that mere growth stories premised upon bland statistics cannot amount to India's diplomatic standpoint but foreign positing with the attribute of a human face, sentiment and hope will form the substratum of India's diplomatic face. The same runs true to the trade quotient embedded in the cultural and trade practicalities of United States with India unassumingly heralding a conjoined front for the twin rule of law abiding, liberal and constitutionally Democratic nationalities of India and United States. The initiation and the precursor role of India as a soft power instrumentality and a natural leader, can serve as a recurrent reality for Washington. This is one stolid policy prescription which can be proffered over here.

❐

[66] Chidanad Rajghatta, " PM Narendra Modi Enthralls a Rapturous Crowd at the Madison Square Garden," Times of India, September 8, 2014

[67] Ibid

The Panchashila of India-US Economic Relationship: Future Trajectory in a Post Pandemic World

Pritam Banerjee

Introduction

To contend that the India-US economic relationship is a critical one for India, would be stating the obvious. It lies at the heart of India's economic rise in the last two decades and the US market served as the bedrock of India's IT and IT enabled services revolution. It was this IT and allied services led economic growth in cities like Bengaluru, Hyderabad, Delhi NCR, and Pune that created the young professional middle-class with disposable incomes, which in turn led to the urbanization revolution and rise of the new economy. The construction boom and demand for services associated with food, hospitality, urban transport, healthcare, and education have in turn led to the creation of millions of new urban jobs. The movement of Indian professionals to the US, mostly in IT and allied sectors, but, also prominently in finance, healthcare, and education, have created new people –to-people connections between the two countries with significant economic impact. The flow of skills and investment from Indian origin professionals in the US has been the catalyst for the growth of the technology sector in the country. The story of many successful Indian start-ups traces their financial and entrepreneurial roots in the US.

The US was the predominant market for Indian exports twenty years ago at the start of this century. While having declined in relative importance, it still remains a critical market for Indian exports. Part of the story of India-US trade and investment is associated with a quaint transfer of technology and production know-how. Such transfers, some formal through licensing or payment of royalty, some informal happening through diffusion of know-how and processes, has been an important part of the Indian manufacturing revolution in pharmaceuticals, biotechnology, automobiles and other key sectors.

But this is not a one-way street. The Indian market increasingly represents opportunity for US businesses, and has grown in importance over the last two decades. US ability to access large numbers of Indian skilled professionals have allowed US firms to grow and innovate, and India serves as a critical location for US research and development efforts in some of the most important growth sectors for the future such as pharmaceuticals, IT, renewable energy, robotics among others. For US digital giants, blocked out of the Chinese market, India represents the most important market outside of the US. The focus of firms like Amazon, Google, and Facebook on the Indian market underlines this.

The Indian growth story is therefore critical to future US growth. Nothing underpins this rising importance of India to US economic actors than the defence sector. The defence sector is an important source of export earnings and jobs in the US. India has emerged as one of the most important markets globally for military hardware and technology, and its relative importance will only increase in the future.

In many ways, it is the India-US economic relationship that has underpinned the India-US strategic engagement. It was the realization about the rising economic importance of India at the turn of the century that led to US strategic thinkers re-consider the India-US relationship that had nosedived post Indian nuclear tests in 1997. The bipartisan support for a robust India-US relationship in Washington is driven as much by the economic prospects India presents to US firms and criticality of India to US led value-chains in knowledge industries, as it is by geo-strategic aspects and the rise of a hostile China.

The India-US economic relationship has its own 'Panchashila' or five fundamentals. These are trade in goods and services, investment, movement of people, technology, and defence sector linkages. Section II below will briefly discuss how these five fundamentals have evolved for both these countries in the last two decades since turn of the century, and Section III will pick up the thread to analyse how it will evolve in the coming decades, especially in light of the shocks to the international system due to the Covid pandemic.

I. Past as Prologue: Brief discussion of India-US economic linkages in the last two decades

The India-US economic relationship has matured in the last two decades and has become multi-dimensional. India and the US have a robust trade relationship in goods and especially services. There are strong India-

US investment linkages. There is a very significant movement of skilled workers from India to the US, which is now resulting in the reverse migration of skills back to India in recent times. India and US have developed strong relationships in research and development and technology that also extends to their defence relationship and increasing proximity of their military-industrial establishments. A brief discussion on each of these five areas follows.

Trade in Goods and Services

At the turn of the century in the year 2000, US was the global economic colossus, accounting for 31% of the global GDP (21% in PPP terms), 19% of global imports and close to 14% of its exports. India was a relative minnow, accounting for just 1.4% of global GDP (4.5% in PPP terms), and less than 1% of its import and exports. US was also the pre-dominant export market for India, accounting for 22% of Indian merchandise exports.

Almost twenty years later in 2019, India's relative global heft has increased significantly, while that of the US has declined. This relative US decline is representative of the rise in importance of large Asian countries, especially China, but also India and Korea.

In 2019, US share of global GDP was down to 25% (16% in PPP terms), while its share of imports was down from about fifth of the global share to 13%. US share of exports have held steadier around 10 to 11% of global share through much of the second decade of this century.

In 2019 Indian share of global GDP stood at 3.3% (7% in PPP terms). In PPP terms India now represents the fourth pillar of the global economy after US, China, and the EU. Indian share of exports and imports have also increased to 2.2% and 2.6% respectively.

While US importance has declined in relative terms for India, India's importance to the US has as a market has increased, and the relative trends would accentuate this rising Indian importance to US, with a corresponding relative decline of the US to India[1].

But there is need for further nuance to these numbers. While the US has been replaced by China has India's most pre-eminent export market, with a 16% share of Indian exports in 2019, it still remains important. What is more even more telling is the qualitative transformation Indian merchandise exportsto the US in the last two decades.

In 2000 Indian exports to US were dominated by textiles and apparel, gems and jewellery, carpets, leather and other such relatively low-tech products. By 2019 pharmaceuticals, engineering, automobiles, and electrical machinery were in the list of top export products. Indian exports to the US have therefore become representative of the deep intra-industry linkages and

[1] All data is from World Bank Development Indicators database

value-chain integration between the two economies. This is in sharp contrast with Indian trade with China, where India mostly exports raw-materials or low-tech semi-processed goods of low unit value and imports final good of high unit value[2].

Such deep intra-industry linkage leading to value-chain integration are even more significant for the India-US trade in services. Right from the beginning, the trade in IT and other knowledge services between the two countries underlined the leveraging of Indian skills and their combination with US technology and capital to serve global markets. India's USD 214 billion services exports, a significant contributor to its economy and critical to middle-class job creation for its burgeoning numbers of educated youth, remains dependent on US dominated global tech industry value-chains[3].

The US has thus continued to remain the pre-dominant market for Indian services exports over the last two decades. The presence of a large number of research and development centres and large captive operations of US IT and technology majors in India has continued to drive the trade in intangible services and knowledge products, some of which are not formally captured in official trade figures due to limitations of data collection.

Movement of People

Indian immigration in substantive numbers to the US started in in late 1960s after the Immigration and Nationality Act of 1965 replaced an origin-based quota system to a system that emphasized skills. The 1990s saw Indian immigration to the US take-off based on the rapidly rising demand for skilled IT professionals. The Indian community today represents one of the wealthiest (in per capita terms) and most educated groups in the US. At about 3 million, or roughly 1% of the US population, it is also one of the fastest growing ethnic cohorts in the US.

Apart from these 3 million plus with citizenship and permanent residency status (i.e., green card holders), a very substantial number of Indian reside in the US at any given point of time as temporary workers (on H1, L1 and other such visa categories) and as students. Such temporary workers and students are often absorbed over the medium term into the US workforce and therefore represent the 'supply chain' of skilled immigrants. Between 2010 and 2019 about 1.86 million Indiansgot H1B visas, by far the highest of any country, accounting for 46% of total H1B visas[4]. Their presence in large number in leading firms in the technology, medicine, and financial sectors underscore

[2] All data pertaining to Indian merchandise exports is from Export Import Database of the Ministry of Commerce and Industry, Government of India

[3] Data on services exports is from World Bank Development Indicators Database

[4] All visa related data is from Visa Statistics Database of the Department of State's Bureau of Consular Affairs available at https://travel.state.gov/content/travel/en/legal/visa-law0/visa-statistics.html

their importance to maintain US competitiveness in cutting edge technology.

The significant Indian student presence in US university campuses, and their absorption into US workforce represents mutually beneficial human capital development for the two countries. This cohort is able to be a conduit for ideas, innovation, technology, and management practices between the two countries. Between 2000 and 2010,0.82 million Indian students enrolled in US campuses representing 13.7% of total international enrolment. In the period 2010 to 2019 that number went up to 1.48 million students representing 15.5% of total enrolment. India is second only to China in terms of total enrolment including for graduate schools and high technology programs[5].

Besides the obvious economic implication of remittances by Indian professionals to India (11.7 billion USD in 2017)[6], and network effects on entrepreneurship, investment, and technology transfer between Indian and US firms that arise from such people to people to contacts, there are economic implications of the cultural and lifestyle related aspects as well.

Return immigration to India of Indian origin professionals and students has led to demand for US brands and US type lifestyle services creating opportunities for US brands and lifestyle products in the Indian market, increasingly important globally due to its large and growing middle-class. Similarly, exposure of Americans to their Indian friends and colleagues have led to an increased appreciation of Indian cuisine and lifestyle products related to ayurveda, yoga, and Indian popular music and cinema.

Investment

The United States is a major source of Foreign Direct Investment. More specifically US based firms are as in many cases the actual investment is routed through tax havens such as Cyprus, Singapore, Bermuda, Mauritius etc. United States as an official source of FDI (apart from the amounts routed from tax havens) have more often that not been in the list of top five sources of FDI into India in the last two decades.

Globally, FDI outflows from the US represented a sum of USD 2.24 trillion in the period 2011-19, representing 17% of the global total. As indicated, this excludes US investment, both private and corporate, routed through tax havens.

FDI into India has taken off since opening up of the Indian economy following liberalization in 1991-92, picking up pace from the late 1990s as the Indian economy started to integrate into global value-chains in manufacturing and services. From an extremely modest annual inflow of FDI of USD 3.5 billion in 2000, the corresponding number in 2019 stood at USD 50 billion.

[5] All enrolment data is from the OpenDoors database available at

[6] Data is from Pew Research Centre's Remittance Flows Worldwide 2017 database available at https://www.pewresearch.org/global/interactives/remittance-flows-by-country/

With the maturing of Indian industry over the last two decades, Indian firms are also seeking to acquire technology, locate manufacturing and establish commercial presence in other countries. Outward FDI from India for the year 2000 was a negligible USD 80 million, the corresponding number for 2019 was 12.4 billion. Total outward FDI from India between 2011 and 2019 stood at a substantial USD 81 billion. It also needs to be noted that Indian firms and investors also often tend to use global tax havens for their investments, and therefore this is likely to be an underestimation[7].

While this is still modest by compared to EU, Japan, US, or even China, this incredible increase by a factor of 150 shows the rapidly growing appetite of Indian industry for global opportunities. Of late, significant Indian FDI has gone into the US market.

As a demographically ageing United States seeks investment opportunities that allows its savings to grow, India offers one of the best bets given its market size and relatively mature industrial eco-system. This is especially true light of two developments in China that has caused disquiet among US investors. The first relates to the blatant inflation of sales and revenue numbers by the Chinese start-upLuckin Coffee that had been listed in US financial market. Luckin Coffee was subsequently fined USD 180 million by the US Securities and Exchange Commission (SEC). But this episode has led to calls for far greater scrutiny of Chinese firms listed in US exchanges and application of stricter accounting standards that apply to US firms and independent audits on Chinese firms.

The second relates new regulations associated with China's Corporate Social Credit System or CSCS that creates an architecture for micro-management of corporate operations for all companies operating in China and requires firms to share data with the Chinese government on almost all aspects of their operations and management. The US government has flagged serious concern about the CSCS and considers it a serious threat to US firms that invest and operate in China[8].

Technology Transfer

The global economy is undergoing a massive technological shift. Industrialization 4.0 will automate many blue-collar jobs and artificial intelligence applications would have the same impact for many white-collar ones. Combined with developments in adoption of renewable energy, nanotechnology, materials science and technologies such as 3D printing, this

[7] All FDI data is from UNCTAD World Investment Report, 2020

[8] For details, refer to China's Corporate Social Credit System: Context, Competition, Technology, and Geopolitics by Kendra Schaefer, November 2020. The paper was prepared at the request of the U.S.-China Economic and Security Review Commission to support its deliberations. Available at https://www.uscc.gov/research/chinas-corporate-social-credit-system-context-competition-technology-and-geopolitics

would completely change the nature of manufacturing and global supply chains. Competitiveness would come to depend even more on ability to access technology and having the skills to apply it.

The United States remains the world's pre-eminent technological superpower, followed by Europe. While China, and to an extent India, have made rapid strides in developing a robust technologically advanced industrial eco-system, they are still way behind the US and EU. US based entities earned USD 117 billion USD as payments for intellectual property in 2019, representing 30% of the global total. In contrast China earned USD 6.6 billion and India 0.8 billion respectively. India has spent USD 28 billion to pay for the use IPR in the last decade alone[9].

The US University system which dominates the rankings for the top 200 Universities in science and technology, and their ability to attract global talent to their campuses and research institutes, including from India, would ensure that the US leadership in IPR development remains in place in the foreseeable future.

Thus, for India to succeed in the global economy, it would remain dependent on US (and EU and Japan) for technology inputs. Some of this know-how would organically flow through the highly-skilled Indian diaspora as was discussed earlier. Some would be the result of India-US defence cooperation and joint production as discussed subsequently.

But a large part of the access to technology would actually flow through US investment and collaboration between US and Indian firms in global value-chains. As US firms leverage India's large absolute number of highly trained technical manpower and set up their global research and development centres in India, this would also emerge as another source of diffusion of knowledge and technology.

As in the case of investment, US firms are increasingly reluctant to work in China or with Chinese firms given their predatory tactics to steal technology. India with a more robust legal eco-system that objectively protects IPR, including for foreign IPR holders, is already seen as a more reliable partner by US firms in this regard.

Defence Sector Linkages USD 230 billion in wages and benefits and has total industry revenue of USD 909 billion (roughly amounting to Netherlands GDP)[10]. The impact on local economies of the presence of defence industries is very significant, and legislators from these regions take the interests of the defence industry very seriously.

---

[9] Data for payments to IPR is from World Development Indicators Database

[10] Data is taken from the report 2020 Facts and Figures: US Aerospace and Defense prepared by Aerospace Industries Association (AIA), available at https://www.aia-aerospace.org/wp-content/uploads/2020/09/2020-Facts-and-Figures-U.S.-Aerospace-and-Defense.pdf

The United States defence spending stood at 718 billion USD in 2019 accounting for close to 40% of the world's total. With international weapons and systems sales of USD 266 billion US also accounted for 54% of the global arms trade in 2019, with 48 large US corporations involved in such defence related trade[11]. The US military-industrial complex is therefore a critical factor in technology development, trade and strategic ambitions for the US, besides making legislators extremely sensitive to its continued good health given its impact on local jobs and economy in parts of the US.

India has emerged as the most vibrant market for defence equipment and technology. With defence spending of USD 71 billion in 2019, India ranks third globally with a share of 3.8% of total global spending in defence. With the world's second largest defence economy, China virtually off-limits to US defence sector, India is a very important market. Moreover, as Indian GDP grows, India's quantum of defence spending and its global share of such spending is both expected to increase substantially in the coming decade[12].

The India-US defence relationship has now matured substantially from the days in early 2000s when US sanctions and Indian lack of trust of US suppliers stymied any meaningful relationships from developing. This relationship is directly linked to common threat perceptions and strategic interests of both countries and is likely to grow.

Since defence sector is often the cutting edge of technology which later finds industrial and consumer applications, defence cooperation is often a catalyst for technology transfer with longer-term implications on product development and manufacturing competitiveness. A enlarged India-US defence cooperation canvas will therefore have implications for technology transfer and growth of new industries in India as well.

As India pursues greater self-reliance in defence production, this would also provide opportunities for investment and cooperation between Indian and US firms. Unlike say a China such cooperation, technology transfer and diffusion of know-how will be based on rule of law and strong protection for intellectual property provided under Indian law, and thus will be of mutual interest and not a result of the kind of coercion that US firms have experienced in China.

II. India-US Economic Relationship in the Post Pandemic world order

The story of the global economy in the last two decades, especially from a developing country perspective, has been that of coping with the rise of China. The process of integration of China into the global economy was championed

---

[11] All data on defence spending and arms sales are from the Stockholm International Peace Research Institute (SIPRI) database. https://www.sipri.org/databases

[12] Ibid

by major western powers, including the US in the 1990s. In the famous words of President Clinton, China's integration into the global economy would be a 'historic step towards continued prosperity in America, reform in China, and peace in the world'.

Subsequent events were to prove the naivety of these assumptions. The state-sponsored Chinese economic machine surreptitiously broke every single rule in the global trading rule book established by the World Trade Organization (WTO). Warning signs about Chinese malpractices on trade and investment started to emerge by early 2000s and complaints about the use of generous subsidies, intellectual property theft, counterfeiting, and use of non-tariff barriers to deny market access to imports into China were beginning to be registered. Many developing economies including India started to feel the impact as Chinese exports eliminated their firms from traditional export markets where they had earlier been competitive suppliers over decades, and even started to dominate their domestic markets.

The developed economies remained relatively cocooned from Chinese competition in the early 2000s since their economies had graduated to the production of technologically sophisticated goods and Chinese manufacturing at that time was concentrated on labour-intensive goods or providing assembly-line mass production services for more sophisticated products that could be used by western firms to cut their production costs.

But by the 2010s, China was beginning to undermine the dominance of western firms even in these technologically sophisticated industries. The west including the US were now forced to reckon with manipulation of the Chinese state and its blatant disregard for global trading rules.

The Covid pandemic has since further underlined the vulnerability of China dependent supply-chains and the dominance of Chinese manufacturing for many key products. This concern will be a key driver of policy actions related to the political economy in the coming decade. US will look to significantly reduce their supply-chain dependence on China and diversity its portfolio of trade and investment.

India will emerge as the key economic partner for the US in this context. As global production becomes more and more tech-driven, a large consumption economy like India stands to gain as it has much more leverage in being able to attract technology transfer. In addition, India's relatively credible legal institutions and independent judicial system would inspire confidence in global technology rights holders to engage with Indian industry. It also needs to be noted that very few countries have the absolute numbers of skilled personnel essential to successful technology adoption and innovation that India has. Human resource development trajectories indicate that China and India would have the largest pools of technically qualified human resources in the world in the near future. The newly announced National Education Policy (NEP) will help to ensure the depth, expanse, and quality of such human resources.

India is, therefore, the critical force-multiplier for sustaining a democratic and rules-based global orderalong with the US, Japan and major European economies like Germany, UK, and France. British Prime Minster Boris Johnson's decision to convene an alliance of the most powerful democracies, being labelled as the D10 alliance consisting of United States, UK, Japan, France, Germany, Italy, Canada, India, Australia, and Korea underlines that this geo-political shift is already underway.

What is significant is that the D10 is considered a much more relevant forum to the G7 which did not include powerful market economies and democracies like India and Korea, and was therefore a relic of the cold war era. What is also significant that none of the G7 member countries have objected to this, and in fact the popular media and think-tank communities in all these countries have welcomed this strategic shift.

The US would be the biggest beneficiary of a rising India that is economically and strategically committed to such an alliance of democracies. The size of the Indian market and its investment heft provides the most potent alternative to China in South Asia, South East Asia, Eastern Africa, and the Middle-East. An India centric regional value-chains in South and South East Asia would be able to counter or at the very least reduce the influence of China backed Belt and Road Initiative (BRI). An India centric regional value-chain will be based on market economy principles and would be governed by rule of law and reciprocity. This dovetails with the economic and strategic priorities of the D10 member countries, especially that of the US.

US firms would stand to benefit most from the rising appetite of an Indian market expected to become the world's second largest in PPP terms within the next 15 years. As the US economy becomes even more knowledge intensive due to the paradigm shifts in production technology, it would be even more sensitive to ensuring that it gets a fair return to the intellectual property produced by US firms and individuals. By 2035, India will be the largest such market where US firms and investors can operate under the protection of transparent laws and fair access to a judicial process.

The fundamentals that would make the India-US economic relationship the defining one for both countries in 21st century is in place. As discussed in Section I, the 'Panchashila' of trade, investment, movement of people, technology, and military-industrial relationship are in place. But there is need for focused engagement between the two countries in all these five aspects of this Panchashila.

There is need for sustained track II diplomacy to develop the modalities and rules of engagement in each of these five areas. There are irritants in trade in terms of protection of sensitive sectors by both countries, there are issues associated with movement of people and visas. US firms have long complained about opening up Indian market for investment in areas like retail and banking. India has some ways to go in defining a strategic military industrial development plan that goes beyond a offset policy for domestic procurement by foreign military hardware suppliers.

New areas of irritants such as data protection and localization and protection of digital services markets are emerging. And there is always the off-chance that US domestic activism that holds India-US economic relationship hostage to imaginary violations of environmental, labour or human rights. This is particularly egregious given that by impeding trade with a democracy like India, such activists actually create economic space for Chinese economic players, and the Chinese regime is a confirmed violator of human, environmental, and labour rights. Such Track II diplomacy needs to focus on establishing the rules of the game that address such irritants and anticipates the institutional frameworks within which such rules would be implemented. These inputs from track II would be officially formalized incrementally. Some of this formalization of rules and institutions would be bilateral, others can take a more plurilateral framework, for e.g., as a part of a D10 agreement.

To illustrate, a long-term objective for India and US could be a Comprehensive Economic Partnership Agreement (CECA) that would address all of the five aspects of the Panchashila discussed earlier. In the short-term the building blocks can be individual bilateral agreements regulating the movement of people (Visas), data localization and protection (a safe harbour agreement that allows free movement of data between two countries based on some conditions), and specific safeguards on protection of IPR in automation, manufacturing and defence related fields. In some areas, such as labour and environment, or the modalities through which democratic free-market economies can protect their markets from predatory investment, digital invasion, and technology piracy, the D10 can provide the forum to develop the governing principles through framework agreements.

Conclusion

In conclusion, it can be said that there is much work ahead for economic and strategic thinkers in both countries, and their policy-makers. The India-US economic relationship is a large house under construction floor by floor. There is no debate about the absolute need for this house to be built. What needs to be ensured is that the construction does not stop and all the floors get built and in good time.

❐

President Trump's South Asia Strategy: An Analysis

Dr Vivek Kumar Mishra
Assistant Professor & Head of the Department,
Political Science and International Relations,
Gautam Buddha University, Greater Noida.

Abstract

President Donald J. Trump administration announced two new foreign policy strategies in August 2017. The first is the"South Asia Strategy", which focuses on handling the Afghanistan war situation and considering the importance of Pakistan and India to tackle it. The South Asia Strategy has designed by Trump's inner circle of advisers to avoid losing rather than winning in Afghanistan.South Asia strategy is based on two main objectives in South Asia.The first is working out a way to withdraw troops from Afghanistan; the other is strengthening India's relationship.The second foreign policy strategy is the "Free and open Indo-Pacific", based on expanding the US geographic scope in the Asian region, including India. Both of the strategies reflect substantial continuity with the previous US administration's policies. Both strategies, have, been designed to keep the view of the rise of China, which, has forced the Trump administration to reexamine its foreign policy priorities towards South Asia and adopt new strategies.

Introduction

Trump's South Asia Strategy presents three priorities.The first is based on providing security and stability in Afghanistan through possible political negotiations. The second seeks better cooperation and support from Pakistan to contain terrorism in the region. The last priority deals with the role of India, as, a development and economic partner in Afghanistan. In the larger context of such a background, the article attempts to analyse Prez. Trump's South Asia policy.

US President Donald Trump announced his administration's new "South Asia Strategy" in a televised address at Fort Myer military baseon August 21, 2017.[1] After the announcement of a new policy in South Asia, multiple efforts have been undertaken to spot the policy's changes and continuities. The new strategy presented three priorities: one, creating security and stability in Afghanistan; two, seeking greater cooperation from Pakistan to contain terrorism and three, an explicit role for India as a development and economic partner in Afghanistan. Trump's South Asia strategy departed from the Obama administration Afghanistan strategy of 2009. It has changed the dynamics of the US relationship towards Indian and Pakistani engagement in Afghanistanunder the Trump Administration.

The much vaunted Trump administration in 2017, has, changed its approach to Pakistan and, with that, its approach to India's role in Afghanistan. In a speech, President Trump publicly chastised Pakistan for accepting American foreign aid while sheltering the very terrorists the US was fighting.[2]With the new South Asia policy, the United States suspended all security assistance and economic assistance to Pakistan to dratepressure on Pakistan to change its policy towards Afghanistan; parallelly, the Trump administration has sought to develop its strategic partnership with India.He called upon India to "do more with Afghanistan, especially in the area of economic assistance and development."[3]

Trump Afghanistan Strategy

Post-September 11, 2001, Afghanistan emerged as a significant US foreign policy concern. The Trumpian Afghanistan strategy was designed to bring the Afghan conflict end on terms and conditions acceptable to the Afghan people and their international partners. It properly views Afghanistan in a regional context, with a renewed focus on Pakistan, and provides flexibility in shaping the deployment and use of US forces in support of Afghanistan and the counter-terrorism mission.[4] The strategy intends to enable Afghanistan to become a more stable state-one capable of protecting its people with limited outside

1 David Nakamura and Abby Phillip, "Trump announces new strategy for Afghanistan that calls for atroop increase", Washington Post August 21, 2017.

2 "Remarks by President Trump on the Strategy in Afghanistan and South Asia", August 21. 2017.https://www.whitehouse.gov/briefings-statements/remarks-president-trump-strategy-afghanistan-south-asia.

3 Ibid

4 Dr. Bharath Gopalaswamy, Ambassador James Cunningham, Dr. Ashley J. Tellis& others "Review of President Trump's South Asia Strategy: The Way Ahead, One Year In" Atlantic Council (South Asia Centre, October 2018), p.2.

support and lay the foundation for bringing the Taliban to the negotiating table and, ultimately, to end the conflict.[5]

On his Afghanistan strategy,President Trump said that "the consequences of a rapid exit from Afghanistan are both predictable and unacceptable", the administration "will not talk about numbers of troops".[6]He said that the Afghan strategy would be based on ground realities and stated, "from now on, victory will have a clear definition. Attacking our enemies, obliterating ISIS, devastating Al-Qaeda, preventing the Taliban from taking over Afghanistan and stopping mass terror attacks against the United States of America."[7]

TheSouth Asia strategy has focussed on a more significantrole of India in Afghanistan. President Trump applauded India as the largest democracy of the World and key security and economic partner of the United States and appreciated India's significant contributions to stability in Afghanistan.[8] Trump also simultaneously framed India's expectationsregarding a quid pro quo of India's trade turnover with the US.[9] India's has to play an important role in Afghanistan. It would be based on its potential, which will contribute toAfghanistan's development, especially in providing economic support, politically stablility, and socially inclusive Afghanistan.

The Taliban's resurgence in Afghanistan has seen a grave security threat in the South Asian region.Initially, the US reconciliation talks with the Taliban have not gone anywhere substantial to bring a political solution. US and Taliban representatives were very close to a troop withdrawal deal that would also produce commitments from the Taliban on a 10-day cease-fire, a reduction in violence, and talks with the Afghan government.[10]

PresidentTrump had changed its Afghanistan policy at the beginning of 2019 becausethe earlier policy had predicated American presence or withdrawal on conditions on the ground realities rather than 'arbitrary timetables. The new policy has prioritised US peace talks with the Taliban to allow the US to exit Afghanistan, ideally before the US elections 2020.[11] The Policy change has increased Pakistan's leverage with the US once again because Pakistan has viewed as an important

---

5 Ibid.

6 The New York Times, "Full Transcript and Video: Trump"s Speech on Afghanistan," August 21, 2017, https://www.nytimes.com/2017/08/21/world/asia/trump-speech-afghanistan.html, accessed on August 25, 2017.

7 Ibid

8 Ibid

9 Ankit Panda, "No Exit From Afghanistan: Major Takeaways From Trump's Big Speech on America's Longest War," The Diplomat, August 22, 2017, http://thediplomat.com/2017/08/no-exitfrom-afghanistan- major-takeaways-from-trumps-big-speech-on-americas-longest-war/

10 Michael Kugelman, "A Critical moment for US policy in South Asia" Arab News January 25, 2020. https://arab.news/45zbj

11 "Trump And Modi: Prospects For Us-India Burden Sharing", The Asia Foundation, June 2019. https://www.isas.nus.edu.sg/wp-content/uploads/2019/06/isas-trump-modi-pdf-june2019.pdf

player to initiate negotiations with the Taliban. It has led the US administration to backpedal on its earlier, stricter policy towards Pakistan.[12]

On February 29, 2020, The US and Taliban representativesconcluded the "US-Taliban Agreement",which paved the waytowards the withdrawal of USand foreign armed forces from Afghanistan over the next 14 months and talks between Kabul and the Taliban.[13]The accord was signed in Doha by US special envoy Zalmay Khalilzad and Taliban political chief Mullah Abdul Ghani Baradar. Mike Pompeo, U.S. Secretary of State, was also present at the ceremony.[14]The Trump Administration signedthis agreement into direct negotiations with the Taliban without the participation of Afghan government representatives."[15]Ambassador Zalmay Khalilzad, an Afghan-born former US Ambassador to Afghanistan, appointed as a special representative for Afghanistan reconciliation in September 2018. Khalilzad held various continuous series of meetings with Taliban officials in Doha and consultations with the Afghan, Pakistani, and other regional governments for over a year. Finally,on February 29, 2020, the efforts culminated in the form of accord.[16]In accord, both sides agreed to two "interconnected guarantees: the withdrawal of all US and foreign armed forces by May 2021 and unspecified Taliban action to prevent other groups including Al-Qaeda from using Afghan soil to threaten the United States and its allies."[17] The agreement also deals with the US commitments as; facilitating a prisoner exchange between the Taliban and the Afghan government and removing US sanctions on Taliban members.

Since the agreement was signed, The USadministration has asserted that the Taliban are not fulfilling their commitments under the accord, especially about Al-Qaeda.[18] US officials also describe increased Taliban violence as "not consistent" with the agreement. Although no provisions in the agreement address the Taliban reducing or refraining from attacks on US or allied forces, the Taliban reportedly committed not to attack US forces in non-public annexes accompanying the accord.[19] On January 15, 2021, the Trump administration reported that "it had reduced US forces in Afghanistan to 2,500, the lowest

12 Rani D. Mullen, "US-India Cooperation in Afghanistan" in South Asia Discussion Paper (San Francisco:The Asia Foundation and Institute of South Asian Studies), June 2019, p.42.

13 "U.S., Taliban sign peace deal; American troops to leave Afghanistan in 14 months" The Hindu (New Delhi), February 29, 2020.

14 Ibid.

15 Department of Defense, "Enhancing Security and Stability in Afghanistan," June 2017.

16 The text of the agreement is available at https://www.state.gov/wp- content/uploads/2020/02/ Agreement-For-Bringing-Peace-to-Afghanistan-02.29.20.pdf

17 Clayton Thomas, "Afghanistan: Background and U.S. Policy: In Brief", Congressional Research Service March 25, 2021, No.R45122.p.1. https://fas.org/sgp/crs/row/R45122.pdf

18 "Taliban not living up to its commitments, U.S. Defense Secretary says," Reuters, May 5, 2020.

19 "Violence 'Not Consistent' with US-Taliban Deal: US Envoy," TOLOnews, October 13, 2020.

level since 2001, in advance of the potential complete military withdrawal by May 2021 as perthe US-Taliban agreement accord."[20]

Trump Administration insisted that the troop reduction would not significantly change the two complementary US missions in Afghanistan: counter-terrorism and training, advising, and assisting Afghan forces. However, some US Department of Defense officials have statedthat "the troop reduction order was not ideal from the US perspective and might result in some adjustments to US operations and limits to US options."[21] Some international observers havealso questioned the decisionto justify that the US can perform both the training and counter-terrorism missions with acceptable risk with a low force level.[22]

The Trump newapproach provided increased devolution of decision-making powers to the military to tackle terror groups operating in the region more efficiently. It also made armed forces withdrawal contingent upon the fulfilment of certain conditions on the ground, instead of being a time-bound exercise, to compel the insurgents to agree to engage in negotiations to end the conflict. Against this background, the US-Taliban deal and initiation of intra-Afghan talks, after much contention over the issue of prisoner release, marked an apparent success for Trump.[23] Simultaneously, the accord raised severesecurity concerns within the Afghan government vis-a-vis the Taliban's possibility of regaining political power in Afghanistan. Moreover, the agreement compelled a recalibration of strategic postures amongst vital regional stakeholders, particularly in the immediate neighbourhood.

Trump Pakistan Policy

Trump's new strategy for South Asia, announced on August 21, 2017, was a harbinger of change in Pakistan relations. On January 4, 2018, the United States suspended all security-related assistance to Pakistan, including payments through Coalition Support Funds and the transfer of security-related equipment - a punitive measure in response to the alleged provision of sanctuaries by Pakistan to the Afghan Taliban and the Haqqani Network.[24]Debates had been intense in the American beltway as to how the US should deal with Pakistan,

20 Clayton Thomas, "Afghanistan: Background and U.S. Policy: In Brief", Congressional Research Service March 25, 2021, R45122, p.1. https://crsreports.congress.gov

21 General Kenneth F. McKenzie, Jr. Defense One Interview with Katie Bo Williams," U.S. Central Command, December 10, 2020.

22 Afghanistan Study Group Final Report, United States Institute of Peace, February 2021. https://www.usip.org/publications?publication_type%5B0%5D=7#filters

23 Shubhangi Pandey, South Asia: Ending, or Losing, an 'Endless War' in Afghanistan? in Harsh V. Pant How Donald Trump has changed the World (New Delhi:Observer Research Foundation, 2020), p.9.

24 Natasha Tariq, Policy Analysis Pakistan's Economic Vulnerability and the US South Asia Strategy in Light of CPEC, Sustainable Development Policy Institute,No. 19/1- International Relations, 2019. http://hdl.handle.net/11540/9583.

but one whose actions, particularly in counter-terrorism, has hardly aligned with that of the US."Any counter-terrorism effort is bound to face a difficult task, as long as the insurgent groups or the terrorist groups find shelters in other countries."[25]President Trump's taughtstand on Pakistan was echoed even during his National Security Advisor H R McMaster's earlier visit to Pakistan.[26]In his South Asian Strategy, President Trumpemphatically said: "Pakistan has also sheltered the same organisations that try every day to kill American people. We have been paying Pakistan billions and billions of dollars at the same time they are housing the very terrorists that we are fighting."[27]

Pakistan's geo-strategic location and influence over the Taliban compel the US policymaker that the US will not beultimately able to ignore Pakistan. It is because of these reasons,President Trump's predecessors chose to overlook Pakistan's troublesome"role in Afghanistan in favour of using Pakistani territory to supply reinforcements to the US troops in Afghanistan."[28] On the other hand, Trump departed from the convention by imposing military aid cuts on Pakistan. PresidentTrump has stated that Pakistan did not takeaction to dismantlethe terror camps within its territory. However, even President Trump proved incapable of wishing away the importance of Pakistanin the US strategic interest.[29]However, the operationalisation and realisation of this verbal pressure on Pakistan are likely to remain challenging. Until now, the Americans do not have much of an alternative to the Pakistani route for Afghanistan's logistics supply.

President Trump wants to oversee an end to the US long-drawn and costly involvement in Afghanistan, including the withdrawal of troops from the region. Pakistan's leverage over the Talibanis crucial for a breakthrough in the talks, which would facilitate a US exit from the region.[30]Not too long ago, President Trump criticised Pakistan for harbouring and supporting terrorist organisations that operate in Afghanistan. The United States relies on Pakistan for logistics; therefore, the strategic importance of Pakistan has significantly increased for the US view.

---

25 Tourangbam, M., "U.S. Strategy in Afghanistan: Old Wine in Trump's Bottle", The Dossier by IndraStra Vol. 1, Issue No: 1, Sep 2017, Article No: 1, pg.5, http://www.indrastra.com/2017/09/Dossier-Vol-1-Issue- No-1-Sep-2017.html

26 Imtiaz Ahmad and Rezaul H Laskar, "US NSA McMaster tells Pakistan leaders to confront terror in all forms," Hindustan Times, April 18, 2017.

27 "Full Transcript and Video: Trump's Speech on Afghanistan," The New York TimesAugust 21, 2017, https://www.nytimes.com/2017/08/21/world/asia/trump-speech-afghanistan.html, accessed on August 25, 2017.

28 Shubhangi Pandey, South Asia: Ending, or Losing, an 'Endless War' in Afghanistan? in Harsh V. Pant How Donald Trump has changed the World (New Delhi:Observer Research Foundation, 2020), p.9. https://www.orfonline.org/wp-content/uploads/2020/11/ORF_Report_Trump.pdf

29 Ibid.

30 Avishek Jha,Trump's South Asia Policy: Strategic Alignment With Pakistan, Ambivalence Towards India? South Asian Voice, August 22, 2019. https://southasianvoices.org/trumps-south-asia-policy-strategic-alignment-with-pakistan-ambivalence-towards-india/

China has a high stake in Pakistan through the China Pakistan Economic Corridor (CPEC), a flagship project under the Belt and Road Initiative (BRI). Pakistan has increased its reliance on China for military hardware. China is investing in the country through CPEC, and public attitudes in Pakistan are also more favourable toward China.[31]As the US builds closer ties with India, Pakistan's policy has to be gauged in light of the shifting geopolitical landscape and the likely impact on bilateral relations in the South Asia region.[32]Consequently, US leverage over Pakistan, through US assistance, is reduced by strengthened Sino-Pakistan ties.[33]The USopposition to CPEC is a significant hurdle in US-Pakistan relations. James Mattis, the USDefence Secretary, said that theBelt and Road Initiative (BRI) passes through thedisputed territory."[34] It passes through the Pakistan Occupied Jammu and Kashmir region, which Pakistan illegally occupies from India. President Donald Trump has opposed the idea of BRI.[35]Trump's inclination towards India and blaming Pakistan for the instability in Afghanistan has added more complexities in an already fragile balance of power in South Asia.[36]

Trump's on India

For nearly two decades, there has been a steady and incremental advance in relations between the United States and India. The two nations have overcome significant internal political and bureaucratic resistance to advance the relationship. Under the leadership of Indian Prime Minister Modi, the US finds itself peculiar to have a good relationship with India. The security relationship between the two countries has never looked stronger. On the other hand, trade and economic ties between the two sides are headed for a serious crisis. More broadly, the international political context that framed the bilateral relationship is changing rapidly.[37]

---

31 Robert Hathaway, The Leverage Paradox. Pakistan and the United States, The Wilson Center, December 6, 2017.https://www.wilsoncenter.org/sites/default/files/hathaway_leverage_paradox.pdf

32 Natasha Tariq, Policy Analysis Pakistan's Economic Vulnerability and the US South Asia Strategy in Light of CPEC, Sustainable Development Policy Institute,No. 19/1- International Relations, 2019. http://hdl.handle.net/11540/9583.

33 Ibid, p.11.

34 "Pakistan, China Snub US Objection over CPEC Project," Express Tribune, October 7, 2017, https://tribune.com.pk/story/1525336/china-rejects-us-objections-cpec/.

35 Rahim Nasar, "US-Pakistan Relations: A Troubling Scenario for South Asia," Asia Times, February 4, 2018, http://www.atimes.com/us-pak-troubled-relations-south-asianperspective/.

36 Tourangbam, M., "U.S. Strategy in Afghanistan: Old Wine in Trump's Bottle", Indra Stra Global Vol. 3, Issue No: 09 (2017), 0016, http://www.indrastra.com/2017/09/US-Strategy-in-Afghanistan-Old-Wine- TrumpsBottle-003-09-2017-0016.html

37 C. Raja Mohan, "Trump and Modi: Prospect for US-India Burden Sharing" South Asia Discussion Paper (San Francisco:The Asia Foundation and Institute of South Asian Studies), June 2019, p.3.

The UShas encouraged Indian burden-sharing in Afghanistan, including through triangular cooperation with the U.S. India, with US$3 billion in foreign aid committed to Afghanistan, of which approximately US$2 billion has been disbursed to date, is already the most significant regional donor in dollar terms."[38] All of this development assistance has been in the form of grants. Indian aid to Afghanistan is even larger when measured in terms of purchasing power parity (PPP), bringing Indian commitments to Afghanistan closer to US$13 billion in PPP dollars.[39]In his new South Asia strategy, Trump said that "India makes billions of dollars in trade with the United States, and we want them to help us more with Afghanistan."[40]

In reality, India has done plenty in Afghanistan. New Delhi is one of Kabul's most significant bilateral donors, and it has provided about US$3 billion in assistance. Washington and New Delhi get along more than well enough to cooperate in Afghanistan, despite their disagreements. Thanks in significant part to a rapidly growing defence partnership, the US-India relationship is blessed with enough goodwill to withstand tensions generated by Trump's times to time easily. The other important reason why US-India cooperation is possible in Afghanistan is to agree on desired endgames in Afghanistan. The reason is that both seek an end to the war and a post-war political arrangement with limited Pakistani influence. Both want Taliban safe havens in Pakistan to be eliminated and for international terror groups to be denied space in Afghanistan. Ultimately, both wish for Afghanistan to be more stable and prosperous.[41]India and the US have a shared interest in a democratic, stable, and sovereign Afghanistan. While India has been the fifth-largest donor to Afghanistan over the past decade, India's security and its economy have also benefitted from the US security umbrella in Afghanistan. Therefore, India's strategic interest is to devote more significant resources to Afghanistan.

The United States' direct negotiations with the Taliban negate India's ardent insistence on an "Afghan-led, Afghan-owned and Afghan-controlled" peace process. The United States deal with the Taliban endanger years of India cultivating ties with a democratic Afghanistan; the possible entry of the Taliban in its political structures could severely dent India's future prospects in the country since the Taliban have strong ties to Islamabad and Rawalpindi. India's enhanced uncertainty about the United States, coupled with fear over

38 Rani D. Mullen, "US-India Cooperation in Afghanistan" in South Asia Discussion Paper (San Francisco:The Asia Foundation and Institute of South Asian Studies), June 2019, p.49.

39 Rani D. Mullen, "US-India Cooperation in Afghanistan" in South Asia Discussion Paper (San Francisco:The Asia Foundation and Institute of South Asian Studies), June 2019, p.50.

40 "Remarks by President Trump on the Strategy in Afghanistan and South Asia", August 21, 2017. https://www.whitehouse.gov/briefings-statements/remarks-president-trump-strategy-afghanistan-south- asia/

41 Michael Kugelman "Prospects for US-India Cooperation in Afghanistan: Limited but Real" in "Trump and Modi: Prospect for US-India Burden Sharing" South Asia Discussion Paper (San Francisco:The Asia Foundation and Institute of South Asian Studies), June 2019.

the effects of troop withdrawal from Afghanistan, may have pushed India's hand vis-a-vis the abrogation of Jammu and Kashmir's special status in the Indian Union.

Counter-terrorism and intelligence sharing are the necessaryarrangements of long-term US-India partnership, particularly given their potential to help manage security risks.Accordingly, the United States and India should share information about the movements and locations of terrorists who threaten their respective interests in Afghanistan.[42] It is also crucial for India that the US should help New Delhi track Pakistan-sponsored terrorist organisations that may take advantage of worsening insecurity in Afghanistan and carve out new bastions to plan attacks in India.

India was on the priority list of President Trump. He released advanced weapons systems, such as unmanned aerial vehicles, for sale to New Delhi. Trump decision to treat India on par with NATO allies where strategic technology release is concerned isfavourable toward India.[43]India has, accordingly, responded with bold initiatives of its own. India has applauded the US strategyof a "free and open" Indo-Pacific region-a concept first articulated by Japan's Prime Minister Shinzo Abe, with whom Modi enjoys an exceptionally close relationship.[44]

US and India have begun to exchange serious intelligence information, undertake joint military exercises and discuss the acquisition of advanced military technologies that would help both states cope with the expanding Chinese military presence, especially in the Indian Ocean.[45] In September 2018, the two countries signed the Communications Compatibility and Security Agreement, which allows the United States to share advanced secure communications technology and that the Obama administration could not finalise.[46]

Its national interests have driven these evolutionary but significant shifts in India's strategic posture, but in every instance, they advance America's

[42] Michael Kugelman "Prospects for US-India Cooperation in Afghanistan: Limited but Real" in "Trump and Modi: Prospect for US-India Burden Sharing" South Asia Discussion Paper (San Francisco:The Asia Foundation and Institute of South Asian Studies), June 2019.https://www.isas.nus.edu.sg/wp- content/uploads/2019/06/isas-trump-modi-pdf-june2019.pdf

43 Ankit Panda, "Strategic Trade Authorization: A Fillip for India's 'Major Defense Partner' Status with the U.S.," Diplomat, August 1, 2018, http://thediplomat.com/2018/08/strategic-trade-authorization-a-filip-for- indias -major-defense-partner-status-with-the-us.

44 Pallavi Aiyar, "Modi, Abe Back 'Free Indo-Pacific,'" Hindu, October 30, 2018, http://thehindu.com/news/national/modi-abe-back-free-indo-pacific/article25364481.ece

45 Pallavi Aiyar, "Modi, Abe Back 'Free Indo-Pacific,'" Hindu, October 30, 2018, http://thehindu.com/news/national/modi-abe-back-free-indo-pacific/article25364481.ece

46 Jeff Smith, "COMCASA: Another Step Forward for the United States and India," Diplomat, September 11, 2018, http://thediplomat.com/2018/09/comcasa-another -step-forward-for-the-united-states-and-india.

strategic objectives as well.[47] President Trump administration has maintained the success story of US-India relations,which George W. Bush Junior initiated. Differences remain in the bilateral relationship over Russia, Iran, and visa issue. On March 4, 2019, Trump notified Congress that the United States intends to stop preferential treatment for Indian goods that now enter the country duty-free.[48] But the president deserves credit for promoting strategic ties with India in a sustained manner.Despite the unpredictability of the Trump administration, India-US relations have been consolidated. It reflected most visibly in defence and counter-terrorism cooperation.

Afghanistan issue is not the core focus of US- India bilateral relations. Despite Trump's comments on Kashmir mediation, India has found support from the United States in the United Nations Security Council's closed-door meeting over the abrogation of Article 370 from Jammu and Kashmir. India has remained firm on its commitment to its strategic partnership with the US. This relationship continues to be central to the US strategic objectives in South Asia as well.[49] While prioritisingIndia's national interest, the Indian policymaker would move from strategic autonomy to issue-based alignment, strategic transactions and pragmatism in its relations with the United States.

Conclusion

President Trump argued that India should be viewed as part of an Afghan imbroglio solution in his South Asia strategy. It is based on an understanding of the strategic utility and constraints encompassing US-Pakistan and US-India relations. The importance of Pakistan has not been completely ignored by former President Trump because of its geo-strategic location and influence over the Taliban. President Trump adopted a separate policy between India and Pakistan.The peace process in Afghanistan demands a different US foreign policy approach vis-a-vis India and Pakistan in South Asia and beyond. Trump's South Asia strategy emphatically and repeatedly focus on Pakistan's responsibility to end the presence of terrorist groups on its soil. However, it can be argued that there is nothing special in Trump'sstrategy, except a realisation of the limits of what the US can do in Afghanistan and the extent to which it can impact the approach of other regional players.

47 Richard Fontaine, "U.S.-India Relations: The Trump Administration's Foreign Policy Bright Spot," War on the Rocks, January 24, 2019, http://warontherocks.com /2019/01/u-s-india-relations-the-trump-administrations-foreign-policy-bright-spot.

48 Niha Masih, "It's Official: India Is Trump's Next Target in the Trade Wars," *Washington Post*, March 5, 2019,http://washingtonpost.com/world/asia_pacific/its-official-india-is-trumps-next-target-in-the-trade-wars/2019/03/05/39000298-3f34-11e9-a44b -42f4df262a4c_story.html; Blackwill and Tellis, forthcoming Foreign Affairs article

49 Robert D. Blackwill, "Trump's Foreign Policies Are Better Than They Seem", Council on Foreign Relations Report (New York: April 2019). CSR 84_Blackwill_Trump.pdf

South Asia's importance for the US until the end of the Cold War was limited. Now the region is far more relevant to the United States for geopolitical, national security, and economic reasons. It requires the US to invest in broader and longer-term regional engagement in which both India and Pakistan have a place. But that place is not next to each other. While India occupies a strategic space, Pakistan has been on shifting sand.

❐

Indian Diaspora's Standing in US in the aftermath of 2014

Dr Shalini Saxena

Abstract

One of the many diasporic groups responsible for the meteoric rise of the United States of America, is the Indian diaspora. Leaving behind their homeland, many Indians have thronged to the American mainland in search for better life and better opportunities. Indians have contributed immensely in all spheres of the American way of life. From aiding in the rise of the American economy to helming key positions in many of the American companies, Indian have deeply entrenched themselves in the American dream. Indian diaspora has proved themselves to valuable asset to the American society so much that in 2016 the current President of USA addressed the Indian diaspora by saying "Ab kibaar Trump sarkar" which is similar to current PM Modiji's 2014 election message. The following proposed paper traces the growth of Indian diaspora post 2014 in USA and its contributions to the American mainland.

Key Words: Diaspora, Asian Indians, Pravasi Bhartiya, Immegrants, Community

Introduction

Academically, there has been a meteoric rise when it comes to the study of diaspora. Studying about a diasporic group and its impact on the host country, whether it is the society, culture or the relation with other societal and political organizations, is complex by nature. When it comes to the study of diaspora, reasons such as the social interactions between the diaspora and the host country, cultural and political relations and the monetary significance they bring to the host country etc., play a pivotal part. Other reasons such as altering oneself to suit the demands of the host society, practising one's religion in the host country, spread of the diasporic language, ethnicity and culture, also, have played a huge part in the growing academic interest.

Globally, the diaspora community is gaining momentum due to the renewed interest being shown in them. The growing interest is so because of the following reasons: Firstly, the rise in skilled personnel from developing countries to developed countries. Secondly, the skilled personnel going these developed countries in turn can serve as a resource base (financially, culturally, socially etc) for the developing countries. Because members of the diaspora community can be contributors, there is a renewed interest in wooing the community.

The term has its roots in the ancient Greek word "Diaspeirein" which signifies "scattering". With the forward passage of time, the term has evolved both in context and meaning and in today's day and age of globalization it connotes to any individual(s) belonging to a particular nationality but residing in a host country to their reasons[1]. According to the Government of India (GOI) definition in 2004, "Indian diaspora consists of people who have migrated to various parts of the globe from the territories residing within the borders of the Republic of India. Indian diaspora also consists of the descendants of those who have migrated to various parts of the globe". In a nutshell, it can be stated that according to the GOI, Indian diaspora are those who are either or temporarily settled in parts of the world and can trace their origin back to India[2].

Under the current government, Indian diaspora are gaining recognition and support that was earlier denied to them. Under the reign of the previous United Progressive Alliance (UPA) government, the Indian diaspora were seen as load and were only brought into the political agenda for economic reasons only. But the Bhartiya Janta Party (BJP), previously in 1998-2004 and now in 2014-2019, see the Indian diasporic community as a national asset. This is very much evident from the current Prime Minister (PM) Modi's foreign trips wherein apart from building strong relationships with other countries, the PM has also initiated community outreach programmes wherein the Indian diaspora is being urged to promote and contribute to India's growing development path[3].

---

[1] Challagalla, Shreya. (2018). The diaspora and India's growth story. *Observer Research Foundation*. pp 1-12.

[2] Ibid. (2018). pp 1-12.

[3] Ibid. (2018). pp 1-12.

A point to be noted here is that, in-spite of being settled in areas having different socio-cultural and socio-political norms, the Indian diasporic community have made a name for themselves and in turn have aided in the development of the host society/country. A prominent example will that of Indians residing within the borders of United States of America (USA). Indo-Americans or formally known as Asian Indians (so as to avoid confusion with the native Indian tribes)[4], the community has created a niche for itself in the ever-growing cosmopolitan society of USA. Be it politics, medicine, infrastructure development, business or even the entertainment industry, the Asian India is present everywhere and is contributing immensely to the American society. The contribution is so much that the current President while on his presidential campaign in order to woo the Asian Indian community, came up with the slogan ***"Abhki baar Trump Sarkar"*** which is similar to the current Indian PM's election slogan. The current chapter is two pronged in nature. On one hand, it traces the growth of the Asian Indian community in USA and on the other it looks into the reasons behind the community outreach programmes put forth by the current BJP led government.

India's Diaspora Policy

Post-independence, India's connection with its diasporic community has somewhat been cold. The Late PM of Independent India, Shri Jawaharlal Nehru believed that connecting with the Indian diaspora in various parts of the world would be unwise as it would rather harm India's relations with those countries than build them. However, in today's day and age, the Indian diaspora is an integral part of the ever changing dimensions of the Indian foreign policy programme. Under the aegis of the current BJP government, the current PM is rewriting India's foreign policy. And one of the major components that is being included into the evolution foreign policy is the growing engagement with the Indian diaspora globally. According to the United Nations (UN), the Indian diasporic community is the world's largest community[5]. The Indian diaspora is a growing factor when it comes to India's monetary and social growth. With the Indian economy surging ahead, the need to connect with the Indian diaspora has become more of a necessity than just a photo-op.

The urge to connect with the Indian diaspora began during the tenure of late PM Shri Atal Bihari Vajpayee, who belonged to BJP. Under his able leadership, the government established the framework of an organized approach via the setting up of a high-level committee on the Indian diaspora in September 2000. The policy was forward by nature and was devised in such a manner that under the BJP led government the policy has served as a

[4] Baniwal, Madhulika. (2018). Factoring Indian diaspora in the Indo-US relationship. *Indian Council of World Affairs*. pp 1-6.

[5] Chaulia, Sreeram. (2016). How Modi mobilizes Indian diaspora. *The Globalist*. Accessed from: https://www.theglobalist.com/narendra-modi-indian-diaspora-politics-india/.

launchpad for various other policies aimed towards working with the Indian diaspora community such as Pravasi Bharitya Divas (PBD), Pravasi Samman awards and lastly the Overseas Citizen of India (OCI) and the Person of Indian Origin (PIO) cards[6].

The Diaspora Services Division (DSD) under the Ministry of External Affairs (MEA), India deals with all matters and issues pertaining to the Indian diaspora community. Policies and programmes such as Voting Rights to Non-Resident Indians (NRI's), Overseas Citizenship of India (OCI), Pravasi Bhartiya Divas (PBD), Pravasi Samman Awards, Know India Programme (KIP), Scholarship Programme for Diaspora Children (SPDC) and various other policies legal and financial assistance to the Indian diaspora are being implemented on a daily basis in order to build an everlasting bridge between the Indian homeland and the Indian diaspora community.

Indian Diaspora in the USA

Among the many diasporic communities residing in USA, the India diasporic community stands out from the rest. The Asian Indian (as mentioned beforehand) is one of the most diverse and growing community whose member are active in all spheres of the American culture and society. From being numbered to a few in the 1970's and 80's to now becoming one of the most affluent groups in the American society, Asian Indians have created a niche for themselves. Indians, migrating from India, started to settle in the Land of the Free in the 19th century and at that time only a handful of them were migrating to the States because of laws prevalent. With certain amendment in the immigration laws in 1965, Indians started to settle prominently in the States in large numbers and started to out grew other diasporic communities monetarily, economically, socially and even politically[7]. Figure 1 shows the growing trend in the number of Indian diaspora group in USA:

[6] Duttagupta, Ishani. (2018). Reaching out to the overseas Indians was part of Atal Bihari Vajpayee's legacy. *The Economic Times*. Accessed from: https://economictimes.indiatimes.com/news/politics-and-nation/reaching-out-to-the-overseas-indians-was-part-of-atal-bihari-vajpayees-legacy/articleshow/65445017.cms?from=mdr.

[7] Gottschlich, Pierre. (2008). Indian diaspora in the United States of America: An emerging political force? In Raghuram, Parvati; Sahoo, Ajay Kumar; Maharaj, Brij & Sangha, Dave. (eds.). *Tracing an Indian diaspora*. Sage Publications. pp 156-170.

Figure 1. Indian Immigrant Population in the United States, 1980-2015

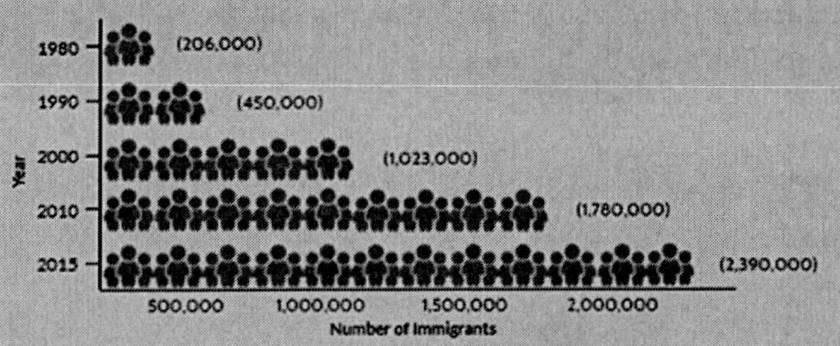

Sources: Data from U.S. Census Bureau 2010 and 2015 American Community Surveys (ACS), and 1980, 1990, and 2000 Decennial Census.

Figure 2. Top Destination States for Indian Immigrants in the United States, 2011-15

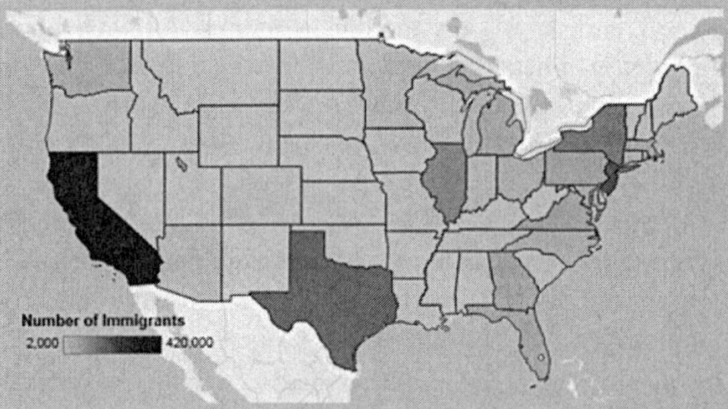

Note: Pooled 2011-15 ACS data were used to get statistically valid estimates at the state level for smaller-population geographies. Not shown are populations in Alaska and Hawaii, which are small in size; for details, visit the Migration Policy Institute (MPI) Data Hub for an interactive map showing geographic distribution of immigrants by state and county, available online.
Source: MPI tabulation of data from U.S. Census Bureau pooled 2011-15 ACS.

According to a 2014 report, 2.6 million Indian immigrants and their children have settled in USA. The Indian diasporic community is the 3rd largest immigrant community in the country. In spite of being an up and coming immigrant group, the community has cemented itself strongly into the American society which in turn puts them above the country's national average and also above other immigrant groups. Indian immigrants are spread throughout the length and breadth of the United States of America as shown in Figure 2. Indian diaspora either settled/immigrated or native born are better educated due to which they have access to better employment opportunities and thus in turn have better household incomes.

Indian Diaspora after 2014

2014 saw the BJP wining the Lok Sabha elections and thereby becoming the party to gain majority single handily. One of the important the current PM did after resuming office was to immediately connect with the Indian diaspora living in various host countries. During visits to USA, PM Modi has interacted with the diaspora in order to harness their energy and assets for the development of India itself. By giving speeches in prominent parts of USA, the government aims to turn every Indian in USA a representative of the Indian motherland. The PM has urged the diaspora to invest economically, financially and culturally, in India in order to elevate the stature of the country and thereby aiding in the fulfilment of the government agenda as per their 2014 election manifesto. An important milestone reached was when the Former US president Barack Obama and current PM of India Modi met in the national capital, Delhi and led to the formation of The Indian Diaspora Investment Initiative that aimed at helping Indian Americans to invest in India[8]. Unlike any other PM before, PM Modi in his diaspora outreach programmes has not connected with those who are at the very top of the community but also with the rest of the community members. In short, the PM has addressed everyone to become the eyes and ears of the Indian state in USA and work towards the development of the Indian state on one hand and on the other promote India's national interests in the States.

Apart from the PM himself, various members of the government including the Vice President (VP) of India, Shri M. Venkaiah Naidu has called upon the Indian diaspora in USA to come together and work with the current government in building a new and resurgent India[9].

In recent past, the prime minister, Shri Narendra Modi, has made a concerted effort to harness the energy and assets of Indian communities around the world. He started with flashy speeches in places such as New York'sMedison square Garden , aimed at turning every Indian abroad into an ambassador. Since then he has repeatedly urged the community abroad to contribute money, time and technical expertise to his signature programmes, including cleaning up the Ganges river, making India garbage-free and building rural toilets. He called upon Indians living abroad to urge families in their adopted countries to visit India every year to boost tourism, and he asked organisers of the Madison Square Garden event last autumn to donate $30,000 to Indian villages.

---

[8] PTI. (2015). Indian Diaspora Investment Initiative would create jobs: USAID administrator Raj Shah. *The Economic Times*. Accessed from: https://economictimes.indiatimes.com/news/politics-and-nation/Indian-diaspora-investment-initiative-would-create-jobs-usaid-administrator-raj-shah/articleshow/46028826.cms

[9] (2018). Vice President calls on Indian diaspora in USA to join hands in building a new and resurgent India. *ProWellnessIndia*. Accessed from:prowellnessindia.com/2018/09/09/vice-president-calls-on-indian-diaspora-in-usa-to-join-hands-in-building-a-new-and-resurgent-india/.

For the first time, India's foreign minister is focusing on Indian affairs overseas. The government has decided on a single identity card to make it easier for the diaspora to connect with the homeland, secure lifelong Indian visas, avoid checks at local police stations during visits, and own land. India also allowed visitors from 43 countries, including the United States, Australia and Fiji, to receive visas upon arrival, replacing the previous process, which took weeks. So, in order to attract the diaspora, the current government has handed out a single identity card in order to make the Indian diaspora community feel at ease when it comes to visiting the country, securing lifelong visas, avoiding police checks and lastly granting the ability to buy land. The Indian diaspora community now get Indian visa on arrival when was not the case in earlier government regimes. Present government is also following up on the recent Supreme Court ruling to allow Indian citizens living abroad to vote in Indian elections.

Now many say they feel closer to India. "Many of us in the diaspora who felt like a severed entity felt reconnected to the Indian mother ship when Prime Minister ShriNarendraModi reached out and embraced us the way he did in New York," said Saureen Shah, a 33-year-old engineer and Indian-American citizen in San Francisco who came to India to work for Modi's election campaign last year. "It was like pressing the restart button in our relationship with India."ShriNarendraModi's affinity for the diaspora is not only strategic, but also personal.

The Indian government perspective over the years has slightly changed. Now Indian economy has gradually opened for foreign investments, but investors were facing procedural limitations and challenges. The government amended banking regulations to facilitate the diaspora investment in Indian Companies. Now Indian policies seem encouraging for diaspora investment in India.

Another reason as to why the current Prime Minister is working hand in hand with the Indian diaspora community in India is the fact when the PM was the Chief Minister (CM) of the Indian state of Gujarat, he was denied a visa for the USA in 2002.During those days, it was the Indian diaspora community in USA that stood behind the current PM. It because of this support shown, the PM is reciprocating the love back and working hard with the community to realise his and their common vision which is to build and support a developed and growing India.

Conclusion

Over the past few decades, governments across the world are connecting with their diasporic populations across the world. This connection has led to growth in the home country while at the same time aided in making the diasporic population feel at ease and being at home. Such is the case with the

Indian diaspora in USA and all across the globe. Years of negligence has made them feel neglected and created uneasiness among them. The BJP government under the aegis of the Late PM Vajpayee ji and currently under PM Shri Narendra Modi has sought to reverse this situation. In order with the diaspora community in USA and around the world, the Modi government has introduced a plethora of initiatives and has repackaged old plans. Programmes such as "Know India Programme (KIP)" that was launched during the Vajpayee period has been refurbished and relaunched under Modi government. Procurement of passports has been simple for those who want to USA or any other part of the world. Further assistance is also provided in order for Indian diaspora to grow and flourish in various parts of the world including the United States of America. The current government it is very necessary to connect with the Indian diaspora living in developed parts of the world such as USA as those in the developed countries are up to date with the latest developments in the field of science and technology and it with the help of those settled, we can have transfer of technology with in turn can fulfil the BJP party's election manifesto and agenda. Policies and programmes can only be implemented to their fullest extent when the Indian diaspora and the Indian government cooperate at the highest level. Aspirations of the diasporic group need to fulfilled and in turn they can promote our national interest in host countries such as USA when then will translate in to a win-win situation of Indian diaspora and India itself. Therefore, keeping this in mind the interaction between PM Modi and the Indian diaspora in USA is necessary as for us the diaspora is strategic asset while for the diaspora the current India government is a boon in disguise[10].

The Indian diaspora has immeslybenefiitedInda by transferring the money and by making investments and also by sharing skills and new technology , social and professional networks that they have developed in the US.

Bibliography

- Chaulia, Sreeram. (2016). *Modi doctrine: The foreign policy of India's Prime Minister*. Bloomsbury Publication.
- Sahay, Anjali. (2009). *Indian diaspora in the United States: Brain drain or gain?* Lexington Books.
- Raghuram, Parvati; Sahoo, Ajay Kumar; Maharaj, Brij & Sangha, Dave. (eds.). (2008). *Tracing an Indian diaspora.* Sage Publications.
- Kumar, R. Gopa. (eds.). (2003). *Indian diaspora and the giving patterns of Indian Americans in USA*. CAF India.
- Naujoks, Daniel. (2013). *Migration, citizenship and development: Diasporic membership policies and overseas Indians in the United States*. Oxford University Press.

[10] Challagalla, Shreya. (2018). The diaspora and India's growth story. *Observer Research Foundation*. pp 1-12.

- Challagalla, Shreya. (2018). The diaspora and India's growth story. *Observer Research Foundation.*
- Baniwal, Madhulika. (2018). Factoring Indian diaspora in the Indo-US relationship. *Indian Council of World Affairs*.
- Naujoks, "Emigration, Immigration, and Diaspora Relations in India"; Naujoks, *Migration and Development*,

  https://www.migrationpolicy.org/article/indian-immigrants-united-states

  https://www.theguardian.com/world/2015/mar/02/narendra-modi-india-overseas-diaspora-united-states

❐

Climate Change: A Prospect for India-U.S. Cooperation

Dr. Shyamli Singh
Faculty and Coordinator Centre for Environment,
Climate Change and Drought Administration
Indian Institute of Public Administration, New Delhi

Introduction

Climate change will affect every American in the coming decades, the question is, to what degree?

"People asked, so the climate is getting warmer. Who cares?" said Michael B. McElroy, the Gilbert Butler Professor of Environmental Studies at Harvard University. "And scientists are partly to blame for that because of how we've described climate change." It's been challenging to get Americans apprehensive about a 1-degree surge in temperature over a 100-year period[1], particularly when most of the imagery concomitant with global warming — collapsing ice sheets or a solitary polar bear padding across a melted backdrop, feel so distant.

Across the United States, people are already living through the impact of climate change. Rising seas, augmented droughts, more penetrating heatwaves, forest fires and stronger storms threaten American cities and towns and their economies. Sans climate action, they will only get worse. In general, the withdrawal of the U.S. from the Paris Agreement will not alter the growth of low-carbon technologies and the

1 Burrows, L. (2017, September 13). From sea to rising sea: Climate change in America. Harvard SEAS – Harvard University. Retrieved April 2,2020, from https://www.seas.harvard.edu/news/2017/09/sea-rising-sea-climate-change-america

trend of the universal climate domination system. [2] Still, the majority of Americans did not have faith that climate change would harm them personally, according to a Yale University study. That connect between climate change and human health has been, in large part, absent from public dialogue and political deliberations in America today.

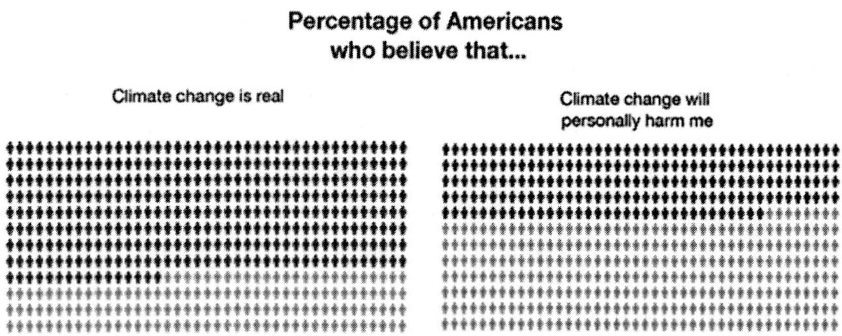

Source: Howe, PeterD., Matto Mildenberger, JenniferR. Marlon, and Anthony Leiser owitz(2015)

Investigators at the Harvard John A. Paulson School of Engineering and Applied Sciences (SEAS), are exploring the connect between human health and a changing climate. Research findings suggest that in Pennsylvania, days with precariously high surface ozone levels could upsurge by 100 percent in the approaching decades, increasing the perils of asthma and other respiratory ailments in children. [3] Wildfires in Washington obstruct thickly occupied areas for days with thick, harmful smoke. Several storms in Texas, Oklahoma, Nebraska, Iowa, the Dakotas and adjoining states could diminish shielding ozone in the stratosphere, baring humans, livestock and crops to harmful ultraviolet radiation.

The Eastern U.S: Heat on the Rise

If the biosphere were to cut all of its carbon releases tomorrow, temperatures are already high enough to cause more severe and protracted heat waves. Extreme heat has solemn impact on human health. Depending on humidity levels, prolonged exposure to 100-plus degree days can lead to heat stroke

[2] Mulugetta, Y., & Urban, F. (2010). Deliberating on low carbon development. *Energy Policy*, *38*(12), 7546-7549.

[3] Anderson, J. G., & Clapp, C. E. (2018). Coupling free radical catalysis, climate change, and human health. *Physical Chemistry Chemical Physics*, *20*(16), 10569-10587.

and dehydration, as well as cardiovascular, respiratory, and cerebrovascular diseases. In the past decade, hundreds of people have succumbed in U.S to extreme heat waves, mostly elderly and poor in urban areas, and have costed huge damage. Northern cities, such as Chicago, New York, Philadelphia and Boston, which are less primed to deal with excessive temperatures, will probably face the brunt of the public health burden of heat waves in coming years.

With little ability to stop future heat waves, the best option to mitigate damage is preparation. Refining the ability to accurately predict heat waves can save lives. Most current models cannot forecast beyond about 10 days and seasonal models have limited ability to predict extreme events. In 2012, for example, the National Weather Service's Climate Prediction Centre forecasted normal summer temperatures in the Northeast and Midwest U.S.[4] Instead, the regions experienced three separate record- breaking heat events in June and July that resulted in more than 100 deaths.

Earth and Planetary Sciences in the Department of Earth and Planetary Sciences and of Environmental Science and Engineering at SEAS, is operational in understanding and predicting these deadly temperature spikes. Sea surface temperature patterns are like a fingerprint on the surface of Pacific Ocean which generally precede the heatwaves in eastern U.S, can be used as a handy tool in predicting the same up to 50 days in advance.

It is established that the lack of precipitation, which is known to add to heat waves, is also associated with this finger print, known as the Pacific Extreme Pattern5. While the pattern is no guarantee that a heat wave will strike, it significantly increases the odds of one occurring. This technique has precedence of predicting previous heat waves, including the heat waves of 2012. The research in this direction is continued in this connection, asserting the prospect on forecasting summer heat waves in the eastern U.S. With ample time in hand, there can be sufficient power options to cope up with spiked demands, crop loss can be averted through altered irrigation practices, homeless people can be tracked. With the warming up of the air due to global climate change, North-eastern urban and suburban areas could also witness a spike in ground level ozone, the chemical compound responsible for majority of smog, especially in summer. Ozone is causative behind severe respiratory

4 Gao, Y., Fu, J. S., Drake, J. B., Liu, Y., & Lamarque, J. F. (2012). Projected changes of extreme weather events in the eastern United States based on a high resolution climate modeling system. Environmental Research Letters, 7(4), 044025.

5 Hegyi, B. M., & Deng, Y. (2011). A dynamical fingerprint of tropical Pacific sea surface temperatures on the decadal□scale variability of cool□season Arctic precipitation. Journal of Geophysical Research: Atmospheres, 116(D20).

illness and is specifically hazardous for children, seniors, and people suffering from asthma[6].

It is a long known established fact that temperature and ozone are linked — the hotter the temperature, the higher the ozone levels. It has also been established that if the temperatures rise above the mid-90s Fahrenheit, this relationship snaps. The question of how to handle ozone episodes persists. This would eventually transform into health emergency situation in U.S., the admissions in hospital and emergency department visits would surge and there would be an equal upsurge in morbidity and mortality due to respiratory diseases.

Concocting Storms in Midwest

With the increase in temperature and release of water vapour into the atmosphere, the storms would be of frequent occurrence with more intensity specifically in the Midwest. Loss and damage associated with the Flooding with these storms is a menace to the lives and livelihood of the 60 million people living in the Midwestern states, especially farmers who are reliant on predictable rainfall patterns. The intensity of these storms, clubbed with factors unique to the region, may also damage the protective ozone layer.[7] These reactions, conditional to the temperature of the stratosphere, could elicit a 12- to 17-percent decrease in ozone in the lower stratosphere. This corresponds to a 2- to 3-percent reduction in stratospheric ozone in the region of enhanced water vapour[8]. Even a 1-percent decrease in stratospheric ozone can lead to a 3-percent increase in skin cancer in humans[9].

Burning West

In 2016 alone, more than 67,000 wildfires burned over 5.5 million acres in the U.S., an area equivalent to the size of New Jersey[10]. If global warming remains on the same pace, the models foresee that by 2050 the wildfire season

[6] Norval, M., Lucas, R. M., Cullen, A. P., De Gruijl, F. R., Longstreth, J., Takizawa, Y., & Van Der Leun, J. C. (2011). The human health effects of ozone depletion and interactions with climate change. Photochemical & Photobiological Sciences, 10(2), 199-225.

[7] McNamara, K. E., Bronen, R., Fernando, N., & Klepp, S. (2018). The complex decision-making of climate-induced relocation: Adaptation and loss and damage. Climate Policy, 18(1), 111-117.

[8] Crutzen, P. J. (1974). Estimates of possible variations in total ozone due to natural causes and human activities. Ambio, 201-210.

[9] Hoffman, J. S., & Longstreth, J. D. (1988). Ultraviolet Radiation and Melanoma: With a Special Focus on Assessing the Risks of Stratospheric Ozone Depletion (Vol. 87). US Environmental Protection Agency, Office of Air and Radiation.

[10] Werf, G. R., Randerson, J. T., Giglio, L., Leeuwen, T. T. V., Chen, Y., Rogers, B. M., ... & Kasibhatla, P. S. (2017). Global fire emissions estimates during 1997–2016. Earth System Science Data, 9(2), 697-720.

in the western U.S. will be about three weeks longer, twice as smoky, and will burn more area. In the coming decades, the area burned in August could increase by 65 percent in the Pacific Northwest; could nearly double in the Eastern Rocky Mountains/Great Plains; and quadruple in the Rocky Mountains Forest region.

But wildfires threaten more than land and homes. The smoke they produce contains particles that can contaminate the air hundreds of miles away. As wildfires increase in frequency and intensity, more and more communities are at risk of extended exposure to harmful levels of smoke, including heavily populated areas such as California's San Francisco, Alameda, and Contra Costa counties, and King County in Washington. The future decades would witness massive fires, the reason may range from a lightning or human carelessness[11].

Pollution Knows No Border

It's not just the continental U.S. that is facing concerns from global climate change. The changes are far and wide ranging from Alaska, Hawaii and many American territories to the developing regimes are on the front lines of climate change. The Atom mission, in partnership with NASA, will fly a total of four trips around the world. The data it collects will help improve the accuracy of the environmental models that inform climate policies.

That first leg gave the research team a sobering view of the scope of climate change in America and American territories. Several hours after leaving the searing heat and wildfires of California, the team flew over Alaska, where large dark pools of water disrupted what should have been a continuous sheet of white, polar ice[12].

However, the long-term goal mouths and trans-national collaboration on climate change will be affected by budget cuts in American climate change exploration and the annulment of contributions from the multidimensional environmental reserve e of the U.S. The international community has primed or the withdrawal of the U.S. from the Paris Agreement as per the current US policies on Climate Change. However, the ceremonial affirmations of pulling out still caused wide-reaching reaction. America will set he pulling out to shape its administrative repute and to renegotiate the Paris Agreement despite its deleterious effects on the political integrity, international connexions, and prospective along-term economic growth of the U.S. If the Paris Agreement is renegotiated, the common but differentiated principle of responsibility of the United Nations Framework Convention on Climate Change will be confronted

[11] Williams, A. P., Abatzoglou, J. T., Gershunov, A., Guzman Morales, J., Bishop, D. A., Balch, J. K., & Lettenmaier, D. P. (2019). Observed impacts of anthropogenic climate change on wildfire in California. Earth's Future, 7(8), 892-910.

[12] Kirchmeier Young, M. C., Gillett, N. P., Zwiers, F. W., Cannon, A. J., & Anslow, F. S. (2019). Attribution of the influence of human induced climate change on an extreme fire season. Earth's Future, 7(1), 2-10.

again. Nevertheless, climate change governance remains a main theme of future sustainable development. Instead of national governments, local governments and non-governmental organizations will develop strategies for technical innovation an deemphasis reasonable cooperation, thus expanding their roles in climate change governance[13]. The capacity building on climate change research and public consciousness should be boosted as along-term objective of global climate change governance. Several steps forward were taken under Clinton and Obama only to suffer sharp reversals under the second Bush and sharpest of all under the current Administration. But there is a hope that that this cycle is about to change. Why? Because in 1965, 1995, and even 2015, climate change appeared still off in the impending, hypothetical, something that could be denied altogether, and to the bestcould leave for later. No longer. The transferral from "future problem" to "now crisis" is being powered by epic scientificstories and chartbuster real-world cataclysms.

America has been witnessing the bearing of extreme weather, as a heating planet faces winds, odds and isolation. Populations like Mexico Beach, Florida, are factually blustered to their foundations. Although hurricanes have been witnessed before, but, the storms are just a little more recurrent and more forceful than before and it's testing to overlook the fact that the scale of technology and the emissions from fossil fuels are a cause of what we are witnessing. The IPCC's most current report has tens the program for climate impacts, while the science of climate change continues to be questioned by people determined to maintain their obstinate obliviousness.14 The profound challenge to our existence of life is not engendered by bombers above or radical detonations which can be seen and heard, but by the delicate movement of temperature. Technology has altered our abilities, conduct and statistics. We cannot modestly get back to the land and, live as implelife "a tone with nature." There's too many of us and not abundant nature. Moreover, we don't have the legacy of our great grandparents. We have lost our traditional knowledge of making our own food, clothing and shelter. We are reliant on the technology that is imperilling the planet.

People in the developed world are reluctant to change how they live and people in the developing world are desperate to live like people in the developed world. The political pressure created by the widespread demand for modern technology and economic well- be irresistible. The leaders of the world, both democratic and autocratic, feel this pressure and have little choice but respond to it. The solution to the problems created by your technology

[13] Climate Change 2014: Mitigation of Climate Change. IPCC Working Group III Contribution to AR5; Cambridge University Press, Cambridge, UK and New York, USA pp.283-350 (2014)

[14] Allen, M., Antwi-Agyei, P., Aragon-Durand, F., Babiker, M., Bertoldi, P., Bind, M., ... & Zickfeld, K. (2019). Technical Summary: Global warming of 1.5° C. An IPCC Special Report on the impacts of global warming of 1.5°C above pre-industrial levels and related global greenhouse gas emission pathways, in the context of strengthening the global response to the threat of climate change, sustainable development, and efforts to eradicate poverty.

can only credibly be disentangled by novel technology. While evolving colossal philosophies, leaders also risk to make evolution on more diffident but decisive building blocks. With clean energy employment design thriving, climate dogmas are not so cool to terminate as "job-killing" any longer. With the political embrace to revolutionize the grid, endorse renewables and competence, restraint methane waste and effluence, move to generation next refrigerants. Such actions could move in be embraced and tread towards a climate smarter America. India a super emerging power and a leader that can be emulated in all its climate action can shake hands with America and tread towards a smoother climate risk resilient path[15].

India's energy needs and fluid consensus

Reasonably priced and reliable energy remains a high precedence for the current government, without which growth will remain sluggish. Simultaneously, the government recognizes that an elite focus on fossil fuels would impair local air pollution and further threaten India's climate security. As the world's fourth largest greenhouse gas emitter, India must shoulder responsibility of any solution to the climate crisis. But, since global climate change has several dimensions added to it—particularly the massive current and historic contributions of developed nations—she is reluctant to take a leadership role, particularly in global climate diplomacy with forward-thinking economies. India has followed a principle of Common but Differentiated Responsibilities (CBDR), by which India would only commit to emissions cuts when others reach India' slow per capita emissions level. Apprehensions about parity are indeed valid. Still, the accord within India has begun to shift toward a more avant-garde position in both addressing the causes of climate change, and also getting ready for a warmer climate. Indian Leadership and scientific community do recognize that climate change affects India directly, through rising sea levels, declining monsoon rainfalls, unpredictable Himalayan melts etc[16]. Moreover, other large emitters have started to slash emissions. The United States and China have each taken encouraging steps lately. Given India's yearning to play a leadership role in global bodies, India can benefit from taking a more forward-leaning position.

15 Markkanen, S., & Anger-Kraavi, A. (2019). Social impacts of climate change mitigation policies and their implications for inequality. Climate Policy, 19(7), 827-844.

16 Jha, S. K., Negi, A. K., Alatalo, J. M., Negi, R. S., & Patasaraiya, M. K. (2020). Assessment of climate change pattern in the Pauri Garhwal of the Western Himalayan Region: based on climate parameters and perceptions of forest-dependent communities. Environmental Monitoring and Assessment, 192(10), 1-15.

Liaising on home grown programs

Prime Minister Modi comes to New Delhi straight from having served as a chief minister. He also comes profoundly aware of energy and climate change policy. That the home work will be cherished not only in governing India, but also in consorting with the United States. Principal to Prime Minister Modi's success in Gujarat was his restructuring of the state's energy system by jettisoning subsidies and thereby swelling electricity production and dissemination. He is also became well versed in both the science of climate change, and efforts to slow green-house gas emissions. As a result, the Nationally Determined Contributions witness the prioritization of solar power, and self-published a book on his "Convenient actions."[17]

One opportunity for Central Administration may be to use the experience as a state-level administration and to apply it at PAN India level. The principle of Common but Differentiated Responsibilities can be prototyped and piloted throughout the nation. What should be "common" is the obligation for each state to act. What should be different is the level of responsibility. The U.S. Environmental Protection Agency has embraced this methodology in scheming carbon reduction targets for states, as has the European Union when allocating reduction targets across its member states, and has China when conniving its regional pilot programs. India can share best practices with the United States and the other major, complex, federal and provincial governments[18].

India and the U.S. : Analogous visions on sovereignty

After the establishment of a domestic plan of action, India is set and empowered to shine globally. This begins with the vision, to make India as a world power marching ahead towards not looking to, open rational cooperation. Starting with local actions will allow the Indian government to avoid anxieties that it has sacrificed Indian sovereignty. Just as in the United States, many in India panic that the U.N. process will lead to a global body that will set emissions targets. Instead, India and the U.S. share a concern in ensuring that targets develop from the bottom up—as they should. The U.S. guards sits sovereignty as heedfully as India does. The U.N. process should not decree obligations[19].

17 Albert, J. R., & Vanaja, D. S. (2020). Solar Energy Assessment in Various Regions of Indian Sub-continent. In Solar Cells. IntechOpen.

18 Dulal, H. B. (2019). Cities in Asia: how are they adapting to climate change?. Journal of Environmental Studies and Sciences, 9(1), 13-24.

19 Carr, W. A., & Yung, L. (2018). Perceptions of climate engineering in the South Pacific, Sub-

US must exhibit that it can act

As the U.S. and India work together, U.S officials must validate that they feel responsible to act a sparingly to cut greenhouse gas emissions, given America's level of economic development and the current size and historic volume of U.S. emissions.

In advance of climate negotiations, the U.S. must keep India abreast about progress on America's climate program—both building confidence and sharing best practices. The U.S. must also demonstrate that it understands the needs of developing countries—in growing their economies, in improving the resilience to a changing environment, and in slowing their own emissions[20].

❐

Saharan Africa, and North American Arctic. Climatic Change, 147(1), 119-132.

20 Zhang, Y. X., Chao, Q. C., Zheng, Q. H., & Huang, L. (2017). The withdrawal of the US from the Paris Agreement and its impact on global climate change governance. Advances in Climate Change Research, 8(4), 213-219.

US-Pak Relations in the Backdrop of Rising China

Sudhir Singh
Faculty, Delhi University

During cold war era, US-Pakistan relations were considered one of the best "cordials" in Asia. In post-cold war era, US- Pakistan relations have been turbulent and ups and downs remain the morale of the story.**Sino-Indian relation have also witnessed many ups and down within this stipulated period. Pakistan and United States had been close associates during cold war era and it was very popular in the Pakistani corridors of power that Pakistan was being governed by AAA { Army, Allah and America}.**

In the post 9/11 scenario, when America was forced to launch operation 'Enduring Freedom' to flush out Taliban and Al-Qaeda from Afghanistan after the Taliban's refusal to take decisive action against the Al-Qaeda. Its leader, Osama Bin Laden was killed by US Navy seals in May 2011 at Abbottabad. Pakistan was sustainable to proclaim that Osama is hiding in Afghanistan but his killing in Pakistan vindicated the fact that he was under the protection of the Pakistani army. Elimination of Osama has dented US-Pak relations at the bottom and since then trust deficit is prevails between both cold war era partners. This paper is intended to dwell upon this issue in a comprehensive manner.

For the last few years India and US participated in joint naval exercises in Indian Ocean. The Malabar naval exercise in which India and US participated, was, not well received in China. 20,000 troops and 25 ships exhibited their fire power right at the doorstep of China. China thinks South China Sea, an adjacent area to Indian Ocean, as it's core national interest and Yellow Sea, as, its military operation zone. How could it bear such a naval extravaganza in its own den? Sino-Indian relations are also influenced by a two different set of thinking by US and China. US as part of its grand strategy, is, harping about a uni-polar world and multi-polar Asia, where, both China and India share an equitable military strength. Also, it thinks to be the sole security anchor in Asia ranging from Vietnam to Pakistan. Now that India is engaged through the historic 123 Agreement, US wants to influence PRC by being closer to India.

China on the other hand, thinks of a triangle of power structure, involving India and Russia to live true to the tenet of a multi-polar world. In the present day international system, China thinks that US has a marginal role to play in Asia, particularly near the dicey Chinese doorstep. China believes that its military might be able to counter any US strategic ambition. This Chinese strategic calculation was tested, when, the Indian air force targeted terrorist training center at Balakot in Mansera district through where CPEC is also passing. China was forced to openly side with Pakistan and vetoed the American and the French move at the UN to declare Masood Azhar (J-e-M), as global terrorist. This sequence was tested after Kargil (1999) and the talloned Chinese, had, to choose the Pakistani side. It has resulted into lowering the much required, trust deficit between India and China.

In the backdrop of the Doklam crisis between India and China, which lasted for 70 days, PM Modi and Chinese President Xi met at Wuhan in April 2018 for summit level talk and a trendy and utilitarian level playing field was prepared. It was decided that China and India will move together on many global issues and settle bilateral issues through dialogue only. PM Modi visited China in April 2018 for a summit level talk with the Chinese President, Xi Jinping. Both leaders had six rounds of exclusive summit level talks. President Xi Jinping sought to open a "new chapter" in relations between China and India as he hosted Prime Minister Narendra Modi in the last week of April 2018 for a summit aimed at mending ties strained by a border dispute.

PM Modi thanked Xi for meeting him twice outside Beijing, telling the Chinese leader: "This in itself shows love and affection towards India." With 40 percent of the world's population, India and China have a responsibility to fix the world's many problems, Modi said, adding that the meeting was a "great opportunity" to do so. Invoking Xi's political slogan and his own, Modi said: "Together your 'new era' dream and our 'new India' effort will be the right step for the benefit of the world." But, neither leader directly mentioned the border row or other sources of tension in their remarks.[1]

The Wuhan process was not duly reciprocated by China by blocking the US move to designate Azhar as global terrorist I then post Pulwama/Balakot scenario. Wuhan and Azhar finally could not co-exist together.

1 Xi Jinping meets Modi, eyes ' new chapter in China-India ties, Dawn, Karachi, 27 April 2018.

US Security Policy towards South Asia after 9/11: A Changing US Strategy

The US-India rapprochement and cooling US-Pakistan relations in the late 1990s were driven principally by a number of factors. With the end of the Cold War, and, the demise of the Soviet Union, the principal obstacle of a US-India relationship was removed and the value of Pakistan in containing the Soviets suddenly disappeared. Secondly, India's economic growth made it an important trade and investment partner for the United States. Its strong Information Technology industry strengthened India's position on the world economic scene. In contrast, the Pakistani economy has not picked up and survives nascently only on debts.

The growing Indian-American community, one of the wealthiest immigrant communities in the United States, plays an increasingly important role in bi-polar American politics. By way of contrast, Pakistani-Americans are far weaker as a political force in the American society. The increasing strategic importance of the Indian Ocean which connects the oil-rich Persian Gulf with growing energy markets in East Asia has further emboldened the Indo-US relations. From a geopolitical perspective, the subcontinent and the Indian Ocean connects Washington's European-Atlantic strategy with its Asia-Pacific strategy. But, as the United States began to contemplate the need for a new European-Asian strategy to deal with potential threats stemming from the uncertain futures of both Russia and China, it was India—not Pakistan—that could play a key role in this new strategy. India and Pakistan have different images in Washington eyes.

India was greeted as an emerging power with a 500 million strong middle class and a vibrant democracy, while, Pakistan was regarded as an extremely vulnerable state, besieged with economic problems and a military hegemony. The US viewed India as a potential counterweight to balance a rising China along the PRC's southern frontier. Important in this regard, border disputes and historical bitterness complicated relations between India and China, who were competitors in the myriad and inter related economic, political and geostrategic respects.

Since PM A.B. Vajpayee, visited Beijing in June 2003, to till date 21 round of high voltage talk have transpired, but, the thorny border issue remains unresolved. Different from China and Russia (which have many strategic points of divergence with the US), improving relations with India, however, was the best way for the US to break through a possible Sino-Russian-Indian strategic triangle, which was first mooted by the then Russian Premier Primakov in 1999. In recent years, due to increasing Chinese-Russian bonhomie, Russia-Pakistan relations have also smoothened but the quaint "bilaterals" have negligent appeal in contrast to India which has spent \$ 58 billion in military expenditure and Pakistan only manages to allocate \$ 11 billion in FY 2018-19.

New US Interests in South Asia After 9/11

George W. Bush Administration continued the Clinton policy of engagement in South Asia, with a special emphasis on US-India relations. The terrorist attacks in New York and Washington in September 2001, however, changed US agenda in South Asia dramatically, as, the United States for the first time found itself in the unaccustomed position of having good relations with both India and Pakistan: India offered its 'full support' for US counter-terrorism efforts and Pakistan decided to align itself with the United States. The September 11 incident provided an infrequent opportunity for Washington to build a partnership with Islamabad and a strategic relationship with New Delhi on different bases.

US and Pakistan: New Trust Deficit

The immediate consequences of the attacks of September 11, particularly for Pakistan, were clear and profound. The campaign, in the name of Operation Enduring Freedom in Afghanistan, made Pakistan a frontline state in the US-led counter-terror campaign. Two factors contributed to Pakistan's renewed significance in US eyes: first, Pakistan shared a border with Afghanistan and was among the few countries that had a formal diplomatic relationship with the Taliban regime. Second, Pakistan itself "combine[d] the two major security threats to the United States: Weapons of Mass Destruction and perceived links with terrorism."[2] On the Pakistani side, General Pervez Musharraf correctly calculated that if Pakistan did not cooperate with the United States, his nation, at the very least, would be marginalised and isolated by the US and the international community; at worst, Pakistan itself could be targeted because of its support of, and close relationship with, the Taliban.

In a speech to the nation on September 19, 2001, Musharraf explained that his decision to support the US, was, based on four key Pakistani interests: the country's security; its economic revival; the need to safeguard its "strategic nuclear and missile assets"; and the Kashmir cause. He also identified economic and social reform as critical priorities for his government. The United States recognised Pakistan's role as a frontline state in the global campaign against terrorism and expressed gratitude for Pakistan's vital support in the international campaign.[3] On the occasion of Musharraf's visit to the United States in February 2002, President Bush announced new bilateral programmes which included: debt relief; democracy assistance; strengthening education; expanded defence cooperation; and cooperation in law enforcement, science

[2] Cohen, Stephen P., and Sunil Dasgupta, "US-South Asia: Relations Under Bush", Foreign Policy Studies. 2001. The Brookings Institution, at www.brook.edu/dybdocroot/views/articles/cohens/2001oa.htm.

[3] "Joint Statement for the Visit of Pakistani President Pervez Musharraf to New York", White House Office of the Press Secretary, November 10, 2001.

and technology.[4] But, soon US had realized that Pakistan is playing a double game in Afghanistan. Pakistan's open proximity with the Haqqani network which has been detrimental for US led NATO forces in Afghanistan, cautioned the US.

It is vindicated with the following statement of Ahmed Rashid, eminent Pakistani strategic analyst of Afghan affairs

"As the US military surge got under way in early 2010 in Helmand and Kanadhar province , there was increasing US pressure for Pakistan to do more to ' capture of kill' Afghan Taliban leaders. The Army , which was now fully convinced that it had to eliminate the Pakistani Taliban in FATA, and deployed 1,40,000 troops to do so , but it still refused to go after Haqqani's base in North Waziristan."[5] The Pakistani army and the Jehadi factory super headed by Haqqani's have been interlinked since the Soviet intervention era. These so called non state actors had been the masterminded for the Mumbai(2008) carnage and gamut of attacks made against the Indian interests in Afghanistan recently. Some elements of the jehadi umbrella have inflicted bloodshed in Pakistan also. Some are linked with the sectarian divide as well. Despite all those acts, Pakistan has yet not snapped ties with these groups."

Pervez Mushraaf's regime played a double game with the US, in, a very tacit manner. Even General Zia-Ul- Haq also played the same game with the US. According to a book ' Duty; Memories of a Secretary at War' written by former US defense secretary Robert Gates, he commented "I gave him a list of specific actions we wanted Pakistan to take. The US also instructed Musharraf to disrupt certain major infiltration routes across the border; enhance intelligence cooperation and streamline Pakistani decision making on targeting. Musharraf kept a straight face and pretended to take all this seriously.[6]" In her book *'The Wrong Enemy; America in Afghanistan 2001-2004,'* senior American journalist Carlotta Gall who has spent ten years in Afghanistan has concluded that "The embassy bombing was on operation by rouge ISI agents acting on their own. It was sanctioned and monitored by the most senior officials in Pakistani intelligence." The evidence was so damming that the Bush administration dispatched the deputy chief of the CIA, Stephen Kappes, to Islamabad to remonstrate with Pakistanis. The bomber struck before Kappes reached Islamabad. Gall writes "Investigators found the bomber's cell phone in the wreckage of his exploded car. They tracked down his collaborators in Kabul, the man who had provided the logistics for the attack. The facilitator, an Afghan, had been in direct contact with Pakistan by telephone."[7]

---

[4] Fact Sheet: Official Working Visit of Pakistani President Pervez Musharraf to New York. White House Office of the Press Secretary, February 13, 2002.

[5] Mushraaf refused to act Against Al-Qaeda, Taliban; US ex-defense secretary, PTI, The Indian Express, New Delhi, P-12, January 12, 2014.

[6] Ibid

[7] Lalit K. Jha, ISI executed Kabul Indian Embassy attack, US couldn't stop it, The Indian Express, New Delhi March 24, 2014.

According to Gall, as, the Afghan government investigated the attack, they became convinced that "the ISI was working with al Qaeda, the Taliban, the Haqqanis, and Pakistani groups such as Lashkar-e-Taiba. Gall concludes "At the core of Pakistan's thinking was an obsessive desire to dominate Afghanistan in order to protect its own rear flank from India. In that way of thinking, the Taliban were guarantors of Pakistan's national strategic interests.[8]" President Donald Trump was perhaps maiden US president who openly admitted this double game through his tweet comments on Pakistan in January 2018.

Post Pulwama/ Balakot Scenario

Immediately as an aftermath of the Pulwama attack (February 2019), it was estimated by strategic analysts that India will retaliate. Pakistan issued a statement and warned that any act of aggression will not only jeopardise Indo-Pak relations but derail the Afghan peace process, as well. The respondent, Afghan foreign ministry reacted sharply and summoned Pakistan's Ambassador to Kabul. In a statement issued after the meeting with Ambassador Zahid Nasrullah, the Foreign Ministry (Afghan) said it deemed his comments to be "in contradiction with Pakistan's commitments with regards to realising peace in Afghanistan". Nasrullah said that any attack by India would "affect the stability of the entire region and impact the momentum" of the Afghan peace effort. At the same time, a former deputy Afghan defense minister, stated, that Nasrullah's remarks would anger local government officials, saying it played into fears that the country's long-running civil war is a proxy for rivalries by regional powers.[9]

Right from November 2018, the Afghan peace talks with the Taliban is on and Pakistan was acting as a de-rigueur, facilitator. Pakistan was hopeful that due to its durable interest, the, US will support it or remain neutral after Pulwama/ Balakot. But the US response has disappointed Pakistan. It is confessed by a reputed strategic analyst of Pakistan. According to Ambassador Munir Akram, an eminent Pakistani strategic thinker,[10] "Although its positions are tendentious, India is likely to secure selective support for its demands because of its size and the general desire of major powers, to, placate it after its self-inflicted military and political debacle. The US in particular can be expected to press for several of India's demands. In fact, National Security Adviser John Bolton's reference to India's "right of self-defence" after Pulwama, virtually endorsed India's ensuing military aggression.

The Islamic Republic of Pakistan will have to work hard to persuade Washington to adopt a more balanced posture. No doubt the US is now aligned with India in the context of its rivalry with China. But, the US is also reliant on

---

[8] Ibid

[9] Afghanistan rebukes pak envoy over Pulwama attack remarks, Reuters, February 21, 2019.

[10] Munir Akram, Now, the diplomatic battle, Dawn, Karachi, March 3, 2019.

Pakistan's facilitation to secure respectable agreement with the Afghan Taliban. Its recent signals of friendship towards Pakistan were missing in the Pulwama crisis. Islamabad needs to establish a stronger reciprocal linkage between its facilitation of US-Taliban talks and the US posture on Pakistan-India issues." Through Balakot, India has used a right of hot pursuit as a strategic option to fight terror, on large scale, calling Pakistan's bluff through its repeated nuclear blackmail. Here, it is important to mention that many powerful countries have already used it, even India used it in Myanmar. When Indian army executed 'Hot Pursuit' in July 2018 after Naga insurgents killed 18 soldiers of the Indian army in which 38 terrorists were eliminated, Pakistan gave a statement that Pakistan is not Myanmar. Balakot strike by air force on terror training facility proved the determination of political and military establishment leadership and proved that Pakistan is also Myanmar. This strikes across the border established India's right of response to terror attacks. Through this attack, India has proved that it will be using same options to retaliate future terror attacks and bring India in the line of the US and Israel who have zero tolerance policy against terrorists. Due to proactive foreign policy of Modi government, India has achieved a major diplomatic success in isolating Pakistan. Iran, Afghanistan and Bangladesh and many other important countries including Russia have strongly supported India in targeting Pakistan based terror training center and needless to say that it has established the fact that Pakistan is the major source of international terrorism. Pakistan all weather friend China also kept stony silence initially and only gave sagacious advice to resolve the problem peacefully.

In the post-Pulwama times, France and the US moved a resolution in the UN to declare J-e-M supremo, Masood Azhar as 'global terrorist' under the relevant and exiting provisions of the UN. China blocked the move 4th time in row since last few years. But the US has moved the resolution again despite huge Chinese protest. The United States vowed on April 3, 2019 to utilise "all available avenues" to ensure Masood Azhar was held accountable but China warned Washington that this attitude could complicate an already tense situation in South Asia.[11] Chinese opposed the move. According to the Chinese foreign ministry spokesperson "We hope South Asia could maintain peace and stability and we hope India and Pakistan will engage in dialogue and through dialogue and consultation resolve outstanding issues," said Chinese Foreign Ministry spokesman Geng Shuang.[12]

India-US, all round relations are growing sharply in a positive strain. India-US strategic relations are also deepening. In the midst of Pulwama/ Balakot crisis, the United States had approved the sale of 24 MH-60R helicopters to India, significantly boosting its emerging ally's firepower to target submarines

11 Anwar Iqbal, US move not conducive to peace in South Asia; China, Dawn, Karachi, April 4, 2019.

12 Ibid

as China expands in the Indian Ocean. In a quick response to an Indian request submitted late 2018, the US State Department said it was informing the US Congress as legally required that it was giving the green light for India to buy the 24 helicopters worth a total of $2.6 billion.[13]

The Modi government signed defence contracts apart from the helicopter deal with the US like for example the $3 billion deal for 15 Chinook utility helicopters, 22 Apache helicopter gunships and Rs 5,000 crores for 145 M-777 howitzers, Rs 7 billion contract to supply 72,000 assault rifles and is in talks for US MH-60R Naval Utility Helicopters and Sea Guardian armed drones, all worth $4 billion.[14]

Since the end of the cold war every US President visited India. Bilateral relations have depended so much and slated to further deepen due to convergences of interests. Right from NSG till Massod Azhar issue, US has taken side with Indian line. US nomenclature of Indo-Pacific further underlined importance of India on Asian security architecture. Although China is aware that Pakistan based terror groups are behind Xinxiang turbulence but due to their increasing urge to contain India within South Asia, they are supporting Pakistan. This Chinese attitude is also going to be sustainable due to prevailing contours of security architecture of the Asia-Pacific. This all-round Chinese support to Pakistan is bound to sustain because India's rise has remained sustainable. India has gamut of challenges arises through this nexus. Through its proactive foreign policy in Asia-Pacific, India could meet these emerging challenges and ensure national interests.

China perceives India as the only challenge in Asia. PM Modi has given exclusive twist to India-U.S relations. Japan, ASEAN and at certain extent Australia has also joined the group in a tacit manner. It is evident through Chinese behaviour on Pakistan front. Till 2013 China was trying to be neutral in Indo-Pak conflict but since the arrival of Modi has taken direct steps to help Pakistan to contain India within South Asia.

The resurgent Chinese behaviour towards India is further vindicated by eminent Pakistani strategic thinker Hoodbhoy comment "the international situation has changed hugely from when the United States loomed large over Pakistan. US pressure after 9/11 forced Pakistan to end its support to the Taliban and LeT, albeit only formally. But today China — not America — is Pakistan's principal economic benefactor as well as its supplier of military hardware.

China, in spite of its problematic Muslim Uighur movement, does not mind much the extra-state actors that keep India off balance in Kashmir. It has repeatedly vetoed India's efforts to get Maulana Masood Azhar onto a UN

13 US approves anti-submarine helicopter sale to India, Dawn, Karachi, April 3, 2019.

14 The 'foreign hand ' in India's election 2019, Rediff com, March 27, 2019.

list of individual leaders linked to Al Qaeda. While China is a signatory to the BRICS declaration against militant groups allegedly harboured in Pakistan, for Pakistan to now give America the finger appears reasonably safe."[15]

Concluding Remarks

United States – Pakistan relations are changing rapidly. Elimination of Osama in May 2011 was turning point and since then trust deficit is soaring between both oldest friends since cold war era. Kautilya stated that foreign policy keeps changing as per the requirements of the national interests. India has emerged as the 6th largest global economy and slated to become 5th very soon. In Asia where locus of global politics is traversing since last one decade, India has emerged as an important strategic power as well. The nomenclature of Indo-Pacific given by the US indicates their priority. Pakistan has not used its excellent geo strategic location to score maximum dividends and even today is not capable to do so. The China factor, is, also important in terms of understanding US-India-Pakistan trilateral relationship. It may be safely stated that Indo-US relations is bound to propel and at the same time Pakistan-US relations is bound to stagnant and China-Pakistan relations at the same time bound to propel.

15 Pervez Hoodbhoy, Mainstreaming Jihad; Why Now?, Dawn, Karachi, December 17, 2017.

India-U.S. Cooperation in the Field of Education and Skill Development

Dr. Vijay Kumar Yadav,
Faculty, Delhi University

Introduction

The relations between India and the U.S. have transformed into one of the defining bilateral relations in the 21st Century. Based on the shared democratic values and convergence of bilateral, regional & global ambitions, India - U.S. relations have evolved into a global strategic partnership. The emphasis on development and good governance on both sides of India & U.S. has created an opportunity to reinvigorate bilateral ties and enhance cooperation under the motto of "Sanjha Prayaas; Sabka Vikas" (Shared Effort; Progress for All) as adopted during the 2014 and 2015 summits of Indian Prime Minister Narendra Modi and U.S. President Barack Obama. The release of a joint statement at the 2016 summit has reaffirmed the strong relationship between India and United States as an "Enduring Global Partners of the 21st Century".

The India-U.S. bilateral cooperation is broad-based, ever-enlarging, encapsulating multi-sectors from health, education, agriculture, clean energy to science & technology, cyber security, & space technology. The partnership has been nurtured by the vibrant people-to-people interactions and positive vibes from across the political spectrums in both India and the United States. Regular visits & meetings of high-level politicians and wide-ranging and ever-expanding dialogue architecture have established a long-term framework for the India-U.S. engagement & it's enlargement.

Education has always played an indispensable role in the development of both India and the United States, and also in the development of the partnership between them. Education has became the preeminent pillar of the India - U.S.

strategic partnership. Both India and the U.S. recognizes the essential role of higher education and vocational training in the economic development, and they are strengthening their exchange programs of students, scholars, and technical knowledge. Cooperation in the education sector has been made an integral part of the strategic partnership between the two countries. In anticipation of annual bilateral Higher Education Dialogue, both the countries are creating and expanding programs to build capacity for curriculum and teacher development. These programs are enabling Indian administrators and officials with responsibilities for higher education and skill development to gain expertise in community college and vocational training administration, and in developing a replicable and suitable model for cooperation with U.S. institutions in vocational skills training.

India-U.S. Cooperation in the Higher Education

India and the United States share strong linkages and a history of collaboration in the field of higher education. The United States is the most preferred destination for Indian students, with more than 130,000 Indian students pursuing advanced degrees in the United States. "India-U.S. Higher Education Summit" had been organized in October 2011 in acknowledgement of strong interest among academic communities in both the countries, which ultimately led to the establishment of an annual bilateral higher education dialogue. The Higher Education Dialogue has had four meetings since 2011 and has laid out a clear road map for facilitating student and faculty exchanges, promoting strategic institutional partnerships, deepening collaboration in research and development, implementing technology-enabled education strategies, fostering partnership in vocational education and collaborating on faculty development, etc.

In the third India-U.S. Higher Education Dialogue, which was held on November 17th, 2014 in New Delhi, the two sides emphasized the key role of education and skill development in the people-to-people relationships and the United States and India. The commitment to promote and encourage greater collaboration in higher education and skill development underscores our shared belief that education will drive the future economic growth and development in both nations and increase the innovation and entrepreneurship necessary to address the common challenges of the 21st century. The two sides reiterated the importance of the Higher Education Dialogue to promote enhanced opportunities for the student and scholar exchanges and faculty collaboration between India and the United States, including our ongoing collaboration on community colleges, workforce training, expansion of research and teaching exchanges, collaboration in the education technology and innovation, and industry-academia linkages in higher education. Both the countries had agreed to share best practices in linking industry needs to the curriculum development to enhance better employability. India and the U.S., both the governments asserted the importance of the community college collaborations to meet Prime Minister Narendra Modi's national skills development goals. They encouraged the binational task force on community colleges to develop a plan for implementation of the Memorandum of Understanding signed between the All India Council for Technical Education (AICTE) & the American Association of Community Colleges (AACC). They appreciated the launch of a new program for Indian education leaders for advanced training on community college administration in the U.S. educational institutions.

In the third India-U.S. Higher Education Dialogue, both sides appreciated the importance of the student exchange programs for strengthening people-to-people linkages between the two countries. It was reported in the 2014 Open Doors Report on International Education Exchange that over 102,000 Indian students are studying in the United States, an increase of a six percentage over the previous year. The U.S. Department of State in collaboration with the Ohio State University has launched the new passport to India website www.PassportToIndia.com to support the University Grants Commission's "Connect to India" program, which aims to attract foreign students to India. The Passport to India initiative encourages young Americans to pursue higher studies and internship opportunities in India. The portal will help American students / youth to identify these opportunities and realize their career aspirations.

Appreciating the great accomplishments of alumni from the Indian Institute of Technology (IIT) as remarkable, both Indian and U.S. governments felt proud of their prior collaborations in the developments of Indian IITs. U.S. is collaborating with India to establish a new Indian Institute of Technology in Ahmedabad, Gujarat. It was also agreed to commit to enter technical level discussions and agreements to explore possible U.S. - India collaborations in the establishment and development of new IIT campuses in India. Both the governments have agreed to enhance the cooperation in faculty development and agreed to cooperate on the "India's Global Initiatives of Academic Network (GIAN)" to facilitate the participation of U.S. faculty to take up teaching and research programs in Indian institutes. Under this 'Global Initiative of Academic Networks (GIAN)', up-to a thousand American academicians will be invited and hosted each year by the government of India to teach in Indian Universities at their expedience.

India is learning from the vast expertise of U.S. community colleges to enhance human resources to meet our demands for skill in employability. It has been agreed to collaborate with U.S. Institutions in the area of technology-enabled learning and Massive Open On-line Courses (MOOCs) to expand the reach of education in India. The dialogue encouraged departments and ministries on either side to continue to evolve ambitious plans to further the partnership.

India-U.S. Cooperation in Higher Education through Exchange Programs

Exchange of Students and Scholars: Sustained interaction between students and scholars of India and the U.S. is keystone to our shared future. Proliferating partnerships and joint projects between India and U.S. higher educational institutions has produced immeasurable advances in various fields like science, business, health, agriculture, and other sectors while strengthening the social fabrics of our nations. The United States has become the most favored destination for Indian students, with around 130,000 Indian students pursuing higher education/ internships in the United States. Contemporary developments in the institutional standards has transformed India into an incredible destination for research in diverse fields for the American students and scholars.

Obama-Singh 21st Century Knowledge Initiative Awards: In November 2009, the then President Barack Obama and Prime Minister Manmohan Singh started the "Obama-Singh 21st Century Knowledge Initiative" to fund institutional partnerships between Indian and U.S. institutions of higher education through faculty exchanges and research collaborations in the priority areas of food security, sustainable health, public health, and climate change. Both the countries have contributed $5 millions each for the initiative and grants up to the tune of $250,000 to select projects. Eight projects were selected in the first round of awards in 2012 and eight more awards were announced during the second higher education dialogue of 2013.

Fulbright-Nehru Partnership: The Fulbright-Nehru program has been implemented through the United States-India Education Foundation (USIEF) since its inception in 1950 and it has tripled in it's operational size with approximately 300 students and scholars from the United States and India participating annually, benefiting more than 18,000 Indian and American students and scholars for exchanges in a full range of academic disciplines with support from both Indian and U.S. governments. The U.S. government exchanges more faculty with India than any other country under this program. With collaboration under the Global Initiative of Academic Networks (GIAN) program of the Ministry of Human Resources Development, both India and U.S. have announced their intent in 2016 to expand the Fulbright Specialist Program to allow more American professors the opportunity to conduct training and workshops in Indian institutes of higher education furthering our cooperation in research and technical exchanges.

Raman Fellowship: During "India-U.S. Higher Education Dialogue" of 2011, the C. V. Raman Fellowship program has been announced with the aim to place Indian junior faculty members for post-doctoral research in the U.S. higher educational institutions. The Raman Fellowships provide an excellent opportunity to Indian researchers to interact with the American academic and scientific community and acquaint themselves with new academic and scientific research methods and to participate in collaborative research projects. This Raman fellowships, awarded for a period of 12 months, is called as "Post Doctoral Research Fellowships" to be awarded by the University Grants Commission of India.

Development of Community Colleges: A high-level Indian delegation visited the United States in 2012 to study the American Community College System. The Ministry of Human Resource Development has organized a seminar on Community Colleges in New Delhi on February, 6-7, 2013 to enlighten its importance. The Ministry of Human Resource Development of India has finalized a framework for the establishment of community colleges in India. The American Association of Community Colleges is actively facilitating cooperation and strengthening capacity building efforts between Indian and American partner institutions. The United States of American intends to host a series of delegations of community college leaders from India to the United States for capacity building and professional empowerment.

Connect India Program: The "Connect India Program" was inducted during the "India-U.S. Higher Education Dialogue-2012", with envisioned to provide placement opportunities to around 200 U.S. students at Indian higher educational institutions for at least a semester of study. Their course of study will be integrated with other extra-curricular activities, providing exposure to Indian culture and society, its economy, & interaction with political representatives of India.

Centre of Excellence on Cyber Systems: India is actively collaborating with the U.S. higher educational institutions to establish a Centre of Excellence on Cyber Systems at the Indian Institute of Technology, Delhi. An Indian delegation plans to travel to the U.S. to identify potential areas of cooperation and collaboration in the field of Cyber Systems & Cyber Security.

India-Support for Technical Education Program (In-STEP): The India-Support for Technical Education Program (In-STEP) is a joint project between the Ministry of Human Resource Development and the United States agency for International Development (USAID) to raise the capacity of teacher education in India. Under the program, India intends to send two groups of fifty teachers to attend a three-month customized training program at a U.S. university. The training includes capacity building activities like pedagogy, observation of in-service and pre-service teacher education and assessment techniques, etc. Every teacher educator would be assigned to prepare a proposal for reforms of a specific area of teacher education in their university/ institution back home. Upon return, the teacher educators are expected to utilize their new expertise to bring positive reforms in their classrooms & institutions, resulting in improving of the teacher and institutional standards. The U.S. Department of State is providing additional opportunities for more than fifty U.S. and Indian teachers each year through its various exchange programs to further expertise in their respective subject domains and enhance their teaching skills, participate in individual projects, conduct research, and follow courses for professional development.

Passport to India: The U.S. government has launched the "Passport To India Initiative" to the develop the next generation American business, sciences, and political leadership. By 2020, the United States is poised to have the highest proportion of college graduates in the world. Thus, the "Passport To India" initiative seeks to increase the number of U.S. students and scholars in India. Administering in partnership with Ohio State University, "Passport To India" works with the private sectors and non-governmental organizations to increase the number of internship, service learning, and study abroad opportunities in India, so more American students and scholars have the cultural understanding and language skills that underpin academic, social, and economic ties, as well as effective diplomacy. The initiative complements the U.S. Department of State' s support for around 170 U.S. higher educational institutions' students to study in India and help learn Indian languages through its Gilman Scholarship Program, Critical Language Program, the National Security Language Initiative for Youth and the Kennedy-Lugar Youth Exchange and Study Program. Under the "Passport To India" initiative, a Massive Open On-line Course (MOOC) has been launched for American students interested in learning about India.

Education USA: The "Education USA" initiative provides Indian students with accurate, comprehensive, and contemporary information about study, research, & internship opportunities at accredited institutions of the United States of America. The U.S. Department of State has taken a significant interest in expanding its advising services under Education USA program in India with virtual advising, launching a new mobile application, improving social media outreach and providing a nationwide advising hotline to reach-out to every aspiring candidature.

The U.S. Embassy and Consulates in India have together issued around 76,000 student visas in the fiscal year of 2015. With Indian students constituting the second-largest group of foreign students studying in the United States in the 2014-2015 academic year, the number of students from India in the United States increasing by over 29 percent to a record high of 133,000. These pictures along with the growing potential for exchange of students under the "Passport To India" program depicts the growing academic links between India and the United States. The sustained cooperation on 32 educational partnerships since 2012 and the announcement of eight educational partnership projects between India and the United States for the fifth and final round of the India-U.S. 21st Century Knowledge Initiative in various focused fields of education and educational reforms; energy, climate change and environmental studies; studies; public health; sustainable development; and international relations and strategic studies represents the the enormous potential for University linkages between the two nations. Building on the long-established partnership and support for the Indian Institute of Technologies (IITs), the U.S. Agency for International Development (USAID) intends to support the Indian Institute of Technology, Gandhinagar-Gujarat. By convening the expertise of the U.S. higher educational institutions, USAID is advancing the goal of the January- 2015 bilateral joint declaration of intent on providing support to IITs to intensify cooperation and collaboration in research and development and its engagement with entrepreneurs and industry. The participation of 161 American and 122 Indian students and scholars in the flagship binational Fulbright-Nehru Program, Number of U.S. State Department programs, and presence of more than 19,700 alumni, including the Prime Minister of India - Narendra Modi, of such exchange programs in India has strengthened the cultural and academic interests between these two nations.

India-U.S. Cooperation in the Field of Skill Development

With more than fifty percent of its population under 25 years of age and over two-thirds under the age of 35 years, India is home to the world's largest youth population. This demographic dividend presents a tremendous potential for India to become a global economic leader, and create new and diverse opportunities for the world at large. Prime Minister Narendra Modi's resoluteness to address India's educational and vocational demands - educating nearly 400 million students by 2022 - has provided a necessity to bring-in community college collaborations to the forefront. Cooperation and collaboration on community colleges and vocational training programs provides a key in realizing these aspirations of millions of youth in India.

In a boost to India's ambitious skill development programs, the United States government has agreed to collaborate with it in the education-related projects to help it in realizing its targets of providing employable skills and training to the youth of nearly 400 million in the next decade. The U.S. Department of State's Bureau of Educational and Cultural Affairs has sponsored a new six-week Community College Administration Program in September 2015, though which Indian administrators from vocational and technical institutions and Indian officials with higher educational planning responsibilities assigned to complete a program of professional development with Florida State University and Santa Fe College. This program is designed to share the U.S. expertise in this community college sector and help strengthen participant's ability to plan and manage existing and new technical, vocational, and workforce development programs in India. Both India and U.S. governments have announced a study tour for officials from Indian state-level skill development entities to study the U.S. network of community colleges with the primary objective of developing expertise and contacts to help the state build a more standardized vocational education system in India. Both governments have announced support for a program linking Texas community colleges with the Indian National Skills Development Corporation by providing necessary seed capital and it was also announced that the Montgomery College of Maryland will convene a team of selected U.S. community college subject experts in collaboration with Indian community college educators to build and strengthen capacity in curriculum and syllabus development using best practices in the U.S. community colleges. The Confederation of Indian Industry (CII) and American National Standards Institute (ANSI) have signed a memorandum of understanding to develop India-U.S. cooperation and collaboration on standards and conformity assessment, covering areas like smart cities and infrastructure, renewable energy, water and sanitation.

Conclusion

India, with world's largest young population, has an ambitious target to educate nearly 400 million students by 2020, and the United States on the other hand, is poised to have the highest proportion of college graduates in the world by 2020. Indian students are struggling with enormous costs of higher education, given the acute shortage of quality educational institutions in the country. The vicious cycle of entrance examinations, unreasonable high demand for top marks to get admissions in the top universities, and substandard quality of education, among various reasons, have prompted a very significant number of students opt to study abroad at much higher costs. The high demand for higher education in India and limited supply of quality institutions reflects the slow pace of development of higher education sector in India. The problem could become catastrophic in view of India's demographics. Lack of access to quality higher education over the next decade could alter India's demographic dividend into a demographic disaster. Thus United States, with its vast standard higher educational institutions, quality research facilities, and its advancement in the new spheres of science, provides enormous potential for providing quality higher education to aspiring Indians, and cooperation, collaboration for standardizing higher educational institutions in India. India and the United States have several collaborations in the field of higher education that mutually benefits the two liberal democracies. In their first bilateral summit in September 214, Indian Prime Minister Narendra Modi and U.S. President Barack Obama committed themselves to a new path for the India-U.S. relationship as- "Chalein Saath Saath" (Forward Together We Go). The joint declaration has endorsed the first vision statement for the strategic partnership between the two countries in various sectors, including higher education. The U.S. Agency for International Development (USAID) has been entrusted with the task of providing a range of high level analytical, diagnostic, and organizational developmental services to support the efforts of Indian Ministry of Human Resource Development (MHRD), that includes faculty development, exchange programs, and partnerships with U.S. higher educational institutions. The U.S. government re-launched the 'Passport to India' initiative to work with private and Non-governmental organizations to increase internship opportunities, and study-abroad opportunities in India.

Beyond these developments, "Employability" is a key concern facing India and sustained efforts have to be made to motivate new certificate programs, knowledge sharing, and public-private partnerships at various levels of the two countries. President Barack Obama has placed a special emphasis on community colleges given their critical role in providing enormous economic opportunities for the poor and middle class Americans. Thus there are significant potential gains to be made through cooperation and collaboration between U.S. community colleges and Indian institutions, adopting models of best practices in skill development. The existing arrangements like the agreement between the All Indian Council of Technological Education (AICTE) and the American Association of Community College for curriculum development and adopting industry demands to train the youth has to be proliferated.

From India's standpoint, the comprehensive objective of the bilateral collaboration with the United States is to bring improvements in access to quality higher education for students and strengthening capacity for research and teaching among faculty in actualizing the promise of a demographic dividend. There are abound potential ideas and areas for cooperation between India and the United States that could be jointly explored for the mutual benefit. The two governments underscored the need to enhance the scope of collaboration and identify new ways to encourage linkages and exchange programs. The potential of India-U.S. partnership will be underutilized until India steps up reforms to bring about fundamental changes to the regulatory framework of its higher education sector on priority basis by transforming institutions such as the University Grants Commission (UGC), All India Council for Technical Education (AICTE), and the Medical Council of India (MCI) by making them more competent to regulate the higher education sector and exploring new models like 'Meta Universities' for "educational institutions for the 21st century" in the country.

Both India and the United States acknowledged the immense possibilities for further collaborations between the two countries given the inherent dynamism and numerous opportunities in new fields for sharing and developing together. The fruitful collaboration between India and the United States in the areas of education, research, and innovation has contributed to the development of new technologies, skills, and knowledge-based societies in both the countries. Both India and the United States need to enhance this collaboration to ride high the partnership for the 21st century.

Bibliography

- "Brief on India-U.S. Relations", *The Ministry of External Affairs, Government of India,* June, 2017, https://www.mea.gov.in/Portal/ForeignRelation/India_US_brief.pdf
- "Fact Sheet: U.S.-India Economic Cooperation and People-to-People Ties (June 7, 2016)", *US Embassy and Consulates in India,* June, 2016, https://in.usembassy.gov/fact-sheet-u-s-india-economic-cooperation-people-people-ties-june-7-2016/
- "FACT SHEET: U.S.-India Higher Education and Skills Development Cooperation", *US Embassy and Consulates in India,* September, 2015, https://in.usembassy.gov/fact-sheet-u-s-india-higher-education-and-skills-development-cooperation/
- "India-U.S. Higher Education Dialogue", Ministry of Human Resource Development, Government of India, *Press Information Bureau,* November, 2014, http://pib.nic.in/newsite/PrintRelease.aspx?relid=111498
- "JOINT STATEMENT: India-U.S. Higher Education Dialogue", *Ministry of Human Resource Development, Government of India,* November, 2014, http://mhrd.gov.in/sites/upload_files/mhrd/files/HED%202014%20Joint%20Statement_clean%20%282%29.pdf
- Shamika Ravi, "India-US relations: Higher education", *The Brookings Institution*, June, 2016, https://www.brookings.edu/opinions/india-us-relations-higher-education/
- "US to help provide skills training to 400 million Indians", *The Indian Express*, December, 2018, https://indianexpress.com/article/india/india-news-india/us-to-help-provide-skills-training-to-400-million-indians/
- "U.S.-India Joint Fact Sheet: U.S.-India Cooperation In Higher Education", *U.S. Department of State,* June, 2013, https://2009-2017.state.gov/r/pa/prs/ps/2013/06/211019.htm

❐

India US Obfuscations on Intellectual Property Rights

Dr. Pawan Singh,
Research Scholar, African Studies Deptt,
Delhi University and Guest Faculty,
Satyawati College, DU

Abstract

The safety of intellectual property rights (IPR) is one of the most disputed international trade negotiations. Ever since, discussion on a multilateral agreement on Intellectual Property Rights started in the 1980s, which is now a significant bone of contention between the developed and developing world. India and the US are major trading partners, but intellectual property rights create hurdles in a more inclusive economic partnership. Where USA wants India to take strict measure to secure IPR, India on the other side, have shown more signs of competition, not just in domestic implementation but also in terms of opposing and seeking alternatives to US-induced global IP norms. This chapter focuses on the US's relationship with India in IPR. We furthermore find the US in the process of strengthening its external IP policy. It also explains the growing consensus between India and the USA for a more holistic IPR regime.

Keywords: IPR, Multilateral, Innovation, Economic, etc.

Introduction

In the globalized modern world, one of the most valuable property is the intangible property resulting from human intellect and skill. Inventions are the creation of inventive thinking, which is promoted by science and technology. Intangible properties are referred as intellectual properties such as copyrights, trademarks, design, trade secret etc. due to the importance of intellectual property, nations become the part of international treaties to protect different types of intellectual property under IPR laws, such as Paris convention for the Industrial property protection in 1883, Madrid agreement in 1891. Global forums like WIPO (The World Intellectual Property Organization), WTO, TRIPS to deal with the mechanism and policy regulation for Intellectual property rights. The vital work of these organizations are to balance the effective growth of innovation and creativity for the smooth functioning of trade.

Intellectual Property laws generally offer exploitation to provide a reward to the innovator and a right of exclusive use to give other innovators an incentive and bring into the public domain innovative information that might otherwise remain as trade secrets. Competition authorities regulate mergers, near-monopolies and commercial agreements in the market to maintain effective competition. Such regulation sometimes results in restrictions being posed on the free exercise of the exclusive freedom granted by IPR laws.

The defense of the intellectual property system can also be traced in Locke's 'theory of property. Locke writes that "every man has a property in his person". Locke claims that individual labour also belongs to that individual". However, Locke's property theory is subject to slightly different interpretations. One explanation of his idea is that society prizes labour with things chastely on the instrumental grounds that we must provide rewards to get labour. In contrast, a normative explanation of his idea of labour theory says that labour should be rewarded. The work of Intellectual Property Rights are to encourage various kinds of innovation and investments. Only few firms would invest in Research and Development if no incentive exists and others take a complementary ride on it. Further, at the national level patent offices publish patent claims and applications, even before the patent expires, the protected invention can be legally used by others for research and development, although not for commercial manufacture or sale.

IPR Laws in India

Due to rapid interconnectedness and opening up of the Indian economy, "Intellectual Capital" is now one of the important wealth drivers in existing international trade. IPR are now significantly noticeable on the legal prospect of India both in terms of judicial pronouncements. and new statutes. India ratified the WTO's agreement, which contains the Agreement on Trade Related Aspects of Intellectual Property Rights (TRIPS). Indian Statutes, enforcement provisions, and dispute resolution methods concerning intellectual property (IP) protection are now fully TRIPS-compliant.

India has laws covering various areas of intellectual property as enumerated herein below:

- Copyrights and Related Rights
- Data Protection

- Geographical Indications
- Industrial Designs
- Information Technology and Cyber crimes
- Layout Designs of Integrated Circuits
- Patents
- Plant Varieties
- Trade Marks

Broadly, the following acts deal with the protection of intellectual property:

- The Copyright Act, 1957
- The Designs Act, 2000
- The Geographical Indications of Goods (Registration and Protection) Act, 1999
- The Information Technology Act, 2000
- The Patents Act, 1970 (amended in 2005)
- The Protection of Plant Varieties and Farmers' Right Act, 2001
- The Semiconductor Integrated Circuits Layout Design Act, 2000
- Trade Marks Act, 1999

At the preliminary stage, there were many problems related to IPR such as the policies, implementation, Act/Rules, and governmental support.

Formerly, inventors and companies were also not cognizant of IPR, so the risk of infringement was alarming without a system. Keeping in view these glitches, India took strong steps in solidification of Intellectual Property Rights in the country. As, in 1856 India's first Patent Law came. Further, there are significant modifications from time to time by Indian patent system.

After independence, new patent laws were made in the form of the Indian Patent Act 1970. They were revised in compliance with the provision under TRIPS. In 2005, Changes were made in Intellectual Property Rights. Although the procedure of amendments in IPR was going on, India joined the Paris Convention, Budapest Treaty, and Patent Cooperation Treaty and finally signed the TRIPS agreement to fulfil the Indian and International standards. Lately, the "Madrid Protocol" was signed by India, which also boosts the Trademarks applicability in 89 nations. Further, the interest of Indian industries, Small and Medium Enterprises (SMEs), technologist, inventors and scientists are the achievements in this field. Research-oriented people are filing their inventions in high numbers on a large scale. There a rapid increase in the number of foreign companies that are now instituting their in-house centres of research

& development in India, which is a positive indication of IPR encouragement.

The first Compulsory License (CL) of country against the "Bayer cancer drug" "NEXAVAR" highlights the Indian Intellectual property rights regime at the global window. This CL gives a ray of hope to Indian Pharma INC, which cannot produce life-saving medicines and now able to manufacture such drugs at a meager cost. This nature of CL is giving boosts to the country's health industry. Due to this, high-end drugs can be in production and delivered to the patients at an affordable rate which is a sign of a disease-free society. A recent survey estimated that the number of Trademark and Patent filings had increased 20 times from previous years.

Despite having the above achievements, our IPR system is still in enact stage, and the constant efforts of Indian policymakers gives pace to the intellectual regime, but there is the need for more policies to be taken to overcome challenges that restrict IPR from reaching the international standards.

Challenges in IPR: Indian Perspective

Today, IPR has a significant role in every sector and has become a vital aspect of research for medical and research-oriented businesses. The government's constant efforts in policy establishment, infrastructure, IT protection IPR search portals, and manpower made an important growth. In consideration of all the triumphs, our industry sector is still facing many challenges at the domestic sphere and international one. IPR in India has issues in remote areas and these areas are considered to be the hotbed of innovation. Many people are still not aware about IPR laws and their benefits in taking rights for their intellectual property. In such cases, the government should significant role in promoting the awareness of IPR in such areas. The large number of camps for awareness and educational hubs should be organized for the inventors to spread skilled impart of knowledge. legal issues also plays an important role in IPR situation in the country. Today there are various trademark and patent infringement matters which are gaining their significance in the legal story of the country. In such kind of increase in IPR matter India needs a skilled team of law persons and IPR professionals. Apart from the above issues.

Previously, when the Patent system of India was not in compliance with TRIPS, it had a risk of a healthy Patent protection facility in India. However, now the condition has been changed totally. India has now become a TRIPS member, and our patent system is fully submissive with the TRIPS. Even though Indian Patent Act has all the TRIPS flexibilities, the relevant provisions also require fine-tuning, mainly related to patent protection, compulsory license, and government use.

In India, it is multilateral behavior that has often been inconsistent. Most notably, while India co-led coalitions are opposing the linking of IP and trade and seeking flexibilities within TRIPS throughout the 1980s and 1990s, it failed to co-sponsor development agendas at WIPO and other IOs in the mid-2000s. The latter is linked to a brief period around 2005 when the Singh government and some sectors of the bureaucracy attempted to strengthen IP to improve innovation. This endeavour failed due to substantial domestic opposition, and India returned to its more traditional opposition to strong IP protection.

India's domestic practice on the other hand has been unlike other developing countries are more coherent, in particular the behaviour of the IPO. The IPO has made huge strides in improving its administrative capacities by rapidly increasing personnel and expertise through enhanced cooperation with the Trilaterals, especially USPTO.67 Curiously, despite the IPO taking part in these horizontal structures, in particular training of patent examiners, its patenting practices remain the most controversial among emerging economies.68 The most famous example is the IPO's application of section 3(d) of the 2005 Indian patent act, refusing to grant a patent to Novartis on its drug Gleevec, arguing that it failed to pass the innovativeness test. The IPO's conservative approach to the issue of patentability makes it a rather unique actor in the developing world; its practices are increasingly scrutinized and even diffuse to other emerging countries.

This departure from EU/US norms is mainly a result of a strong developmentalist ideology70 and vested economic interests.71 The former is observable at least since the Ayyangar Committee Report, which was commissioned by the government to evaluate the effects of patent law on development and culminated in the 1970 Patent Act. On this basis, India shelved part of the patent legislation it inherited from the British colonial administration and successfully developed a domestic pharmaceutical industry based on generics and reverse engineering. With WTO (TRIPS) membership, the business model of the Indian generics industry faced a major challenge that threatened its very existence. The generics industry has as a result become a powerful lobby opposing maximalist IP interpretations and has played a crucial role in India's domestic and international IP positions.

IPR Laws in the USA

Innovation has been a vital component of the American success story. In fact, the Joint Economic Committee of the U.S. Congress estimates that as much as 50% of all economic growth in the US over the past half-century can be attributed to productivity gains resulting from innovation.2 Patents have, therefore, been integral to the United States' approach to incentivizing innovation by ensuring that innovators enjoy exclusive rights to the commercial gains from their inventions.

The US patent and copyright systems derive from the "intellectual property clause" of the US Constitution 2 and the governing statutes are codified in Titles

35 and 17, respectively the United States Code. The federal Trademark system derives from the Commerce Clause and the governing statute is the Lanham Act which is codified in Title 15 of the United States Code. The United States has had a patent statute since 1790 and a formal patent examination system since 1836. The 1952 Act, codified in Title 35 U.S. Code is the governing legislation. The United States Court of Appeals for the Federal Circuit and the United States Patent and Trademark Office (PTO) are the two most important institutions in the modern patent system.

US foreign IP policy has unfolded since the end of the 1980s under strong influence from the private sector, especially the technology-intensive pharmaceutical, software and phonogram industries.13 Pushed by these interests, the US has over the years put strong emphasis on using hierarchical (coercive) instruments, but has also intensified horizontal (network-based) efforts to promote IP protection abroad. On the hierarchical side, the main unilateral measure has been the US' Special 301' approach which – drawing on the 1974 US Foreign Trade Act and the 1988 Omnibus Act – tasks the US Trade Representative (USTR) to evaluate foreign countries' IPR policies annually since 1989. Depending on the severity of IP violation and the impact on the US economy, countries may be placed on the '301' Watch List (WL), the more imminent Priority Watch List (PWL), or even flagged as Priority Foreign Country (PFC), the latter leading to an in-depth investigation which may ultimately result in trade sanctions.14 The '301' placement of foreign countries usually closely follows prior recommendations submitted by business associations such as the International Intellectual Property Alliance (IIPA).

Multilaterally, the US-induced WTO TRIPS agreement made it possible to sue non-compliant countries via the Dispute Settlement Understanding (DSU), which may authorize retaliatory measures such as quotas against IPR infringing third countries.16 Furthermore, the US has pushed maximalist IP legislation through negotiations of bi- and plurilateral FTAs, from NAFTA in the early 1990s to the more recent Trans-Pacific Partnership (TPP) negotiations.

In terms of horizontal strategies, the US has addressed IP-relevant issues through regular bilateral consultation fora such as economic dialogues; technical assistance and capacity building programmes; and through deployment of IP experts to US embassies in order to boost advocacy of IP protection in host countries.17 In the area of patents, an important programme of transgovernmental cooperation has been the 'trilateral hub', where the patent offices of the United States (USPTO), the European Union (EPO) and Japan (JPO) have shaped a global system of patent administration since 1983.18 Horizontal cooperation also takes place within multilateral settings, in particular through the Patent Cooperation Treaty (PCT), which aims at promoting cooperation among patent office's so that patents granted by one PCT signatory will be recognized by other members.

Issues of conflict between India and the USA

India continues to be on the 'Priority Watch List' of the United States Trade Representative (USTR) for lack of adequate intellectual property (IP) rights protection and enforcement, the USTR said in its Annual Special 301 Report, released on Wednesday. India remained one of the most challenging economies for IP enforcement and protection, the report said, using language it has used previously. Algeria, Argentina, Chile, China, Indonesia, Russia, Saudi Arabia, Ukraine and Venezuela are also on the Priority Watch List. While India made "meaningful progress" to enhance IP protection and enforcement in some areas over the past year, it did not resolve recent and long-standing challenges, and created new ones, the report said. The same assessment was made in the 2019 report.

For US observer's Patent issues continue to be of particular concern in India as long-standing issues remain for innovative industries. The potential threat of patent revocations, lack of presumption of patent validity, and the narrow patentability criteria under the India Patents Act burden companies across different sectors. Moreover, patent applicants continue to confront costly and time-consuming pre- and post-grant oppositions, long waiting periods to receive patent approval, and excessive reporting requirements. Stakeholders continue to express concerns over vagueness in the interpretation of the India Patents Act.

In 2020 US blamed registered their disagreement that Copyright holders continue to report high levels of piracy, particularly online. Court cases and government memoranda also raise concerns that a broad range of published works will not be afforded meaningful copyright protection in India. In 2019, the Department for Promotion of Industry and Internal Trade (DPIIT) proposed draft Copyright Amendment Rules that would broaden the scope of statutory licensing to encompass not only radio and television broadcasting but also online transmissions, despite a high court ruling earlier in 2019 that held that statutory broadcast licensing does not include online transmissions.

Path of Collaboration

While India made meaningful progress to promote IP protection and enforcement in some areas over the past year, it failed to resolve recent and long-standing challenges, and it created new concerns for right holders.

India's accession to the World Intellectual Property Organization (WIPO) Internet Treaties in 2018 and the Nice Agreement in 2019 were positive steps. However, amendments to the Copyright Act needed to bring India's domestic legislation into alignment with international best practices are absent. The United States is monitoring India's next steps, including DPIIT's December

2020 solicitation of public comments on amending the Copyright Act. The December 2018 draft Cinematograph Act (Amendment) Bill containing promising provisions to criminalize illicit camcording of films continues to await Parliament's approval.

India took steps to address stakeholder concerns over burdensome patent reporting requirements by issuing a revised Manual of Patent Office Practice and Procedure in November 2019 and revised Form 27 on patent working in October 2020. The Manual includes the requirement for patent examiners to look to the WIPO Centralized Access to Search and Examination (CASE) system and Digital Access Service (DAS) to find information filed by patent applicants in other jurisdictions, with the aim of eliminating the need for applicants to file redundant information with India. While some stakeholders have welcomed the revised version of Form 27, concerns remain with respect to whether Indian authorities will treat as confidential sensitive business information that parties are required to disclose on Form 27.

Among other positive developments, in September 2019, the Nice Agreement for the classification of goods and services for the purposes of registering trademarks came into force, and India continues to work on guidelines for its implementation. The Cell for IPR Promotion and Management (CIPAM) continues to promote IP awareness, commercialization, and enforcement throughout India. In December 2020, the United States Patent and Trademark Office and DPIIT signed a new Memorandum of Understanding relating to IP technical cooperation mechanisms.

In March 2021, the United States and India, along with Australia and Japan, announced the Quad Vaccine Partnership. They are taking shared action necessary to expand safe and effective COVID-19 vaccine manufacturing in 2021 and are working together to strengthen and assist countries in the Indo-Pacific with vaccination, in close coordination with the existing relevant multilateral mechanisms including the World Health Organization (WHO) and COVID-19 Vaccines Global Access (COVAX). In addition, Indian manufacturers have entered into voluntary licensing agreements with international partners to produce billions of COVID-19 vaccine doses. The United States intends to continue to engage with India on IP matters, including through the United States-India Trade Policy Forum's Intellectual Property Working Group.

❐

An Ode to the US Philanthropy Or Is It?

Dr. Saket Bihari,
Associate Professor,
Development Studies, IIPA

Introduction

Though US takes pride on it being the purveyor of liberty, happiness and freedom of expression but nations of the order of United States have always utilized the instrument of Food aid and other genres of dole outs with an intent to keep the receptacle nations dependent on the central provider nation state. Also, the stratagem of Aid diplomacy, initiated through the Truman Doctrine and Marshall plan initiated by the United States in the aftermath of the world war II came to stay in the geo economics of Europe and later on the larger world reflected by the receptacle nation states in the poverty ridden states of Asia and Africa.

The Marshall Plan initiated by the United States of America in a post World War II scenario can be surmised as below. A renowned American history portal reminds us and enumerates that, " In the immediate post-World War II period, Europe remained ravaged by war and thus susceptible to exploitation by an internal and external Communist threat. In a June 5, 1947, speech to the graduating class at Harvard University, Secretary of State George C. Marshall issued a call for a comprehensive program to rebuild Europe. Fanned by the fear of Communist expansion and the rapid deterioration of European economies in the winter of 1946–1947, Congress passed the Economic Cooperation Act in March 1948 and approved funding that would eventually rise to over $12 billion for the rebuilding of Western Europe."[1]

[1] URL; https://history.state.gov/milestones/1945-1952/marshall-plan (Online: Web), Accessed on 10 May, 2021

The US History portal further informs us that, " Thus the Marshall Plan was applied solely to Western Europe, precluding any measure of Soviet Bloc cooperation. Increasingly, the economic revival of Western Europe, especially West Germany, was viewed suspiciously in Moscow. Economic historians have debated the precise impact of the Marshall Plan on Western Europe, but these differing opinions do not detract from the fact that the Marshall Plan has been recognized as a great humanitarian effort. Secretary of State Marshall became the only general ever to receive a Nobel Prize for peace. The Marshall Plan also institutionalized and legitimized the concept of U.S. foreign aid programs, which have become a integral part of U.S. foreign policy."[2] Thus, it was deft and strategically safe and effective initiation of the American nation and its leaders to lift the European counterparts out of war losses and damages caused by the violent and deadly conflict which nearly engulfed the entire international system with US being a slight exception to the rule. Thus, the war hewn impoverishment heaped on the international comity of states had to be countered which began with the poverty eradication and equity enhancing instrumentalities of the order of World Trade organization and the International Monetary fund. Thus, power engenders the spread of resource richness and heady and gainful pelf and prosperity as one can discern the tirade of the plight of the nations of the order of Great Britain, France, Scandinavia and other player states in Europe as they ge0- economically hobbled on from a much tom tommed Allied victory.

The Truman Doctrine

President Harry S. Truman established that the United States would provide political, military and economic assistance to all democratic nations under threat from external or internal authoritarian forces. The Truman Doctrine effectively reoriented U.S. foreign policy, away from its usual stance of withdrawal from regional conflicts not directly involving the United States, to one of possible intervention in far away conflicts.

The US History website reports that, "The Truman Doctrine arose from a speech delivered by President Truman before a joint session of Congress on March 12, 1947. The immediate cause for the speech was a recent announcement by the British Government that, as of March 31, it would no longer provide military and economic assistance to the Greek Government in its civil war against the Greek Communist Party. Truman asked Congress to support the Greek Government against the Communists. He also asked Congress to provide assistance for Turkey, since that nation, too, had previously been dependent on British aid."[3]

[2] Ibid 1

[3] US Government Press, Truman Doctrine, 1947.

The add on narrative is furthered as follows, "At the time, the U.S. Government believed that the Soviet Union supported the Greek Communist war effort and worried that if the Communists prevailed in the Greek civil war, the Soviets would ultimately influence Greek policy. In fact, Soviet leader Joseph Stalin had deliberately refrained from providing any support to the Greek Communists and had forced Yugoslav Prime Minister Josip Tito to follow suit, much to the detriment of Soviet-Yugoslav relations."[4] However, a number of other foreign policy problems also influenced President Truman's decision to actively aid Greece and Turkey. The legendart Truman Doctrine further notes that, "In 1946, four setbacks, in particular, had served to effectively torpedo any chance of achieving a durable post-war rapprochement with the Soviet Union: the Soviets' failure to withdraw their troops from northern Iran in early 1946 (as per the terms of the Tehran Declaration of 1943); Soviet attempts to pressure the Iranian Government into granting them oil concessions while supposedly fomenting irredentism by Azerbaijani separatists in northern Iran; Soviet efforts to force the Turkish Government into granting them base and transit rights through the Turkish Straits; and, the Soviet Government's rejection of the Baruch plan for international control over nuclear energy and weapons in June 1946."[5] The Truman plan was directly linked to the eradication and annulment of poverty and mass impoverishment heaped on and faced by a nation or a region due to a myriad array of factors such war, rebellion or a national emergency, humanitarian disaster or a natural catastrophe.

Development Studies are the sine-quo-non of human security deliberations and discussions. Any eclectic approach to human security still cannot be clubbed under the nomenclature of Development Studies. Development Studies though owes its origins from the paradigm of sustainability with the entire ambit of human security concerns such as gender empowerment, literacy, nutrition, human rights and Poverty alleviation are the order of the day as far as sustainability is concerned.

The hallowed Development Studies portals contends that, " Development Studies is a diverse field of study that takes 'development' as its central concern. 'Development' is a contested concept, which encompasses two broad sets of concerns. The first concerns processes of social, cultural, ecological, economic and political change. Development in this sense can be a normative concept that implies *progressive* change, as well as a focus of critique, with attention to the uneven, contradictory and potentially negative consequences of development-related change."[6]

The Development portal further contends that, "The second set of concerns relates to the architecture focused on meeting certain goals, often based around improving the well-being of people and sustainable use of natural resources.

---

[4] Ibid

[5] Ibid 1

[6] "What is Development Studies,"URL: https://www.developmentstudies.asn.au/driving-home/about/ (Online: Web), Accessed on September 1, 2021

This 'architecture entails a diverse set of actors, including states, multilateral organisations, non-government organisations, multinational corporations, small-scale enterprises, community-based organisations, local volunteers and more. The study of *intentional* development can be oriented towards working with these groups and individuals to improve development practice, and/or efforts to reveal the unintended and potentially negative consequences of development. Although these two sets of concerns can be studied separately, they are intimately connected and arguably should be studied together. Intentional development is part of broader processes of change; efforts to understand these processes in their historical and contemporary context are vital to improving development practice and revealing its consequences. All notions of development are relational *global* processes that occur in and between *all countries* and are influenced by, and have consequences at, *local* and *individual* scales."[7] *It's all about a hybrid and amalgamative approach, where–in, the eclectic notion development comes to the fore which ensconces the narrative ranging from micro that is, individual scales and all the way to the larger ambit of macro receptacles, such as the ones premised upon the larger societal concerns, nation-hood formulaic and the community fulcrum taken as a whole.*

The London school of economics portal informs us that, "The societal and critical functions of Development are numerous and too many. The rate of growth of societities and economic development are the order of the day. In a manner the critique of the menace of capitalism and arcane feudal society are the components of the order of the day as far as the sustainability crescent of the debate is concerned."[8] Since times immemorial, the dictum of development and economic growth of nations and societies all the way percolating to the idiom of individual centers of survival, forms the staple fare as far as the growth and progress of a nation, community and its denizens are concerned which also happens to be the core issue and theme which the realm of Development Studies aims to target.

Through development studies, we seek to bring a critical perspective to applied real world problems, and the policies, programmes and practices behind these. Historically, our focus was on poorer countries in Africa, Asia and Latin America. This now extends to development issues worldwide. We particularly aim to understand the interconnections between global, regional, national and local processes of change. Because real life is complex, development studies brings together diverse disciplines. With roots in anthropology, economics, sociology, politics and geography, it may also combine with others such as psychology, law, management, natural science, history, agriculture or engineering.[9]

---

[7] Ibid

[8] Emmanuel Kuranzia, "An Overview of Development Studies: Background Paper," Working Paper 2, 2007

[9] "About Development Studies," URL: https://www.devstud.org.uk/about/what-is-development-

Development research aims to build partnerships between the people most directly affected by social, economic, technological and environmental change, and academics, policy-makers and practitioners. Equitable collaboration between those based in the global South and global North is particularly important. Working in partnership leads to more insightful and creative theory and more sustainable and equitable practice.[10]

We need to gravitate away from the Silo of national, community and individual scale progress and growth both in the sphere of plain-jane human security and growth. Thus, the Global impact and the international ramifications of development are the order of the day as far as the present deliberations and confabulations are concerned. International development looks at improving the lives of individuals worldwide through areas of need and interest. With areas such as health, education, democracy, sustainability, and economics, people are better equipped to live more equitable lives with greater opportunities. The United Nation, through the UNDP, works on Sustainable Development Goals (SDG), in order to "end poverty, protect the planet, and ensure that all people enjoy peace and prosperity by 2030". Countries are working to ensure that poverty, AIDS, and discrimination against women and girls are addressed in over 170 countries and territories. [11]

Why is International Development Important?

- 10% of the world's population, 700 million people, live in extreme poverty with some regions live on less than $1.90 per day.
- 781 million people lack basic water-drinking services, with 144 million people dependent on surface water.
- 35% of women in the world have experienced physical or sexual violence from a non-partner at some point, while 70% of women have experienced violence from an intimate partner.
- 263 million children, adolescents, and youth are not currently in school.
- Approximately 38 million people worldwide are living with HIV/AIDS, with 1.8 million children.
- 1 billion children between the ages 2-17 have experienced physical, sexual, or emotional violence or neglect within the past year.

The Narrative of Global Careers in International Development

The idea behind every education happens to be that of furnishing the pupil and the student with a must get profession and vocations in order to sustain the population and make them earn a living for themselves. Thus, a rewarding

studies/ (Online: Web), Accessed on 1 September, 2021

[10] Ibid

[11]https://www.netimpact.org/careers/international-development/big-picture?gclid=EAIaIQobChMI-tyOi5fi8gIVbJlmAh0nRwecEAAYAiAAEgLA9vD_BwE

career in Development Studies both, in the Government organizations and the International Non Government Organizations. Thus all the sustainability goals and objectives are torn asunder as deliverables in order to look beyond a country specific comprehension of Development. International development professionals work to reduce or eliminate poverty in developing countries. Practitioners in this vast field target issues ranging from global health to emerging market investment opportunities, at scales ranging from village-based enterprises to country-wide financial and government infrastructures.

There are a variety of different careers that offer experience with international development. Some opportunities to consider are positions with internationally-focused non-governmental organizations (NGOs), the Peace Corps. Multilateral donor organizations, and partners in non-profit and private sectors. With such a wide range of issues that international development focuses on, a wide array of jobs are available. Some of the job titles that a person interested in international development can pursue include advocacy, communications, consulting, fundraising, policy, and research.[12]

Embrace the unfamiliar

Because international development often means spending time in developing countries, you might just find yourself immersed in unfamiliar environments and cultures. If you're not adaptable in these situations, this might not be the career for you. Grow a thick skin No matter how hard you work and how great your ideas are, you're going to encounter situations that are emotionally challenging and roadblocks that seem senseless...sometimes even infuriating. Resilience, dedication, and the ability to roll with the punches are essential to making a lasting impact.[13] Because international development often requires immersion in other cultures, professionals need to be careful they don't swoop in thinking they know all the answers.

Conclusion

The most successful solutions stem from genuine collaboration with local communities, so if you're often sure you know what's best for others, you might want to consider a different line of work. The moot question is that can United States of America live up to its Global philanthropic responsibilities by adhering to Global commons and arriving at Global solutions in order to stem the tide of the grand and stuttering American decline. The besieged nation needs to be back with the Global Climate change Regime along with the idiom of sustsnaibility including Disarmament and proliferation concerns. Only Then!

❐

[12] Ibid

[13] Ibid 1

America's 'Other War' with China on IP Theft

Makhan Saikia,
Senior Journalist,
PhD, TISS, Mumbai

Introduction

This article proposes to unearth the reasons behind China's massive Intellectual Property (IP) theft mostly from American conglomerates operating in that country. Further, it will also discuss why China does it either in the name of collaborating or partnering with the foreign firms. The author tries to map out what legal remedies are being adopted both by China and the US to stop the menace of the IP theft. Finally, the research work offers a pragmatic framework to prevent the growing cases of missing IPs of American enterprises operating in China.

Before we discuss China's massive IP theft from the American and other conglomerates, it is worthwhile to understand the rise of the global governance of IP. It is all but simple to delineate that with the arrival of globalization, we have experienced a borderless world. And in this new realm, we all are fast entering into a newly defined world of social interconnectedness, economic integration, political mobilization etc largely determined by an expanse of information and communication technologies.

Globalization is a multi-dimensional process (Saikia 2017: 1). From the very beginning, globalization has been regarded as a force and a process which has brought a new age. Globalization has pushed IP and operations related to it to a new high. IP has become an economic tool for global business and development. IP has been rightly defined by the World Intellectual Property Organization (WIPO), the nodal agency of the UN like this: 'IP refers to creations of the mind such as inventions; literary and artistic and symbols, names, images and designs used in commerce'. More particularly, the IP refers to a broad collection of rights relating to such matters as works of authorship, which are protected under copyright law, inventions which are protected under patent law, marks which are protected under trademark law as well as trade secrets, industrial designs and other related rights (ibid: 16). Further, the Convention establishing the WIPO concluded in Stockholm on July 14, 1967 (Article 2) clearly outlines various sections of the IP practiced all over the world. It is well understood that IP system refers to a set of laws and procedures which is implemented or enforced by established institutions in each country. Beyond their legal concerns, the IP rights also aim to promote social, economic and cultural well-being of a nation.

Besides the WIPO, the establishment of the World Trade Organization (WTO) in January 1995 and the very unveiling of the most unique Trade Related Aspects in Intellectual Property Rights (TRIPS) of the organization has completely changed the global IP governance system of the world.

Origin

The roots of China's twisting of the global IP system dates back to the onset of its entry into the WTO and even much before, when it started opening its economy cautiously. It must be noted that the West has largely misunderstood the intentions of the Chinese leaders. China knows very well that a new knowledge economy would soon envelope the whole world. And this new economic paradigm would be absolutely ruled by the most advanced tools of information and communication technologies. Precisely, the 21st century has been already set to overrule or rather replace the other giant economic tools like the hardcore industries of the yesteryears. Alikhan and Mashelkar rightly note: 'Leadership of the world in the 21st century will increasingly be in the hands of those who create and harness knowledge. This century, often called, the century of knowledge, is indeed the century of the mind' (2009). Probably, an economically resurgent China might have realised how it could utilise its money, muscle power and manoeuvring ability to the best of its limit to take the centre stage of globality. Though it all started from the early days of legendary Deng Xiaoping, who was known as the architect of modern China, yet the country's journey to the market economy passed through two other significant regimes of Jiang Zemin (1989-2002) and Hu Jintao (2002-2012). Deng, the second paramount leader, must be credited for his pragmatic approach unlike the founder of the great People's Republic of China (PRC), Mao Zedong, who ruled the country from 1949-1976. The quiet and unassuming death of Mao in 1976, and a brief period of instability had helped Deng to take over the leadership of the Chinese nation in 1978 and continued till 1989. Since he launched the opening up policy in 1978, China has transformed itself from a backward agrarian economy and politically isolated state into the world's second largest economy and an important player with global interests and influences. Since 1978, China's GDP has averaged almost 10 per cent a year and more than 800 million people have been lifted out of poverty. There have also been significant improvements in access to health, education and other services over the same period. Even Jiang's term was equally evincing positive resolves to shape China into a WTO-run world trade order. Both Jiang and his premier Zhu Rongji were hopeful that the country's entry into the global trade body would force to carry out domestic economic reforms in the days to come.

Eventually China accepted far more rigorous terms than any other new member that entered into the WTO. Therefore, the Chinese state media also highlighted that this membership would spur the 'cleaning up of laws, regulations, and policies; facilitate the establishment of an impartial, efficient judicial system and bring much needed external competition to the country's inefficient state-owned enterprises' (Tan 2021). It needs to be stressed that China's state-led mercantilist trade regime was proved purely incompatible with the global trade order envisioned by the WTO. It has gradually become clear that the hope of a changing market-led economic order and extensive political reforms in China were largely overblown in the years followed by 2001. Since then, the last two decades what the international community has experienced is a purely robust state capitalist economic model supported by a rigid authoritarian leadership fully immune from any influence from the western liberal economic and political framework. Sadly, China is making all desperate moves to export this model to the rest of the world. Alas! there are very few takers.

Finally, after Hu, Xi Jinping, the current President took over in 2012 and since then, his anti-Western and aggressive economic and military agenda have taken the centre stage of his regime. His great 'China Dream' followed by the gargantuan 'One-Belt-One-Road' (OBOR) has been truly bringing tremors to its neighbours and to the rest of the world. Further, the COVID-19 pandemic and the bundles of allegations making China the creators of the killer virus have made Xi a villain all around the world. However, it is yet to be confirmed by the UN's top health agency World Health Organization (WHO) that China is the source of origin of the COVID-19. During this pandemic period starting roughly from September 2019 till now, China has largely remained unaffected unlike many of its counterparts and probably enemies such as America, India, Australia etc. It has surely emboldened Xi to claim that China can overcome great pandemics like the COVID-19 and can sustain its growth and development in all sectors.

China has been indicating enough that it wants to set an alternative global rule making system apart from the Western liberal system. And for China, joining the WTO has become a turning point in this regard. In 2001, when the Communist nation joined the world trade body, it almost took 15 long years of negotiation to reach the deal. In fact, it was a 'reflection of the challenge of reconciling China's Communist command economy with global trading rules and of the international community's insistence that China sign on to ambitious commitments and conditions' (Tan 2021). Particularly, the US and other developed nations like Japan had a high hope that this would finally integrate China into the global economic order. Moreover, many liberal economic and trade experts were of the view that this market liberalization would open up the country to gradual democratic reforms. Interestingly, the former US President Bill Clinton called Beijing's accession to the WTO 'the most significant opportunity that we have had to create positive change in China since the 1970s'. And Clinton also advocated that this particular historic event would 'commit China to play by the rules of the international trading system'. However, nowhere we could witness any dramatic change in that socialist country since 2001, except its sharp economic rise despite having massive violation of human rights and suppression of minorities in that country. Its political system and decades old authoritarian practices have remained the same, rather Beijing has demonstrated enough resilience to adapt to the growing market dynamism while maintaining its unique Maoist ethos.

China is not meeting its international obligations to protect the IP rights of foreign business enterprises after joining the WTO-TRIPS. Thus, it is directly hampering the innovative process or network not only in China but elsewhere as well.

Why is it difficult to prevent IP theft in China?

China has overhauled its legal system to a considerable extent in 2020. But global trade experts are of the view that this minor restructuring of its complex and party-controlled legal architecture may not be able to eliminate major hassles confronted by overseas companies within China. It is well understood that China's legal system only enables IP theft. Since China's IP framework is intrinsically linked with the country's legal system, solving issues like trade secrets theft, online infringement and political influence and local protectionism via the court would require a complete structural overhaul. Beijing undoubtedly knows this which means that pledges made in the phase one trade agreement with the United States were at best hollow promises designed to appease Washington' (Rechtschaffen 2020). It would be an uphill task for US and other business entities operating in China to prove that their IP is stolen by local Chinese agents or companies. It is often observed by legal and business experts that the theft of trade secret is extremely difficult to locate and equally a cumbersome process to prove in the court unlike other forms of IPs.

Stolen IP and China

It is well documented that China steals IPs of western business houses doing business in that country. But it does after taking away the most secret business ideas of overseas firms? But many of the trade experts and business leaders are still clueless how China uses these trade secrets after they are pilfered. In 2019, William Schneider Jr, a former Undersecretary of State for Security Assistance, Science and Technology and Chair of the Defence Science Board said: 'China has institutionalised a system that combines legal and illegal means of technology acquisition from abroad'. It is very clearly documented by now that China steals IP from academia, key government institutions and from business enterprises. But it is not well-known how China converts such technologies for both business and military purposes. So far it is learnt that first of all these trade secrets are being sent to one of China's two dozen top science universities. They in turn apply for Chinese patents on technology. Once their claims are certified by the patent office, the Chinese Government distributes the patents to various business enterprises across the country. Thus, the stolen IPs from foreign companies finally appear in public as Chinese origin patents. Precisely, these are well-orchestrated plans by the top policy makers of the Chinese Communist Party (CCP) since the onset of globalization and privatization in the country. It is claimed by many western experts that China's Shenzhen-based controversial telecommunication giant Huawei Industries has been one of the top recipients of such stolen patents. Thus, its new 5G technology and distribution around the world has become a centre of controversy in last few years. It has been so that Huawei's overseas operations were forced to close down in countries like the US, UK and in Australia. The main reason behind the ban on the Huawei in the US is that the companies' founders are having close connections with the Chinese Government and hence it would be easy for the company to leak personal data of different countries to the officials back home. In fact, Schneider highlighted the case of Huawei. A media report published in 2019 confirmed that Huawei acquired 56000 5G and artificial intelligence-related Chinese patents despite spending very little on research and development.

Why is China dreaming 'Big'?

China's quiet rise (hepen jueqi) or peaceful development as highlighted during the reign of Hu Jintao has turned fully violent today. It is ambition to build and in fact reclaim its empire will not be successful. Though Xi Jinping has been able to attain the status of the greatest leader of China only after the legendary Mao Zedong, yet he will have to encounter a world entirely different from what his predecessor did.

With the benefit of hindsight, it is crystal clear that in no time China will adhere to the global rule-making standards. Because simply its President forever Xi is in a hurry. He is also probably emboldened by the precarious state of contemporary democracies and their rulers. Indeed, his calculations are not all imaginary. The last two decades have witnessed not only the decline of democracies but also the growth and strength of authoritarian regimes across the globe. Its not all about their rise. Also we have encountered the sharp growth of their economic performance and military might. Precisely, China under Xi can be ranked as the top performer in this category.

China's struggle and aggressive behaviour to climb up to the top will never be met. Unfortunately, China, especially under Xi Jinping since 2012 has chased this wild dream so far. And it is true for many of the big nations around the world to either reclaim its lost status and power or to set the tone of the global governance order. 'All great powers have a deeply ingrained self-perfection shaped by historical experience, geography, culture, beliefs and myths. Many Chinese today yearn to recover the greatness of a time when they ruled unchallenged at the pinnacle of their civilization, before the century of humiliation' (Kagan, 2021). But China today must realise that it's a globalized and post-globalized scenario wherein all the nations are dependent on each other. Beijing should not think that it is indispensable to the global governance system.

Recent Trends in China's IP Architecture

China, it seems, is planning to work constructively with the top global IP governance body i.e. the WIPO. It is in fact, both a tact for Beijing and also a blanket cover for all its wrongdoings so as not to hamper its massive economic efforts to overtake the US in the near future. The IP governance system of the country has made considerable progress in recent years. This includes establishment of specialised IP courts, a Supreme People's Court IP Tribunal, and finally a rigorous revision of IP laws at all levels.

IP protection in China equally matters to both Beijing and Washington. The reason behind is 'IP is seen as strategically vital by both the nations; China's growing stake in IP and obligations under its phase one trade deal with the US have contributed to advances in its protection'. Under its 14th five-year plan (2021-25), China has rightly prioritised IP protection. It is taken as a part of its strategy to move towards self-reliance in critical technology applications. Only in this April, the economic policy makers of the Central Government published a guidebook detailing how Beijing is intending to strengthen the protection of the IP and raise high value patent ownership over the next five years. Also, the Government has made it clear that only this year it is planning to reveal its strategic plan to make China a global IP power by 2035.

As a part of the phase one trade deal between China and the US, the former agreed to crack down on intellectual property violations. But how far and what China will do to prevent IP violations by the Government, its agencies and business organizations both within and outside the country, is not transparent. It must be noted that last November Xi told the Communist Party Politburo that 'IP is a core factor of international competitiveness and a focus of international dispute'. It simply indicates that he is well aware of the benefits of an IP infrastructure and all possible disputes emerging out of violations or infringements of IP rights.

Now China understands well that IP protection is conducive for economic development and expansion as well. Some China observers say that Beijing must be either coming under international pressure or it must be ramping up all possible strategies to protect its own business behemoths who are all out to invest and do business in foreign soils as a part of its grand OBOR. Therefore, Xi in recent days emphasised that protecting IP is protecting innovation only. It may emerge from the fact that the CCP has a diverse group of members-hailing from executives with international business background to dyed-in-the-wool apparatchiks who blindly follows what their dear President Xi pronounces. It may so happen that the CCP in the coming days may encounter seismic shifts as more and more older generations of leaders are fast ageing and retiring. But then Xi is possibly on board for a longer than usual tenure of presidential terms. Maybe he could set a record beyond what two big paramount leaders-Mao and Deng did in the past.

Xi has become more of a pragmatist than an idealist. Thus, he said that IP protection was critical for China's business environment, the opening up of its economy and the protection of critical technologies with national security implications. In fact, China's stake in the global IP domain has been increasing very fast as its economy is growing and expanding all across the globe. International trade and legal experts are of the view that China is fast shifting from a manufacturing-based economy into a knowledge-based economy.

It has been observed that Beijing's WTO membership forced the country to undertake a formidable legislative, legal and regulatory overhaul in order to make archaic domestic laws and rules into compliance with the global trade regime. But the experience in the last two decades indicate that Beijing has not done enough to check IP stealing and espionage carried out by its own entities, mainly government agencies and private firms from both American and other companies operating in China.

What America is doing?

Washington's game plan is clear, though at times messy. And the rest of the West and other democratic and progressive power centres such as India, Japan, South Korea, Australia, Canada etc. will certainly align with America as all of them are either threatened by Chinese expansionism or by its aggressive military might. Hence, the US must accept its global role and ensure the maintenance and sustenance of the global liberal order.

In 2020, then FBI Director Christopher Wray revealed in a public speech that China is engaged in a generational fight to surpass the US economically and technologically. To that end, the Americans have become victims of information and IP theft. Unfortunately, this dark saga represents 'one of the largest transfers of wealth in human history'. Wray further highlighted that 'The Chinese Government is engaged in a broad, diverse campaign of theft and malign influence and it can execute that campaign with authoritarian efficiency. They are calculating. They are persistent. They are patient. And they are not subject to the righteous constraints of an open, democratic society, or the rule of law. The greatest long-term threats to our nation's information and intellectual property and to our economic vitality is the counterintelligence and economic espionage threat from China'. Thus, he put it bluntly that the American people are going to be victims of China's massive IP theft in the coming days. And stated that the American taxpayers are footing the bill for China's technological development. It has been estimated that the Chinese theft of American IP costs more than $ 600 billion a year annually. During the reign of President Donald Trump, he imposed the harshest ever trade restriction over China. Literally, a full-fledged trade war was launched against China and still it continues under the current President Joe Biden. Major reversals of strategies have not taken place towards China so far.

While addressing the Congress in April this year, US President Joe Biden cautioned that US-China relations 'as a battle for the century', with IP as one the key issues. He said: 'America will stand up to unfair trade practices that undercut American workers and American industries, like subsidies from the state-to-state owned operations and enterprises and the theft of American technology and intellectual property'. This clearly shows how Washington is gearing up to safeguard its interests in the field of IP.

Meanwhile, the US has called China the 'world's principal IP infringer'. A report released by the Office of the US Trade Representative (USTR) in April accused China of not carrying out any measures to check blatant violation and theft of IP in China. Therefore, the USTR flagged emerging concerns in other IP related policies followed by China as well. It attributed more than 80 per cent of US counterfeit seizures from China, including Hong Kong. Incidentally, the USTR Office has kept China on its 'priority watch list' for monitoring all types of IP infringement. Again, the US is also accusing all agencies affiliated to the Chinese Government and its military of infiltrating US companies computer systems to steal IP for the commercial advantage of Chinese business houses. But the Communists in Beijing flatly denies such allegations coming from Washington and its various security agencies in recent days.

Finally, Congress is considering a new bill called the US Innovation and Competition Act (USICA) which will help America to compete technologically with China. Now high concerns are being raised from many quarters that the bill must include strong research security provisions to stop China's rapacious program of acquiring science and technology knowhow. It is stated that the US science and technology programmes are not well-protected from Beijing till date. 'The members of the US Congress must revisit the full range and scope of the CCP's foreign technology and science acquisition programmes and address them in the bill' (Blumenthal and Zhang 2021). It is clear that acquiring foreign technology is not a secondary or incidental objective of China. Rather it has been considered as the central agenda by both the CCP and the Government as a part of its larger goal to overcome the US in its race to become global superpower. Therefore, President Xi himself has declared acquiring 'key core technologies' as one of his foremost goals. His is an agenda of extreme expansion and an open challenge to American domination of the global liberal order. His confrontationist approach will not yield any benefit to Beijing. It is better to make peace and negotiation at the centre of the business and politics between the US and China.

It is well-accepted that engagement will be much better than confrontation with a country like China. Else its authoritarian rulers will avail every opportunity to twist international trade laws and accordingly, make its command economy more inaccessible to the outsiders. It would be a great loss not only for China but also for the rest of the world as well.

Remarks

The afterthought is that Beijing is reluctant to tighten its IP laws. The primary reason behind it is that it might hinder the country's mad race to become global economic superpower in the coming days. The road ahead is clear- the US needs to tighten its legal framework so as to streamline the Chinese IP theft. Moreover, Beijing and its leadership must be brought under global pressure. Else Xi and his cronies are simply thinking that they can do what they want. It must be made clear to China that America is a super-power, whether it likes it or not. Accordingly, Washington needs to check China's irresponsible behaviour in many other fronts like observance of international maritime laws, aggression towards its neighbors, massive expansionism in the name of economic bail out plans (as it is undertaken now in the Taliban controlled Afghanistan). It is time to check China and made it a law-abiding nation.

References

- Alikhan, Shahid and Mashelkar, R. (2009), Intellectual Property & Competitive Strategies in the 21st Century, The Netherlands: Wolters Kluwer.
- Blumenthal, Daniel and Zhang, Linda (2021), China is Stealing Our Technology and Intellectual Property. Congress Must Stop It, National

Review, June 2 (www.nationalreview.com).

- Guo, Baogang and Teng, Chung-chian ed. (2011), China's Quiet Rise, UK: Lexington Books.
- Kagan, Robert (2021), A Superpower, Like It or Not, Foreign Affairs, March-April, Vol 100, Number 2.
- Rechtschaffen, Daniel (2020), How China's Legal System Enables Intellectual Property Theft, The Diplomat (www.thediplomat.com).
- Saikia, Makhan (2017), Globalization and Intellectual Property Rights, Delhi: Atlantic Publishers.
- Tan, Yeling (2021), How the WTO Changed China, Foreign Affairs, March-April, Vol 100, Number 2.

(Dr. Makhan Saikia is an author and expert on Globalization and Intellectual Property Rights. He is the President of the Global Research Foundation. He has done his Master's and M. Phil in Political Science from the Centre for Political Studies, School of Social Sciences, Jawaharlal Nehru University, New Delhi. And, He has completed his Ph.D on Globalization and Intellectual Property Governance from the School of Management and Labour Studies, Tata Institute of Social Sciences, Mumbai).

❐

US-Afghan Relations: Uncertain Future

Dr. Raghubansh Sinha

Introduction

When the new Biden administration in mid-April 2021, in an early review of US foreign policy soon after taking office, announced that it was on track to withdraw from Afghanistan, few had imagined that this decision few months down the line would turn out to be a major political crisis and severely damage the reputation of the US as a military superpower.

Ahead of the planned drawdown of American troops, US president Joe Biden had assured the American people and the world that his administration was on a well thought out calibrated evacuation roadmap that would ensure stability for the Afghan government in Kabul.

There would be "no circumstance where you see people being lifted off the roof" like in Saigon, he said, pointing to the desperate evacuation of American citizens in 1975 in the final days of the Vietnam War.

A Botched Withdrawal

However, on August 15, 2021 live images of US helicopters transporting Americans to Kabul airports for emergency evacuation reminded one of America's failure in Vietnam and the limitation of the US military might today. The fact is that the post-9/11 world has changed dramatically. The USA today feels more secure and confident to prevent a repetition of September 11, 2001.

As such, most US opinion polls and American experts have supported an orderly pull out from the "forever war", and focus on newer political, economic and geostrategic interest. Greater challenges of economic rejuvenation amid the Corona virus pandemic and geopolitical competition with China seems to be uppermost on the mind of American political leadership.

Over the last two decades, US public opinion on withdrawal of American troops from Afghanistan has tended to run along party lines. But there has been a growing realization in the US that effort at "nation making", whether in Afghanistan or Iraq was a mistake.

After 20 years, few in the US had the stomach for a campaign that had killed 2,448 Americans, wounded 20,722 , resulted in unseen trauma to their mental health and expenditure amounting to over a trillion dollars.

Biden was determined to pull out of Afghanistan. "I will not send another generation of Americans to war in Afghanistan with no reasonable expectation of achieving a different outcome," he told global media at the White House.

Taking stock of US counterinsurgent efforts over the last few decades, former US Secretary of State Henry Kissinger highlighted the "inability to define attainable goals and to link them in a way that is sustainable by the American political process".

As a result, even if the US-Taliban deal finalized by the Trump administration in February 2020 was an embarrassment for the sole superpower, it was seen as a necessary step to extricate itself from the two decades Afghan quagmire.

Not surprisingly, as much as the Trump administration was berated by the Democratic Party for its foreign policy failures, particularly for driving away its western allies and creating suspicion among its close partners in Asia, few had the courage to question president Donald Trump on the wisdom of doing a deal with the Taliban, which had once provided shelter to the al-Qaeda chief Osama bin Laden in Afghanistan.

So while the new US administration under president Biden sought to move away from several key foreign policy decisions of his predecessor soon after taking control of the White House on January 20, 2021--such as joining the 2015 Paris Climate treaty and renegotiating the abandoned Iran Nuclear deal--he reaffirmed his decision to withdraw American troops from Afghanistan before the 20th anniversary of the 9/11 attack.

Laying out his rationale for withdrawal, Biden said the US had achieved its key objectives in Afghanistan. "The United States did what we went to do in Afghanistan: to get the terrorists who attacked us on 9/11 and to deliver justice to Osama Bin Laden, and to degrade the terrorist threat to keep Afghanistan from becoming a base from which attacks could be continued against the United States. We achieved those objectives," he underlined.

He argued that the US "did not go to Afghanistan to nation-build," which was "the responsibility of the Afghan people".

But even among those who supported the military operation soon after the morale-sapping attack by the al-Qaeda on the heart of the US homeland, few had imagined that a Siagon like visuals would be telecast worldwide as Taliban fighters marched into Kabul amid confusion and abandonment by president Ashraf Ghani-led government on August 15, 2021.

The US government has been unable to explain how after spending more than $ 1 trillion in Afghanistan, including billions of dollars on training and building a modern fighting force, the Afghan National Defence Security Forces (ANDSF) crumbled like a house of cards within few days. A military force with nearly 300,000 personnel and among the most well equipped air force in the world melted away against a ragtag Taliban militia in sandals moving on motorcycles with AK 47 slung over their shoulders.

Even the US intelligence agency's prediction in late July that the Taliban will be in a position to threaten Kabul within few months was extremely off the mark as the Sunni-dominated terrorist group overran the troubled country and took over the capital within days of the American forces pulling out of the strategic Bagram air base on June 30.

The result was that the CIA chief William Burns made a secret visit to Kabul to negotiate with the Taliban for a 15-day deadline for the evacuation of US embassy staff, American citizens and other key Afghan citizens who were instrumental in the operations with the Taliban over the last two decades, including translators, military and tribal commanders, and intelligence officials in the field.

The US was reduced to a position where American diplomats and spokespersons had to publicly acknowledge the cooperation of the Taliban leadership and thank them for accommodating their demands to facilitate evacuation.

As the last US military plane flew over the Hindu Kush Mountain in the wee hours of the morning of August 31, several questions came to mind as the world awaited the dawn of a new Taliban regime in Kabul.

The more "fundamental concern", for Kissinger is "how America found itself moved to withdraw in a decision taken without much warning or consultation with allies or the people most directly involved in 20 years of sacrifice". Was the US leadership and the generals lulled by the efficient military operation, which ended the Taliban regime within few months and drove them out of Afghanistan? Did the US overreach in its ambition as it sleepwalked itself into a nation building objective? Was the Afghan challenge put in simplistic terms as "a choice between full control of Afghanistan or complete withdrawal?"

Seeking to find a definite answer just months after the US withdrawal would be handful for most experts. Few would venture to provide a nuanced understanding of the events that has destroyed the reputation of the US among friends, allies and even foes.

While these are sad commentaries on the humiliating and messy US pullout process, the more critical questions are the future impact of these events on the US foreign and security policy, the troubled region and Indian interest in the coming months and years?

Land Of Warring Warlords

A society based on tribal and ethno-centric loyalty, Afghans have fiercely opposed any centralization of power. Widely known as the "graveyard of empires", perpetually warring warlords have come together in broad coalitions against foreign invaders, be it the British in the 19th century the Soviets in the 20th century or the Americans in the 21st century.

For these reasons, terror outfits have been attracted to Afghanistan to set up safe haven as ethno/tribal loyalty, instability due to recurring civil war and difficult mountainous terrain prevented the establishment of semblance of modern state.

When the US embarked on 'Operation Enduring Freedom' on October 7, 2001 few had imagined that the mightiest military in history would be bogged down for two decades. Soon after the 2008 financial crisis, there has been growing isolationist opinion among American middle class. It is another matter that successive administration had failed to publicly acknowledge it, resulting in a tsunami of a support for 'America First' espoused by Donald Trump, pushing him into the Oval Office in 2017.

Since 2011, the debate on pulling US forces out of Afghanistan has been ongoing. The abstract nature of the objectives in Afghanistan ensured that no US administration could set a deadline and stick to it. The root cause of the problem was, according to Kissinger, that "The military objectives have been too absolute and unattainable and the political ones too abstract and elusive".

In effect, there has been increasing opinion in the US that it needs to focus inwards, particularly on the economy which has been severely impacted by its declining clout and growing influence of China on the US market and the world at large.

'America is back' is the phrase Biden has used most frequently to portray a resurgent nation as he sought to assure allies and partners of his priorities and global commitment. He has underlined the need for the US "to focus on shoring up America's core strengths to meet the strategic competition with China and other nations that is really going to determine — determine our future".

He stressed that Americans need to prepare "for the next pandemic or biological threat," stay ahead on emerging technologies, so that it could be "more formidable " against its "adversaries and competitors over the long run" to "fight the battles of the next 20 years, not the last 20 years".

The fact is that Biden is preparing for the 2022 mid-term Congressional election. He needs to quickly put in place a plan to rebuild America amid the Covid-19 pandemic devastation and focus on the Indo-Pacific and China. The Chinese Communist Party under president Xi Jinping has stepped up pressure on the US as China, which seeks to replace the US as the dominant world power, increasingly becomes aware of its vulnerability and short window of opportunity to stamp it domination.

And for both the causes—rejuvenation of the American economy and facing the China challenge—Biden needs to free up resources from Afghanistan.

Ahead of the messy withdrawal, pullout from Afghanistan was seen as the right choice by most Americans. A YouGov poll for The Economist between April 17th and April 20th clearly brought out the wide support for president Biden's decision by more than two to one. Some 58% of adults supported his decision to pull out the remaining 2,500 US troops by September 11, in contrast to 25% opposed to the move.

But the chaotic American pullout amid the Taliban takeover has pushed Biden's popularity southwards since August 15. YouGov survey between August 14th and 17th suggested that 33% of American citizens believed the withdrawal from Afghanistan a mistake.

However, most polls suggest that the decision is unlikely to hurt him in the crucial 2022 Congressional midterm election. In effect, Biden is unlikely to pay a heavy political price for the Afghan debacle. Surely there are several landmines on the way. A terrorist attack linked to the Taliban or al-Qaeda or ISIS in the US could be a game changer.

The Pakistan Factor

Among the various factors that brought the US to such a pass is their failure to find a solution to Pakistan dilemma. While harboring the various factions of the Taliban in its tribal areas along the Afghan-Pakistan border, it sought to help the US forces in transportations and logistic supplies along with intelligence for the Nato troops stationed in the landlocked nation. In effect, Pakistan played a critical role in the failure of US objectives in Afghanistan. The US leadership failed to take decisive action against Pakistan which was playing a diabolical double game.

Highlighting the umbilical link between Pakistan's deep state and the Taliban, Kissinger underlined that even though the initial military campaign "prevailed with great effectiveness", the "Taliban survived essentially in Pakistani sanctuaries, from which it carried out insurgency in Afghanistan with the assistance of some Pakistani authorities."(Pakistan's military spy agency, Inter-Services Intelligence). It was easy for US-led Nato forces to contain the Taliban but not eliminate it as the terrorist group found a ready support and hideouts in Pakistan which looked upon them as an asset in Islamabad's quest for strategic dept against more powerful India.

The end of the American military campaign may have ended Western reliance on Pakistan, but Islamabad continues to project itself as the sole honest broker to moderate the fanaticism of the Sunni terror group, discourage the export of terrorism and drugs to the rest of the world.

In the US strategy, Pakistan may prove to be the key to 'Over the Horizon' military operations against terror groups in Afghanistan. Moreover, Pakistan houses several UN/US designated terror groups, which remain anti-US in orientation as well as threats to its western allies and partners, including India. Also, Pakistan's deep link with its "all weather friend" China has the capacity to complicate Indo-Sino relations and push Chinese agenda in the landlocked nation. So even though Pakistan may not be pivotal following the withdrawal of US forces from Afghanistan, "it remains in a position to offer something to the West".

In return, Pakistan has several things to look forward to from the US-led western world.

Though the Taliban victory has cheered the Pakistani deep state as it has cut Indian influence in Afghanistan, Islamabad is aware that instability and religious violence leading to a civil war will have direct impact on Pakistan. Pakistan's declining economic growth, balance of payment and deepening debt crisis linked to Chinese infrastructure projects has put it at the mercy of the international financial institution controlled by the western nations.

Security Threat to India

India is in a dangerous neighbourhood. The Taliban takeover of Afghanistan will provide Pakistan a staging ground for recruitment and launching of Taliban-linked anti-India terror groups such as Lashkar-e-Taiba (LeT), Jamat ud Dawa (JuD), Jaish e Muhammad (JeM) and Hizbul Mujahideen (HM) among others.

A confident India aims to use its clout with western nations to isolate Pakistan on the Kashmir dispute, particularly after ending the special provision of Article 370 and bifurcation of the Jammu and Kashmir into two separate Union territories.

A desperate Pakistan is likely to respond in the best way it has in the past—stepping up support for anti-India terror groups. India needs to prepare for Afghanistan's terrorist potential under the Pakistan control Taliban regime.

During the last two decades, India had earned large amount of goodwill in Afghanistan by investing over $3 billion in creation of critical infrastructure such as dams, hydropower projects, schools, roads, hospitals and landmark parliament building among others.

The long term goal of India has been to build infrastructure and provide stability and prosperity to Afghanistan by making it economically viable.

India also sought to open up economic opportunity for the deadlocked country by boosting connectivity with the neighbouring countries. In the face of Pakistani opposition to direct land route connectivity between Afghanistan and India, New Delhi has made massive investment in Chabahar Port project in Iran to link up with Afghanistan and other Central Asian states. With the Pakistan-supported Taliban takeover in Kabul, India has little diplomatic leverage to push ahead with these ambitious projects.

'Three-Front War'?

For India, the control of Afghanistan by the Taliban, which is increasingly dependent on Pakistan and China, could not have come at a worse moment. The threat of 'two-front war' with China on the northern border and Pakistan on the eastern border could easily become a 'three-front' war for India as Afghanistan turns into a launch pad for Taliban terrorists into Jammu and Kashmir.

Turning the restless Taliban cadres, who have not known anything other than fighting for most of their lives, suits the interest of both Pakistan and China. The resolute determination shown by Indian military against the PLA on the disputed LAC has surprised the Chinese who had grown accustomed to achieving their military objectives without significant costs. Nothing would stop them from pusing the Taliban and various Pakistani terror outfits such as LeT, JuD, JeM and HM into Jammu and Kashmir to tie down the Indian military.

What Now?

In Afghanistan there was never an easy choice for the US. But the chaotic and humiliating US withdrawal from Afghanistan has brought out a key lesson: When the US retreats, the void will be filled by anti-American forces, something dreaded by its western allies and regional partners.

Clearly, the US has undermined its credibility as a reliable partner. At a time when regional and western partners will play a crucial role in overcoming America's future challenges, including pushback against increasingly assertive and authoritarian China and post-pandemic economic rejuvenation, the US needs to follow a more consultative approach so as not to abandon its friends.

In a hurry to leave, the Biden administration overlooked the conditional element of the US-Taliban deal which was to push the Sunni group to negotiate in good faith with the Afghan government for a political settlement. Rather, as was obvious to everyone, the Taliban negotiators were playing a waiting game for the US to leave Afghanistan before it embarked on forceful capture of the troubled country.

Direct US military involvement in Afghanistan has ended, but Washington still remains the biggest player on the diplomatic chess board. Taliban seeks international recognition and economic support to stabilize its regime in the impoverished country, which is dependent on international aid for 80 per cent of its needs. Taliban's two greatest supporters, Pakistan and China, are well aware that a destablised Afghanistan in throes of a civil war meets none of their geostrategic or economic aims.

The US cannot wish away its critical role in keeping the region and the world safe from future terror attacks emanating from Afghanistan. Taliban must be held accountable for fulfilling its commitment for basic human rights for women, children, minorities and all civilians. Taliban and its supporters –Pakistan and China—must be asked to walk the talk amid troubling reports of brutality against women and minorities, public execution of soldiers, and journalists being hounded and browbeaten to follow their dictate.

Evidently, the Taliban leadership has become more sophisticated in their utterances, but there is little to differentiate them from the fundamentalist authoritarian Islamist regime of the 1990s. In such as scenario, the US must not make the mistake it committed following the withdrawal of the Soviet forces from Afghanistan in 1989 after a decade-long intervention Russian military. There are two fears today. One, the US contemplates such an eventuality and second, Afghanistan could yet again turn into a breeding ground for terrorist groups that may target the US homeland. Clearly, the US faces a difficult choice once again.

❐

Bibliography on US Foreign Policy and US Culture

Hemant Khare
Library Assistant, IIPA

- Callinicos, A. (2000). *Equality*. Cambridge, UK: Polity Press.
- Chomsky, N. (1966). *Topics in the theory of generative grammar*. The Hague: Mouton.
- Chomsky, N. (1997). *World orders, old and new*. London: Pluto Press.
- Chomsky, N., & Herman, E. S. (1980). The political economy of human rights. Volume 1. The Washington connection and Third World fascism. Sydney: Hale & Iremonger.
- Chomsky, N., & Lamrani, S. (2005). *Superpower principles: U.S. terrorism against Cuba*. Monroe, Me: Common Courage Press.
- Chomsky, N., & Otero, C. P. (2002). *Chomsky: On democracy & education*. New York: Routledge Falmer.
- Cullen, J. (2001). *Popular culture in American history*. Malden, Mass: Blackwell Publishers.
- Dahl, R. A., & Neubauer, D. E. (1968). *Readings in modern political analysis*. Englewood Cliffs, N.J: Prentice-Hall.
- Diggins, J. P. (2017). *The Liberal Persuasion: Arthur Schlesinger, Jr., and the Challenge of the American Past*. Princeton: Princeton University Press.
- Dwivedi, Manan (2009). *South Asia security*. Delhi: Kalpaz.
- Dwivedi, Manan (2016). *India and China: Negotiating spaces in the narratives*.

- Dwivedi, Manan (2016). *Serendipity and the American dream: United States' foreign policy in a changing global order.*
- Dwivedi, Manan (2019). *American interventions and just cause: The rationale behind the Oregon Trail.*
- Dwivedi, Manan (2020). *Trump's America: Diplomacy and economic policies.*
- Dwivedi, Manan (January 01, 2018). Big Data in the International System: Indian, American, and Other Perspectives.
- Dwivedi, Manan & Chakravarty, D. (2013). *Internal security threats in South Asia*. Delhi: Kalpaz Publications.
- Dwivedi, Manan, & Kacker, U. (October 01, 2013). Re-examining indo-U.S. relations: a paradigm shift in the new global setting. *Journal of Third World Studies, 30,* 2, 137-150.
- Dwivedi, Manan, & Manish, S. (2010). *International Relations: Theoreticians Insights into the Novae Discipline.*
- Dwivedi, Manan, & Richhariya, Katyayinee. (2020). *The Untold tale of an unending border*. South Asia Democratic Forum (SADF).
- Dworkin, R. W. (1996). *The rise of the imperial self: America's culture wars in Augustinian perspective.* Boston: Rowman & Littlefield Publishers.
- Galliani, R., & Besterman, T. (1976). *Studies on Voltaire and the eighteenth century: Volume CLXIII.* Oxford: Voltaire Foundation.
- Ganguly, S. (1999). *The crisis in Kashmir: Portents of war, hopes of peace.* Cambridge: Cambridge University Press.
- Ganguly, S. (2006). *South Asia.* New York: New York University Press.
- Ganguly, S. (2013). *India's foreign policy: Retrospect and prospect.* New Delhi: Oxford University Press.
- Ganguly, S., & Kapur, S. P. (2012). *India, Pakistan, and the bomb: Debating nuclear stability in South Asia.* New York: Columbia University Press.
- Ganguly, S., & Thompson, W. R. (2011). *Asian rivalries: Conflict, escalation, and limitations on two-level games.* Stanford (Calif.: Stanford security series, an imprint of Stanford university press.
- Ganguly, S., Diamond, L. J., & Plattner, M. F. (2009). *The state of India's democracy.* New Delhi: Oxford University Press.
- Ganguly, S., Fair, C. C., & ebrary, Inc. (2008). *Treading on hallowed ground: Counterinsurgency operations in sacred spaces.* New York: Oxford University Press.

- Ganguly, Sumit, and David P. Fidler. 2013. India and counterinsurgency: lessons learned. New York: Taylor & Francis Group.
- Ganguly, S., Shoup, B., & Scobell, A. (2007). *US-Indian strategic cooperation into the 21st century: More than words*. London: Routledge.
- Girvetz, H. K. (1969). *The evolution of liberalism: Introd. by Arthur Schlesinger, Jr*. London: Collier Books.
- Gravel, M., & Chomsky, N. (1971). *The Pentagon papers: The Defense Department history of United States decisionmaking on Vietnam*. Boston: Beacon Press.
- Hunebelle, D., & Hunebelle, D. (1974). *Dear Henry: Begegnungen mit Henry Kissinger*.
- Kissinger, H. (2011). A world restored: Metternich, Castlereagh and the problems of peace, 1812-1822. Whitefish, MT: Literary Licensing.
- Kissinger, H. (1982). *American foreign policy: A global view*. Singapore: Institute of Southeast Asian Studies.
- Kissinger, H. (2004). *Ending the Vietnam War: A history of America's involvement in and extrication from the Vietnam War*. New York: Simon & Schuster.
- Kissinger, H. (2012). *Years of renewal*. London: Simon & Schuster.
- Kissinger, H. (2014). *World order*. New York: Penguin Press.
- Kissinger, H. (2015). *World order: Reflections on the character of nations and the course of history*.
- Kissinger, H. (2019). Nuclear weapons and foreign policy: Double & Company, Inc.
- Kissinger, H., & Burr, W. (1999). *The Kissinger transcripts: The top secret talks with Beijing and Moscow*. New York: New Press.
- Lester, E. (2019). *Liberalism and leadership: The irony of Arthur Schlesinger, Jr*. University of Michigan Press.
- Mahapatra, Chintamani (1990). *American role in the origin & growth of ASEAN*. New Delhi: ABC Pub. House.
- Mahapatra, Chintamani (2007). *US-Philippines strategic relations: Underpinning unequal associations*. New Delhi: Reference Press.
- Mahapatra, Chintamani (2009). *The US approach to the Islamic world in post-9/11 era: Implications for India*. New Delhi: Academic Foundation in association with Observer Research Foundation.
- Mahapatra, Chintamani, & Australian Defence Studies Centre. (1996). *Cooperative efforts in the Indian Ocean*. Canberra: Australian Defence Studies Centre.

- Mahapatra, Chintamani, & Institute for Defence Studies and Analyses. (1998). *Indo-US relations into the 21st century*. New Delhi: Knowledge World in association with Institute for Defence Studies and Analyses.
- Mahapatra, Chintamani, & Tripathy, A. K. (2007). *Transnational terrorism: Perspectives on motives, measures and impacts*. New Delhi [India: Reference Press.
- Nautiyal, A., & Mahapatra, Chintamani (2015). *India-China Relations in the Contemporary Era: Opportunities, Obstacles and Outlooks*. Lanham: Kalpaz Publications.
- Parini, J. (2004). *The Oxford encyclopedia of American literature*. New York: Oxford University Press.
- Parret, H., Chafe, W. L., & Chomsky, N. (1974). *Discussing language: Dialogues with Wallace L. Chafe, Naom Chomsky [etc.]*. The Hague: Mouton.
- Schlesinger, A. M (2018). *Colonial merchants and the american revolution: 1763-1776*. Place of publication not identified: Createspace independent.
- Schlesinger, A. M. (1932). *Political and social history of the United States, 1829-1925*. New York: Macmillan.
- Schlesinger, A. M. (1981). *The birth of the Nation: A portrait of the American people on the eve of independence*. Boston: Houghton Mifflin.
- Schlesinger, A. M. (1994). *The age of Jackson*. Boston: Little, Brown and Co.
- Schlesinger, A. M. (2002). A life in the twentieth century: Innocent beginnings, 1917-1950. Boston: Houghton Mifflin.
- Schlesinger, A. M. (2003). *The age of Roosevelt: 1*. (The age of Roosevelt.) New York: Mariner Books.
- Schlesinger, A. M. (2007). *The disuniting of America: Reflections on multicultural society*. S.l.: an Academic Internet Publishers, AIPI.
- Schlesinger, A. M. (2015). The vital center: The politics of freedom. New Brunswick (N.J.): Transaction Publishers.
- Schlesinger, A. M. (2018). *Robert Kennedy and his times*. London: Futura Publication.
- Schlesinger, A. M., & Bruns, R. A. (1983). *Congress investigates: A documented history, 1792-1974*. New York: Chelsea House Publishers.
- Schlesinger, A. M., & Fox, D. R. (1969). A History of American Lif. New York: Scribner.
- Schlesinger, A. M., & In Schlesinger, J. A. M. (2014). Nothing Stands Still . Cambridge, Mass: Belknap Press of Harvard Univ. Press.

- Schlesinger, A. M., Dallek, R., LaFeber, W., & Burr, R. N. (1983). *The dynamics of world power: A documentary history of United States foreign policy, 1945-1973*. New York: Chelsea House Publishers.
- Sreedhar, & Malakar, S. N. (2004). *The second coming: US war on Iraq 2003 : an Indian perspective*. Delhi: Academic Excellence.
- Tocqueville, A & Virginia. (1963). *Democracy and despotism: An excerpt from part II of Democracy in America*. Richmond: Virginia Commission on Constitutional Government.
- Tocqueville, A. C. H. M., Mayer, J. P., & Lawrence, G. (1981). *Journey to America*. Westport, Conn: Greenwood.
- United States., & Kissinger, H. (1974). *The inter-American relationship*. Washington: Dept. of State, Office of Media Services, Bureau of Public Affairs.

❑❑❑